T0275123

LET'S GO FOR A RIDE

THE WILD LIFE
OF MAINE'S
LONGEST-TENURED
UNDERCOVER
GAME WARDEN

WILLIAM LIVEZEY AND DAREN WORCESTER

Down East Books
CAMDEN, MAINE

Down East Books

Published by Down East Books
An imprint of Globe Pequot, the trade division of
The Rowman & Littlefield Publishing Group, Inc.
4501 Forbes Blvd., Ste. 200
Lanham, MD 20706
www.rowman.com

Distributed by NATIONAL BOOK NETWORK

Copyright © 2022 by William Livezey

All rights reserved. No part of this book may be reproduced in any form or by any electronic or mechanical means, including information storage and retrieval systems, without written permission from the publisher, except by a reviewer who may quote passages in a review.

Library of Congress Cataloging-in-Publication Data

Names: Livezey, William, author. | Worcester, Daren, 1976- author.
Title: Let's go for a ride : the wild life of Maine's longest-tenured
    undercover game warden / William Livezey with Daren Worcester.
Description: Camden, Maine : Down East Books, [2022]
Identifiers: LCCN 2021052264 (print) | LCCN 2021052265 (ebook) | ISBN
    9781684750191 (cloth) | ISBN 9781684750221 (ebook)
Subjects: LCSH: Livezey, William. | Game wardens—Maine—Biography.
Classification: LCC SK354.L58 A3 2022 (print) | LCC SK354.L58 (ebook) |
    DDC 639.9092 [B]—dc23/eng/20211117
LC record available at https://lccn.loc.gov/2021052264
LC ebook record available at https://lccn.loc.gov/2021052265

∞™ The paper used in this publication meets the minimum requirements of American National Standard for Information Sciences—Permanence of Paper for Printed Library Materials, ANSI/NISO Z39.48-1992.

To Gail

CONTENTS

ACKNOWLEDGMENTS

I HAVE TO START BY THANKING MY AWESOME WIFE, GAIL, FOR ENDUR-
ing numerous trials and sacrifices as a game warden's wife, including
the added stress of my undercover work. Gail is my most loyal and best
friend, lover, and encourager. Most importantly, in her frank and to-the-
point way, she has helped me stay grounded and accountable to my Lord
and Savior, Jesus Christ.

To my four amazing children—Amanda, Brooke, Billy, and Morgan—
who had the joys of raising orphaned baby deer, bears, skunks, raccoons,
and other critters, but also endured the hardships of life as a law enforcement officer's kid. Now married, raising their families, and most importantly, living out their faith, I'm so thankful and proud of them!

Thanks to my mom, stepfather Frank, and sister Chris, who supported my dreams and were always there for me!

Thanks to my many mentors, including Grandad Jacobus, Uncle
Paul, and Uncle Dave, for teaching me how to hunt and encouraging my
love and passion for the outdoors. To the patrons at my mom's bar (The
Olde Indian Valley Inn) and the other men who took me hunting and
fishing. Yes, you taught me how to poach. I know you only intended on
showing me a good time, and your "teaching" is probably objectionable
to most people, but you helped me form the skills I would later need to
be a successful game warden and an undercover officer. To my football
and wrestling coaches, all of whom saw I needed a father figure and made
themselves available. To Coach Jim Henning, who sacrificed his time to
minister through Fellowship of Christian Athletes, and taught a wayward
kid like me to surrender to God, completely changing my life's trajec-
tory. To Game Warden John Ford, who took me under his wing while

I attended Unity College and introduced me to the thrill of catching a night hunter. And to the many senior wardens who taught me how to be a game warden and helped me hone my skills.

Thanks to my childhood friends and trapping partners like Steve Cupcheck, Tim O'Brien, Randy Fluck, Durrell Moyer, Victor Lotti, Leo Orloski, and others who spent countless hours roaming through the woods, hunting, fishing, trapping, making campfires, and sleeping in fields watching the stars all night and discussing our dreams. I'll never forget my first stakeout with Leo when we caught my first poacher stealing fur by watching a dead muskrat in one of our traps all day.

Thank you to my Christian friends: Steve Sellars, Jay Strunk, Merlin Benner, Pastor Val Vigue, Pastor Jeff Moody, Pastor Mike Booker, and the many other brothers for challenging me in my faith, holding me accountable, and being patient with me as the Lord transformed my life.

Thanks to all of my law enforcement peers, game wardens, game warden investigators, federal agents, police officers, troopers, and supervisors that shared their lives and friendships through our many adventures together!

Finally, a special thanks to my co-author Daren Worcester, who spent countless hours writing, organizing, and ensuring the stories in this book were accurate and well written!

—Bill Livezey

Thank you, Bill, for entrusting me to help share your life's story and to Gail for supporting the project. Much appreciation to Michael Steere, Hannah Fisher, Alyssa Messenger, and the entire Down East Books team. Thanks to my wonderful wife, Frances, who graciously allows me to squirrel myself away for writing time. And to my boys, Wyatt and Avery, thanks for the joy you give me; I cherish being your dad.

—Daren Worcester

INTRODUCTION

My name is William Livezey, but you can call me Bill. I'm a conservative Christian, a husband to my amazing wife Gail, the father of four beautiful children with kind hearts and good heads on their shoulders, and a proud grandfather. A retired Maine game warden with thirty years of service, I enjoy helping teens and youth figure out life, spending as much time as I can outdoors, and Gail's home cooking.

You can probably already tell that my personal life isn't a page-turner, which is why I'd like to introduce you to my alter ego, Bill Freed. For twenty years, I lived a double life working undercover as the *other* Bill. This moniker wasn't my only alias, but for simplicity, we'll stick with Bill Freed here. I'm the longest-tenured covert operative in the history of the Maine Warden Service, and I suspect there aren't many—if any—conservation officers nationwide who have worked undercover as long as I have. As you'll soon find out, there are good reasons why others haven't matched my longevity.

In some respects, the two Bills are polar opposites. I don't drink or smoke, but Bill Freed will pound beers with the worst of the bad guys. Sort of. We'll get into that more soon as well. However, in more ways than not, Bill Livezey and Bill Freed are two peas in a pod. We're both from Pennsylvania. We both married our high school sweetheart. And we're both avid fans of the Philadelphia Eagles, Phillies, and Flyers, which OSHA should categorize as a job hazard when working undercover in the Maine woods. As you can probably imagine, I've taken my fair share of verbal abuse for my fandom, but it worked. You see, the closer my secret life resembled my actual life, the more real and believable it was.

Even so, the transformation from Bill Livezey to Bill Freed was like walking into a dark room where the furniture had been rearranged. I knew the general layout, but there was no telling what trouble I'd bump into. After twenty years of buddying up to the most egregious wildlife criminals in Maine, Bill Freed has stories to tell. Tales of high-speed car chases, horrific acts of excessive poaching, drug dealing, murder plots, and far too many compromising situations where the curtain between Bill Freed and Bill Livezey was at serious risk of being yanked away. Let me tell you, when a blitzed sociopath comes at you with a razor-sharp boning knife, you question your career choices.

Becoming a game warden was my dream ever since I was a kid, inspired by the television shows *Gentle Ben* and *Flipper*, where the main characters befriend wild animals and work to protect them. Back then, my worldview was that of good guys versus bad guys—an impression also likely formed by television and movies—where each side worked together like two football teams. However, being a game warden opened my eyes to the fact that there's a lot of gray area in between, and the truly bad guys aren't exactly a band of brothers—even when they are, in fact, brothers.

As wardens, we see three types of sportsmen and women. At one end of the spectrum, there's a small percentage of folks who follow the letter of the law and never step out of line. This reality surprises people, but there are fewer of these sports than you might think. Most people fall into the second category—whether they want to admit it or not—of those who generally follow the rules but every now and then, when the conditions are just right, the temptation is too great. Maybe they've hiked into a remote pond that's rarely fished and they don't see the harm in taking a trout or two over the bag limit. Or perhaps they're hunting near their home on the last day of the season when a doe wanders into their line of fire. A uniformed warden will issue a summons if they catch these individuals in the act; however, as an undercover agent, I'd document the infraction, but if it wasn't serious or habitual, then it wasn't worth blowing my cover.

My focus was at the far end of the spectrum on the small percentage of people who do the most damage to Maine's wildlife. The habitual offenders who live by the saying, *If it's brown, it's down.* Some of these individuals are otherwise good people who are addicted to the thrill of the hunt or the cat-and-mouse game with wardens. Many just want something to brag about to their buddies. Then there's those who are rotten to the core. They love killing, and poaching is the tip of the iceberg for their bad-guy rap sheet. They're convicted felons, alcoholics, and drug dealers. Domestic abuse is commonplace. They're all-around dysfunctional, willing to lie, cheat, and steal from those closest to them without a second thought. They were my bread and butter.

It was my job to put the truly bad guys out of business, and for that, I considered myself one of the good guys. That said, thirty years in law enforcement debunked my childhood belief that good and bad banded together. Faith and experience also taught me that painting people in black and white labels is dangerous. That's why I have altered the names of those who ran afoul of the law in this book. They have gone through the judicial system and paid the penalty for their crimes—it's not my intent to drag their names through the mud again. While I'm not naive to the fact that apprehending poachers for a slew of violations may not alter their behavior toward wildlife, people can change. My path growing up was far from straight and narrow.

From personal experience, I believe in second chances.

1
ARMED AND DANGEROUS

BLACK SMOKE BILLOWED OUT OF THE OLD VICTORIAN HOUSE'S second-story windows. Packed shoulder-to-shoulder in a parking lot filled with onlookers, it felt like a high school football game, an electric current surging through the crowd. Except the throng wasn't cheering for tackles and touchdowns. They were out for blood. Yelling obscenities. Urging the police to act. Every few seconds, someone pointed to a window and shouted that they saw the man inside, fueling a chorus of people screaming, "Get him!" and "Blow him away!"

"He's armed and dangerous!" a cop on a bullhorn warned as a line of police officers worked to keep the crowd back. There was a single man in the building, a fugitive drug dealer and suspected murderer who'd been on the run for six months. The police inadvertently ignited the fire by shooting tear gas inside to subdue the man, and as far as they were concerned, it was now a waiting game. Firefighters and paramedics were on the scene, but they were also bystanders, not wanting to get shot by the man whose life they were trying to save.

A serpentine tongue of flames erupted from the window and licked the outside of the building, igniting cheers from the crowd. My sister, Chris, a year and a half my elder, collapsed onto the pavement. She thrashed and shrieked on the ground, but no one paid her any attention. All they cared about was the pariah of their community getting his due.

I just stood there. Numb.

The armed-and-dangerous man inside the building was our father.

I was fifteen.

William Livezey senior wasn't always a bad guy. He started out as an honest worker who owned and operated a lawn mowing and woodcutting business. But even then, he was intimidating. Physically strong from endless hours of hard labor, his stocky, five-foot-eleven stature alone was unnerving. He also had a penetrating glare that could coerce grown men into doing his bidding without uttering a word. But what really put people on edge was his hair-trigger temper. Dad could go from zero to sixty in the blink of an eye, often leaving a trail of destruction in his wake.

One time when Chris (short for Christine) and I were getting ready to attend a Philadelphia Flyers game with him, he got into it with Mom and cannonballed off the deep end. Yelling and screaming obscenities, he repeatedly punched the wall phone until there was nothing left but shattered pieces scattered across the floor. His rampage continued into the den, where there was a fully stocked bar to entertain guests. He proceeded to smash every single bottle of alcohol—there had to have been close to thirty—off the stone fireplace, raining glass throughout the room and onto us kids. The wooden bar stools were next, followed by the coffee table and the couch. When there was nothing left to destroy, his menacing glare turned to us kids.

"Get in the car," he growled through clenched teeth.

That was one side of my father. The other was a man who was tender, thoughtful, and downright mushy with us kids. He typically cleansed his Incredible Hulk outbursts with a heartfelt letter of apology. The night of the Flyers game, we didn't drive far before he started crying—one of the few times I ever witnessed him shedding a tear—and begged forgiveness. He even had the presence of mind to stop at a phone booth to call Mom to apologize and let her know we were okay.

Ultimately, his seesawing moods perpetuated a complicated family dynamic. We all loved him dearly, but we never knew whether to run to him for giant hugs or to cower in the corner.

When I think of the time I spent with my father as a child, my favorite memories are the ones that sparked my love for the outdoors. We'd go catfishing at night in Pennsylvania because he was busy with his lawn mowing and woodcutting business during the day. He'd still have on his steel-toed boots; dirt, grass, and oil-stained canvas work pants;

and a sweat-soaked T-shirt with stuck-on sawdust as we dropped a line into the creek. I was barely big enough to keep the rod upright, so he'd kneel beside me, smelling of an oddly comforting mixture of fresh-cut grass and gasoline, and wrap his thick arms around me to help steady it.

"You watch," he'd tell me. He had the trademark seventies haircut, silky-straight brown hair brushed to the side with the part on his left, along with a babyface and full cheeks that expanded into a broad smile. "When you get a bite, you're going to see the rod go."

Sure enough, there was nothing like the excitement of catching a fish with Dad. But as I got older, things started to change. If I could put my finger on the cause of my father's unraveling, it was his blind ambition. Like a fish, he snagged the bait and swam with the success of his lawn mowing and woodcutting business by investing in several duplex rental buildings, a historic inn and bar, another bar, and a deli. As a family, we took residence in a custom-style stone home with a large living room and den, four bedrooms, two stone fireplaces, a glass-walled porch above the garage, and, most importantly to me, a gigantic yard for playing. We were moving up in the world, but Dad, hooked to his various mortgages, was burning the candle at both ends to make his businesses successful and attend to his employees and tenants.

During those years when Dad was still living with us, but we barely saw him, my love for hunting and fishing continued to grow thanks to Granddad Jake, my mother's father, and my uncles Dave (Mom's brother) and Paul (Dad's half brother) who shared the obsession. I couldn't get enough of the outdoors. Even when I was at home, television shows like *Flipper*, *Gentle Ben*, and *Mutual of Omaha's Wild Kingdom* monopolized my attention. As a result, I often brought home "rescued" animals such as a baby raccoon and even an opossum to care for them. It got to the point that Dad felt it necessary to have a sit-down.

"Billy," he said, "you need to start thinking about something other than animals. You're going to have to get a job someday, and there's no money in wildlife work."

I never got the opportunity to prove him wrong. Bar ownership fast-tracked Dad into a spiral of alcohol and drug abuse, adultery, and his main addiction, money, which he pursued through dealing drugs. Mom didn't stand for it, and they soon divorced. My sister and I moved with her into a small row home in Souderton, Pennsylvania. In the divorce settlement, she'd taken ownership of the Olde Indian Valley Inn, a historic hotel and bar in town. A loving and nurturing person, she wasn't your stereotypical, rough-around-the-edges bar owner—far from it. She was always one to help someone down on their luck, even when it meant letting bar tabs and rental fees lapse much longer than she should. Of course, this meant that she had to work harder to make ends meet. While still married to my father, she'd mostly cooked in the inn's kitchen and tended housekeeping, but once she became the sole owner, she worked her fingers to the bone managing all aspects.

As an adolescent, this left me with little to no supervision, and I took full advantage. Like father, like son, I went down the wrong path at warp speed. By twelve, I was regularly drinking and doing drugs. Back then, you couldn't buy alcohol from convenience stores in Pennsylvania, so people came to the bar to get beer for home. One of my jobs in the mornings before school was to stock the take-out cooler, and in the process, I'd resupply my stashes. Free access to alcohol boosted my popularity with a rough crowd of kids. It was only a matter of time before my buddy Victor and I were arrested for stealing. We'd broken into a drying machine at the laundromat for drug money, but it was the middle of summer, so we'd only gotten about fifteen dollars worth of quarters. We figured that the washing machines were the real money chests, so, like all dumb criminals, we returned to the scene of the crime and were nabbed.

There was also an entire semester in seventh grade where I flunked *all* of my classes. Needless to say, I was the poster child for juvenile delinquency—the kid that good parents warned their children to avoid. Nobody who knew me back then would have bet that I was in line for a law enforcement career. The safe money was picking the other side of the jail bars.

Even when I was partying and getting high, I loved being outdoors. I took long walks in the woods whenever I could to clear my mind, and I'd get up at four in the morning to maintain my trap line before stocking the coolers. I made good money trapping, hauling in eight dollars per muskrat and anywhere from twenty-five to forty for raccoons. But here, too, my behavior went south. With Dad drifting in and out of the picture, bar regulars became my role models. They took me hunting and fishing, and their methods were, well, less than honest. One guy taught me to "fish" with M-80s. He'd have me stand downstream as he lit the supersized firecracker and tossed it into the brook. The green wick was waterproof, so it kept burning, and within a few seconds, a loud explosion was accompanied by a volcanic burst of water. Concussed fish would soon float to the surface, and I'd scoop them out as they came downstream. For a boy entering his teenage years, it was pure awesomeness.

Then there was Tony, a friend of my mom's boyfriend Charlie, a Vietnam veteran for whom poaching was second nature. One time, I showed up at his farm while he was skinning a deer out of season. The next day he took me out, and he killed another deer with a .22 long rifle, which is illegal to use *during* deer season because it requires a perfect shot to take down a deer with such a small caliber. Nothing was out-of-bounds when Tony took me hunting, and I could probably write a book on his escapades alone. I remember coming across a turkey while rabbit hunting and asking myself, *what would Tony do?* He was so proud of me for shooting it. With the lessons I learned from Tony and others, I established a poaching group with friends my age. Even still, I had a personal code of conduct. I might shoot a deer out of season or at night, but I only took one per year, which was the legal limit. It's funny how many people I've encountered later in life as a warden who similarly justify their actions.

For a while after the divorce, Dad tried to maintain some semblance of parental responsibility. The guy who introduced me to M-80s was a convict fresh out of jail who worked on Dad's lawn-mowing crew, and my father freaked out on him when he learned about the firecracker fishing. I also found myself on the wrong side of Dad's temper when he stopped by Mom's place unannounced and caught me smoking pot with friends. He slapped me into the next week and ordered me to call Mom at the bar to fess up.

But then things *really* changed.

Dad's oldest brother Tom was murdered. They co-owned an apartment building together and had life insurance policies for each other, so my dad quickly became the top suspect. His father believed he was in on it, vowing to help the police in any way he could, but Dad had an alibi, and at the time, they couldn't directly connect him to the crime. During the investigation, we were only aware that Dad was uncooperative with the police and refused to take a polygraph test. Deep down, though, I think we all knew. For us, it made an already complicated family dynamic even more strange. As a warden, my colleagues often wondered why kids in dysfunctional homes, especially abused ones, still yearned for their parents. It's not something one can fully understand unless they've lived it. Kids love their parents regardless. It's how we're programmed.

You might say that it was my mother's job to shield us from our father, but he was legally permitted to spend time with us. Besides, that wasn't in her nature. My mother only saw the good in people, and she knew Dad loved us and, even as he spiraled deeper into the drug world, would do anything to protect us. That's what she believed, anyway.

Dad started picking me up in a white Pontiac Trans Am on my visitation days. Silk shirts and white pants replaced his dingy, working-class clothes, and he wore diamond-studded rings and thick gold chains as if he were decorating himself as a Christmas tree. His dad smell became an overdose of cologne, and he even got a perm. All of which was a facade to make people think he was a made man. In hindsight, it's no wonder he got caught. He might as well have put a neon sign on top of the Trans Am that read "Drug Dealer."

As the Bible warns, he gained the world but lost his soul.

Not even a year after slapping me for smoking pot, I tagged along with him to one of his apartments, where he'd piled a mountain of marijuana on the table in clear pound bags. Some guy I'd never seen before with long dark hair and a hollow face came over and they divvied up the stash. After they finished and the stranger left, Dad turned to me, and for the first of many times in my life, I heard those notorious bad guy code words: "Let's go for a ride." His idea of going for a ride was taking his prized Trans Am to the carwash. As we waited our turn, he said my name and nodded to a half-smoked joint in the ashtray. The sting of being slapped for smoking was still fresh in my mind, so I tried to play it cool.

"What's that?"

He rolled his eyes. "You gonna light that thing up or what?"

I did, and we smoked our first joint together, white walling the Trans Am's interior as the carwash jets doused the outside with soap and water. Dad's pot was more potent than what I was getting through friends, and we were both in the clouds by the time the carwash was over. I couldn't wait to get home and brag to my gang of hooligans about getting high with my dad. At fourteen, it was the coolest thing ever, and it was just the beginning.

Not long after that, he drove us out of town—I don't know where— to a house on a remote country road with no streetlights. The long drive-way and both sides of the road were packed with motorcycles and cars as far as I could see, but we found an open spot on the street that was close. Rock music was blaring from the house and people were hooting and hollering in the yard.

"Wait here," he told me.

I was happy to oblige. It was late at night, and aside from the faint glow of lights, I couldn't see the ranch house through the trees. I'd gone inside on a previous drug deal during the daytime, so I knew the layout. One of Dad's primary dealers, a wiry biker in his mid-twenties with decayed teeth, owned the house. They'd gone into a back room, and my father yelled at him while I waited in the living room, standing against the wall. Several other bikers, big men with goatees or full beards, sat on couches around a coffee table smoking pot out of a black gas mask that they'd connected to a bong pipe. There were guns out on the table, but they didn't seem to mind that Dad was yelling at their gang member. The screaming eventually died down, and Dad and his dealer were buddy-buddy again when they came out.

"Billy," Dad said to me, a stoned smile on his face, "you know what happened here, don't you?"

I shook my head no, too afraid to speak.

"This is where those murders occurred." He gave the drug dealer a playful shove. "Ain't that right, Joe?"

"It is." Joe didn't seem to share my dad's amusement. "The kid from next door broke in and killed my whole family. Shot them one by one as they came home and threw their bodies down the basement stairs. I'd probably be dead, too, but I was in jail for trafficking at the time."

"Where's the kid now?" my dad wanted to know.

"Behind bars."

"Maybe he's got your old cell," one of the mask-smoking bikers joked. The murders were real. I'd heard about them on the news. Whether or not that was the actual house, I didn't know, but I believed it, and the story stuck with me as I sat in the dark car waiting for Dad to come back. A parade of rough-looking people with long beards and hair, many dressed in red bandanas, chaps, and leather biker jackets, continued to stagger in and out of the party. One man hunched over and vomited in the middle of the street. I also watched a couple getting frisky against a car until a second woman came out yelling and swinging her purse at the man.

I slunk lower and lower into the Trans Am's black leather seat, but it was so dark that nobody noticed me. Two hours passed, and my dad still hadn't returned. By this time, my mind was racing with worst-case scenarios. I imagined him lying at the bottom of the basement steps. I didn't know what to do. There were handguns in the car—in the glove compartment and under the seat. Wherever we went, Dad always had guns. It was as if he acquired them as part of a drug dealer sales-incentive program. Part of me wondered if I should pack a pistol and go inside looking for him. He'd left the keys in the ignition, so I also contemplated jumping behind the wheel and getting out of dodge. Ultimately, I did nothing but continue to wait.

The sound of screeching tires caused me to look up as my father walked across the street. "Here," he said as he climbed into the car, smelling like a skunk, "hold this." Dad tossed a half-pound bag of purple crystal rock meth into my lap. Amazed, I sat there, staring at it. My friends were never going to believe *this*.

Dad drove us to his bar in Quakertown, which was closed because it was after hours by this point. He let us in and locked the door behind us. It was a typical setup with a long wooden bar in the front of the room, neon beer signs in the windows, several black-and-white box televisions mounted in the corners, a series of wooden tables and chairs, and a pool table and dartboard at the back. Tired, I sunk into a chair at one of the tables and stared absentmindedly at the black ashtray as Dad took the bag of meth behind the bar. It wasn't long before there was a knock at the door.

Dad was busy doing something with the meth (I didn't know what at the time), so he said to me, "Billy, that's probably my guinea pig. Go check. Ask him the password, but only let him in if he says 'Fight, Eagles, fight'—got it?"

"Yeah," I said, but I had no clue what he meant by "guinea pig." I'd learned that it was better not to ask questions.

The man knew the password, so I opened the door. A tall, paper-thin guy with a shaved head and a long, gaunt face filled the doorframe. Fresh scabs like cigarette burns pocked his upper cheeks, and he had a long, unkempt red beard that hung to mid-chest and hid whatever carnage was on the rest of his face. I didn't recognize him as one of Dad's workers, but he wore a baggy green hoodie sweatshirt with a yellow backhoe logo from some construction company. The dark rings under his eyes suggested he hadn't slept in days. He gave me an uneasy feeling, and that was before he grunted at me and proceeded to the bar.

"That your kid?" he asked my father in a disdainful voice as I returned to my seat.

Dad ignored the question. "It's all set," he told the man.

"What about him?" The man nodded in my direction.

"Billy don't care what you shoot into your veins. Don't worry about him."

"If you say so."

The man took off his sweatshirt, followed by his belt. He deliberately turned his back to me so I couldn't see what he was doing, but I saw the belt dangling from his left arm. A moment later, he was groaning and pounding his fist on the bartop.

Then Dad called me over. "Open your mouth." He dipped his index finger into the meth and stuck it on my tongue. The sudden taste of starter fluid caused me to gag and nearly vomit. "Good," I heard him say as I tried in vain to spit it out.

I assume Dad made me try meth because of its vile taste, wanting to scare me away from using it—at least, I hope that was the reason. Ultimately, it didn't work. What he did do by exposing me to the shadowy underworld of illicit drugs, which neither of us realized at the time, was provide me with invaluable training for an undercover agent that I simply couldn't get from the police academy.

It must have been a weeknight because I remember coming home from wrestling practice, sweaty and famished.

"Your father's here," Mom told me the moment I walked through the door. "He's upstairs in your room."

My stomach could wait.

"He's crashing," she warned as I dashed up the stairs.

Dad was passed out on my bed, dead to the world, a loaded Colt .38 Special revolver on the pillow next to his head. Barbara, his girl-friend since the divorce and likely beforehand, sat on the foot of the bed, sobbing. She was dolled up in black slacks and a red halter top as if they were going to a party. Like my mother, Barbara fell for my father's charm. She loved my sister and me dearly and treated us like one of her kids, but there's no sugar-coating the situation. Blue-eyed, blonde, and barrel-chested, Barbara was as much of an accessory to Dad's dealer persona as the Trans Am and diamond-studded rings. It wasn't odd or uncomfortable for Barbara to be in our home because my mother's heart was too big for her own good. Looking back on it now, I suspect that Mom pitied Barbara.

"He's been up for four days straight," Barbara told me. Sadly, I was already familiar with the binge-crash cycle of Dad's meth abuse.

It took Barbara several tries to shake him awake.

"Hey, Billy," Dad managed to say in a hoarse voice. He shielded his eyes from the overhead light with his hand. "What are you doing here?"

"It's my bedroom. What are *you* doing here?"

"Right."

Dad grimaced as he turned himself onto his side to face me. Wearing white pants and a tank top (a black silk shirt was on the floor), he was a ghost of the man who used to take me catfishing. Now more bony than broad and muscular, his face was taut, and his bloodshot eyes had dark-ened puddles underneath as if he'd just gone twelve rounds in a boxing ring. Dad stunk of cigarette smoke and body odor, his fancy permed hair was matted with bedhead, and his hands were visibly shaking. But this skeleton was still my dad, and there was something comforting about simply being with him.

"I came to say goodbye."

"What? Where are you going?"

"I've got a mole at the police station who told me Joe got busted selling to an undercover cop, and he snitched. Now there's a warrant out for my arrest, so I gotta get out of here for a while." He made it sound like the warrant would simply fade away with time.

"For how long?"

"I don't know."

"What are you gonna do?"

"This old dog still has some tricks. They can take everything away from me," he pointed to his temple, "but they can't get what's up here."

Dad reached gingerly into his back pocket and retrieved his wallet, pulling out a Louisiana driver's license. It was obviously a fake because it had his picture with the name Raymond Murphy.

"You can call me Ray," he said, mimicking a popular Natural Light commercial. "Don't tell anyone where I've gone—even your friends—you never know who's a snitch." He looked me hard in the eye to drive-home his point. Only now, as I think back on this conversation, do I see the irony.

"I know some people in Louisiana," he continued, "and they're gonna hook me up with a bartending gig."

"How will you get there? You can't drive your car—you'll get caught."

He smiled, and if I wasn't mistaken, a little proud. "Don't worry about that. I've got a guy to drive me."

"What if he's a snitch?"

"He's not."

"But what if he is? What if you get caught?"

"That's not gonna happen," he said flatly, sitting up. "I can't go back to my house, so I'm taking the guns that I stashed under your bed." He held up the Colt .38 in one hand and a 9mm pistol in the other.

"I'll never surrender."

Six months later, Chris was pounding on my bedroom door. She barged in before I could respond.

"Dad's back!"

"What—where? How do you know?"

"I saw him. He came by the bar, and we played pool for a couple of hours this afternoon."

She wasn't trying to rub it in, but I instantly felt jealous.

"C'mon," she said. "Get ready. He's hiding out at Barbara's place, and he invited us over for dinner."

Barbara lived in an apartment on the second floor of a triplex in Lansdale. It was an old white Victorian house that shared a large parking lot with the town library *and the police station*. I couldn't believe it—Dad was hiding in plain sight! I'd been in awe of his outlaw status, and this made him seem like Billy the Kid or Jesse James.

Chris drove us over in Mom's brown, full-sized station wagon. Along the way, she filled me in on her afternoon with Dad.

"He's sad," she said. "He kept crying while we were playing. He must have said that he's sorry for everything he's put us through a hundred times."

I listened intently to every detail. Dad always had a soft spot for us kids, but what she was describing seemed different from the brazen, success-at-any cost man we'd watched him molt into. Was it possible he was back to turn over a new leaf? Was *that* even possible?

Sirens came on strong behind us, and Chris pulled over to let a pair of police cars pass. A few minutes later, a fire truck blared its horn and flashed its lights, soon followed by an ambulance.

"What's going on?" Chris wondered aloud.

"Wouldn't it be weird if this is because of Dad?"

"Don't say that!" She admonished me, but her nervous tone betrayed her thoughts.

As we neared Barbara's apartment, all routes to it were closed from police roadblocks.

"C'mon!" Chris shouted, slamming her hand on the steering wheel after passing a fourth blocked intersection. Our fears were getting real.

We found a place to park on a side alley and walked back to the roadblock. One of the cops pointed to us and yelled to the other officers, "Hey! That's his kids." He instantly confirmed what we were thinking—*this was about Dad.* Instinctively, I ran around the two police cars blocking the road. The officer who recognized us lunged for me, but I played football and was in good shape despite my drug use. I dashed around him, creating a diversion for Chris to run between the police cars before the remaining officers could react. We sprinted down the street and slipped into the growing mass of people.

"We're good," I said, gasping for breath. "They didn't chase us."

Chris grabbed my arm and pulled me forward. "Let's get closer."

There must have been over five hundred people—maybe even a thousand—packed into the municipal parking lot outside of Barbara's apartment building. We pushed our way closer to the front, but not too close, to avoid getting recognized again. The police had a perimeter set, keeping the crowd a hundred feet from the building. Beyond the line of officers working security, the SWAT team with their helmets and bulletproof vests was assembled and ready for action. Two fire trucks and an ambulance were also parked to the side—the firefighters and EMTs kept their vehicles between the building and themselves in case my father opened fire.

An officer on a bullhorn kept yelling for people to get back. "He's armed and dangerous!"

"I see him," a heavyset woman near us in the crowd yelled. "At the window!"

There were only two windows from Barbara's second-floor apartment facing the parking lot, both of which were closed. It was early evening, just before dark, on an overcast September day, and the lights were out inside, so the only thing to see in the window was the steely reflection of the oak trees at the back of the parking lot. Still, the idea that this woman *might* have seen Dad had me clinging to hope. After six months of wondering where he was, what he was doing, and whether he'd forgotten about me, I just wanted a glimpse.

"What are you waiting for?" a man yelled. "Go get him!"

"Kill him!" someone else shouted.

"Blow him away!"

"Billy," Chris said, "what's gonna happen to Dad?"

A popping explosion followed by smashing glass stole our attention. Another burst followed as the SWAT team shot a second canister of tear gas through the other window.

The crowd erupted in cheers as if the home team had sacked the quarterback.

Moments later, thick black smoke began rolling out of the broken windows. I'd never seen tear gas before, but that obviously wasn't it.

"Let's call Mom," I said. There was a payphone on Main Street at the train station. Chris placed a collect call to the bar, but she was too emotional and her sobbing words were incomprehensible. I took the receiver from her and—somehow—calmly explained that Dad was in a standoff with the police at Barbara's, and they'd fired tear gas into the apartment. "We're okay," I told her, making sure to emphasize this point, "we're outside."

"Billy—" Chris steered my attention back to the Victorian apartment building, which was still visible from the payphone. As if encouraged by the crowd, the black smoke had intensified.

"The apartment's on fire," I told my mother, "and the fire department isn't putting it out."

We pushed our way back into the mob, angrily elbowing anyone who was cheering. Flames now stretched out of both windows and climbed the outside of the building.

"Why aren't they doing anything?" Chris cried out. Lines of black eyeliner streaked down her round cheeks.

"I don't know."

When the flames reached the roof, the fire department finally turned on the hose, lofting a high-arching stream over the building. They weren't trying to extinguish the fire. It was a preventative measure to keep the flames from spreading to the other properties. They were content to let William Livezey, senior, burn alive.

Chris realized it, too, collapsing onto the ground.

I didn't know what to do. I felt cold, detached, as if it were all a dream. The police expected my father to flee from the fire. Several SWAT officers aimed automatic rifles at the windows, and small teams clustered around the doorways. But I knew something they didn't. Dad wasn't coming out. Not one to mince words, when he said he'd never surrender, he meant it. One way or another, Dad was going to die in that building like an outlaw. It was his last stand.

A disturbance at the security line drew the crowd's attention. A petite woman was trying to fight her way past the police. "My children!" she kept yelling. "My kids are in the building!" I recognized my mother's voice, but I was thoroughly confused because I'd told her we weren't inside. The officers were holding her back and trying to calm her down when I reached them.

"Mom!" I grabbed her arm and tried to turn her to me. "We're okay. Chris is with me." She was in hysterics, and it took a moment and several repetitions for what I was saying to sink in. Eventually, she stopped wrestling and simply nodded her recognition. The police released her, and we slipped back into the crowd. We found Chris curled up on the ground, settled into a long, deep sob.

Charlie was there, too. "I think we should go," he collectively said to our remaining family. "There's nothing we can do here."

He was right. The fire was raging, its dragon flames having enveloped the entire apartment building. Thick black smoke extended in a skyscraper column to the heavens. Even the SWAT team was falling back from the building and relaxing their defensive posture.

It was over.

Charlie drove us home in Mom's station wagon. On the way, he stopped at the Olde Indian Valley Inn and retrieved a couple of Michelob Light six-packs from the takeout cooler. That night we huddled around a television, sipping beers in silence as we watched the eleven o'clock news coverage of the standoff. Among the dramatic shots of the mobbed crowd, individual testimonies, police officers, and firefighters, several men carried a blue body bag from the building's charred skeletal remains. That was my last impression of Dad.

When I went to bed that night, the scene was still running on a constant loop in my mind, the loudspeaker warnings that he was armed and dangerous ringing in my ears. In the end, Dad was armed but only dangerous to himself and those closest to him. He put a bullet through his head before the fire claimed him. And he left me in total disarray.

My father was a small-town kingpin; nevertheless, the police leveraged the incident as a significant victory in the war on drugs, touting him as one of the biggest dealers on the East Coast as if he led a New York City syndicate. The newspapers and television reporters ate it up. It was my first exposure to media sensationalism, and it was suffocating. Everywhere I went, people *knew*. My father and I shared the same name, there was an obvious physical resemblance, and we lived in a small town where everyone knew everyone and news spread like wildfire even without the papers stoking the flames.

In public, I could feel the icy stares and condemnation. I sensed what people said behind my back. They *knew* I was no good—just like my father. I don't know whether the whispering occurred or was a figment of my imagination (or a mix of both), but it became a self-fulling prophecy. Like my father, I doubled down on my wayward ways. My drug use escalated from wading in the kiddie pool with recreational drinking and smoking pot to cannonballing into the deep end. I dabbled with mushrooms and coke, but marijuana, crystal meth, speed, quaaludes, and excessive drinking were my go-to pain killers. I also took up the family business, and I'm not talking about lawn mowing or bartending. Back then, it was frighteningly easy for a fifteen-year-old to obtain mass quantities of marijuana and speed—Robin's Eggs, Yellow Jackets, and Crossroads—for resale. I was angry at the police, and walking in Dad's footsteps was a natural way to strike back.

There was also the guilt that formed a one-two punch with my paranoia. Afraid of what people thought of me, I avoided going out in public; however, alone with my thoughts was an even darker hell. I fantasized about bull-rushing into the burning building, fighting my way through the smoke and flames, and saving my father before he put the gun to his head. Why hadn't I done *that*? What kind of son was I? It was irrational,

I know, but the guilt held my mind in a straitjacket. I wish I could say this was rock bottom, but it wasn't.

Five months after my father's death, the police finally solved my uncle's murder. That's when we learned that Dad hired a man to kill his brother. Of course, this precipitated a regurgitation of the news stories detailing my father's downfall.

I couldn't escape it. Why did these things keep happening? It was one kick after another. Throughout most of it all, my coping mechanism was a bottle, pill, or joint. Getting high was the only way I knew to avoid the truth—my life was broken. Still, it was too much for a sixteen-year-old to handle. The intense speed of winging from snorting a line of meth was overwhelming. It gave me the spins and made my skin crawl. I gravitated to quaaludes as my preferred self-medication because it numbed the pain and made me feel indestructible without the spin cycle. On quaaludes, I could get punched in the face and still feel on top of the world.

The cumulative drug use took its toll. I started waking up in the middle of the night, overwhelmed with anxiety, shaking, my body on fire, and the sheets soaked with sweat. One evening, after a string of these episodes, I found myself praying to God. I'd never been to church or had any formal religious education. My grandmother on my mother's side was Christian, and Mom prayed with me when tucking me into bed as a young child, so perhaps they planted the seed. At this time, though, I couldn't have told you the difference between Jesus and Joseph. Something about praying just felt right. I begged God to take away the nightly episodes, and I made a deal, promising to quit drugs.

That was the last night I woke up feeling like I was burning alive.

Still, I was far from getting my life in order. Along this journey, some people tried to help. Victor, my buddy and accomplice in the botched washing machine heist, had a stepfather who worked at Graterford State Prison in Pennsylvania. After we got arrested, his stepfather arranged a visit and tour for us, during which we served hard time in a small room where an inmate yelled at us to straighten out before we ended up in prison for life like him. Shortly after my father's death, the local police took a busload of at-risk kids to the Scared Straight program at Rahway State Prison in New Jersey. There, we had the privilege of more inmates yelling at us to avoid making the same mistakes as them. These initiatives were well-intentioned, and they certainly impressed upon us that prison wasn't a pleasant place. But they missed the mark because they didn't address the issues stewing inside of me.

While I'd quit narcotics, I continued to feel stuck at rock bottom. Almost a year to the day after my father's death, Granddad Jake died in a tragic farming accident, thrown from his tractor while bush hogging a field. He'd been one of the few stable male role models in my life. During the years when Dad was seemingly working around the clock, it was Granddad who took me fishing and hunting. His death was devastating.

Then, in 1981, when I was seventeen, Steve Sellars invited me to attend the Fellowship of Christian Athletes (FCA). Steve was an actual friend—not one of the guys hanging around because I could get free booze—and a football teammate. At the time, life didn't make sense. I'd seen first-hand from my father's example the results of living solely for one's self, and there had to be something more to life than that. The night I prayed to God and struck the deal to stop taking drugs had left a lasting impression upon me. From it, there were two things I believed with certainty: there was a God, and I was a sinner. I agreed to attend the meeting, where I heard the Gospel and decided right then and there to trust Christ. I'll be honest, it was a slow transformation process—the Lord had his work cut out for him with me—but for the first time in my life, I had hope.

As my trespasses were peeled away like rotten layers of an onion, I found another incentive at FCA to keep my life in order.

Her name was Gail.

2

ADDICTED

AWASH IN THE PALE GLOW OF A FULL MOON, THE FIELD WAS FRAMED BY the bristle-brush appearance of the leafless hardwood treeline. Sitting shotgun in Warden John Ford's department truck, which he'd backed into the woods on a bank along the right side of the opening, I stared across the field and its tramped-down grass glistening with frost—waiting, watching.

Smack in the middle of the field and roughly fifty yards from the road were two deer decoys hand-painted by John and held erect by sticks that looked like the real thing. He was a talented artist, and after several hours of staring at the silhouettes of a doe and her fawn, my tired eyes even saw them moving. It struck me how similar a poaching stakeout was to actual hunting. The optimistic excitement of a well-conceived plan, followed by the slow dilution of hope as the hours ticked away and one promising sign after another, turned into nothing. Then, just when we started to think about throwing in the towel—it's go time!

The truck's side windows were cracked open on each side to keep them from fogging and so that we could hear anyone coming. We were bundled up, but it was closing in on four in the morning and we'd been sitting there since well before midnight. The cold air had wormed into my clothes, and I repeatedly wiggled my toes and clenched my hands into fists to soothe the biting sting. While it was tempting to ask John to start the truck and blast the heater, we couldn't chance revealing our position.

"You think this is cold?" John said as he tugged down the ear flaps on his black trapper hat. "Have I told you about the time Warden Allen and I hid amongst pulp logs on a train?" John had thick eyebrows, a stout nose, a whistler's gap between his top front teeth, and chipmunk cheeks with crescent-moon dimples that radiated from the corners of his mouth to his crow's feet like ringlets on a pond. He was showing a sly half-smile, his tell that he was working up something funny to say and couldn't wait to get it out.

"No," I said, thinking I'd remember a train stakeout story.

"Oh, this is a good one," he said with a chuckle. "We'd gotten a tip that the train conductor kept a rifle in the cab, and he was shooting deer on his nightly route and driving back afterward to get them. So we snuck onto the train, and being young and foolish like yourself, we thought the best place to hide was amongst the pulp logs because we could look out if shots were fired. Of course, it wasn't the brightest thing to do because we'd have gotten pancaked if the logs shifted in transit." Being the storyteller that he was, John paused for a moment to let the danger sink in. "But lemme tell you, it was colder than a witch's . . ."

John's story trailed off as we both tuned into the washing sound of a vehicle cruising along the pavement. Headlights soon flooded the road as a full-size truck slowly passed the field. At this time of day, it's easy to tell the poachers from the early commuters because they're the only ones driving *under* the speed limit. My heart practically skipped a beat when the red brake lights glowed and the truck stopped on the shoulder of the road.

"Showtime," John said as if I wasn't already clinging to the edge of my seat.

Using binoculars, I watched the driver get out of the truck with a rifle and walk back to the field. He was a tall man with broad shoulders and a thick chest—probably a construction worker or someone employed in a trade, likely leaving early for the job site to give himself extra time in case he got lucky on the way. A short distance into the field, he raised the rifle to his shoulder, and even though I was expecting it, the booming explosion gave me a jolt. His second shot knocked the doe decoy over.

Knowing the gig was about to be up when the man realized that the fawn didn't move, John immediately started the truck and goosed the accelerator. Our hearts sunk at the whirling sound of the back tires spinning out. The poacher heard us, and he started running back to his truck.

Before John could say anything, I leaped out of the cab and barreled across the field. My heart felt like it was going to pound out of my chest. The cold air stung my cheeks, and the crisp grass crunched like potato chips with each step in rapid-fire succession as I closed in on the poacher.

"Stop!" I yelled at the top of my lungs. "Game warden!"

But here's the thing: I wasn't a game warden. I wasn't even a trainee. I was a student at Unity College, invited by John for ride-alongs to see if I wanted to pursue a warden career. As you might guess, chasing-down an armed poacher who probably had forty pounds on me in the wee hours of the morning wasn't exactly within bounds of departmental policy. As the term "ride-along" implies, my butt should have been planted in the front seat where there was less risk of being shot, stabbed, or pounded to a pulp. But the rules with John were, well, *different*.

Young and foolish? You bet!

I grabbed the man by the shoulders and spun him around, ready for anything—except, perhaps, what happened next. He turned to me and dropped his head, taking a sudden interest in his boot laces. There was a foul stench, and I realized that he soiled himself. Fortunately, I didn't have to guard him long before John arrived with his truck. John told the poacher that we'd take him to Waldo County Jail, and he let the guy sit in his own truck while he called it in. John's plan was for the poacher to ride with him and for me to drive the guy's truck to what John called "the crowbar motel." I could see steam rising out of the cab of the poacher's truck, so I reminded John that he had a load in his pants.

"Good point," John said. "Plan B is we'll let him drive his truck. He's already sitting in it."

On our way to the jail, John gave me a high five and said, "That was unbelievable. You literally scared the crap out of him!" He continued to rib me for it. After my upbringing, I can't even begin to tell you how great it felt to get positive reinforcement—even in the form of good-natured teasing—from a male role model.

This experience was hardly an isolated example of finding myself in the middle of the action during ride-alongs with John. On another occasion, we received a tip from an informant that a husband and wife team of night hunters had just shot a deer. We caught up to their car as it cruised past the field and pulled it over. The wife was driving, but the husband wasn't in the vehicle. John instructed *me* to search the car for firearms and ammunition while he took the wife aside for questioning. I rifled through it, finding an abundance of trash—empty cigarette packs, disposable coffee mugs, fast-food bags stuffed with greasy wrappers and french fry containers—but no evidence.

Borrowing John's baton-length, six-cell Maglite, I expanded the search into the field. As I combed back and forth through the knee-deep grass, I thought about using the Maglite as a weapon if the husband got a jump on me. Close to a hundred yards from the road, I found the deer. It was a good-size doe, around a hundred and fifty pounds. The deer's chest cavity had been cut open, but the poacher hadn't fully extracted its innards. At this distance from the road, he likely snuck into the field to shoot the deer and was probably in the process of dressing it when we arrived. This scenario meant that if we found the guy, he'd likely have blood evidence on him. Excited to share my discovery with John, I ran back to the truck.

"Great work," he said, those two words swelling me with pride. John then handed me his twelve-gauge pump-action shotgun. "Take this and lay down in the field next to the deer. Don't let anyone touch it."

"Okay," I said, eager to carry out his instruction.

As I laid on my back in the field next to the deer, watching my breath rise slowly into mushroom clouds, it occurred to me that the shooter likely hadn't gone far. What would I do if he came back? There was no way I had the authority to apprehend anyone—especially at gunpoint. What if he drew a weapon on me? Today, this kind of thing would be a sure-fire lawsuit. But at the time, I forced myself to push those thoughts aside. For that moment, I was a game warden with a job to do—even if I wasn't.

I was suddenly hyper-aware of the sounds around me—a rustle in the grass, an acorn knocking into branches as it fell within the ghostly trees, the who-who-who hooting of a great-horned owl in the distance. Later in my career, I'd learn that wardens develop a fine-tuned skillset for nighttime observation. I don't know if there's anything to this, but I like to think that we unlock dormant traits in our DNA.

The poacher never returned to the deer that night, but the Warden Service apprehended him with a K-9 team in the morning. For me, it didn't matter. An addiction hooked me as I laid in the field alive with anticipation, tuned into nature's frequency, adrenaline coursing through my veins. The natural high from the thrill of the chase was ten times more potent than any drug I'd experienced. And to think people got paid for this!

At some point, John asked me what I thought of the ride-alongs. "Do you want to become a game warden?"

I couldn't help but laugh. Did I!

What I didn't realize at the time was that getting the Maine Warden Service to want *me* was a different story altogether. That's a lesson I learned the hard way.

"You're not gonna have any friends," my old poaching buddies said when I was home on college break and telling them about my desire to become a game warden. "They'll do a background check," they warned. "You're toast." While I didn't want to hear it, they had a strong point. "Besides, you won't have any time to go hunting or fishing yourself." Another hard truth. They also wouldn't have been my friends without busting my chops. "What are you gonna do, arrest yourself?"

Despite the peanut gallery's well-placed skepticism, I wasn't easily deterred. What they didn't understand was that I'd experienced the thrill of the chase, and I was addicted. In a way, I was lucky. While most of my friends had no idea what they wanted to do for work, I'd found my calling. For me, it was game warden or bust—there was no fallback plan. Of course, there was also the high risk that I was attempting to open a locked door. I refused to nurture that thought, but they'd planted the seed of doubt in the back of my mind.

From talking with John, I had insight into the application process for becoming a game warden. It began with a hundred-and-fifty-question written entrance exam, followed by the physical test and the oral board. The physical consisted of a mile and a half run, sit-ups, bench press (or sometimes push-ups), and a timed, two-hundred-yard swim—the requirements for each varied depending on the participant's age, gender, and weight. Aspiring wardens had to pass the physical and have a combined written and oral test score in the ninetieth percentile or above to proceed to the background investigation and polygraph. The final stage for those invited after the polygraph was an interview with the Colonel.

As a two-sport high-school athlete who was still in good shape, I knew the physical requirements would be easy for me. Not to brag, but I could do eighty-two push-ups in a minute when the benchmark for me was thirty-eight. There was one exception in my ability to pass the physical—swimming. In the water, I sunk like a rock. So I started training by regularly going to the YMCA or area ponds and lakes. It was hard work, but at least it was something I could prepare myself for to alter the result—unlike the polygraph.

The first time I applied for the Maine Warden Service was in 1985 while still enrolled at Unity. I knew the competition would be stiff, but I was shocked to learn there were two thousand applicants! These days, we're lucky if a hundred people try out. I passed the physical (I vomited after the swim); however, I scored in the eighty-ninth percentile of the combined written and oral exam, just missing the cut. Getting so close to passing was frustrating, but John reassured me that the chances of advancing on my first attempt were worse than fishing in a puddle, so I chalked it up as a learning experience overall.

In December of 1986, I finished my associate's degree at Unity. I immediately took a job as a corrections officer at the Maine State Prison in Thomaston as I awaited another opportunity to apply for the Warden Service. What's more, Gail and I were engaged to get married that May, so we needed the money.

My second chance at the Warden Service's entrance exam came in 1987. Over two thousand and six hundred applicants applied this time, but I scored within the ninetieth percentile and advanced to the background and polygraph process. I can't even begin to describe how nervous I was getting hooked up to the polygraph machine. I felt sick to my stomach as they wrapped cold cords around my torso that reminded me of a blood-pressure band, along with clasps on my pointer fingers. All I could think about was the questions I was about to get. I told myself to be honest and let the chips fall where they may. The worst thing I could do was get caught lying.

The interview started simple enough: What was my name? Where was I from? Where did I go to college? All questions intended to calm me down and set a baseline. And then they cut to the chase.

"Have you ever committed a crime?"

It was suddenly boiling in the room, the same one used for interrogations, and I could see myself sweating in the two-way mirror as I wondered if anyone was watching on the other side. I felt like a criminal.

"Yes," I said.

As you might imagine, it wasn't a simple yes or no question, and my answer led to a series of follow-up inquiries that weren't favorable for my chances. I answered them all with complete honesty—the laundromat heist, the drug dealing, the drug usage, and the part I was most nervous about, the poaching. Five and a half hours later, I emerged from the State Police crime lab, my integrity intact but feeling like a wretched human being. The low-life sensation lingered for several weeks as I waited on pins and needles for the results. Every day after work at the prison, I rushed home to check the mail. When the letter from warden headquarters in Augusta finally came, I ripped into the envelope like a kid opening birthday presents.

My eyes fixated on the intoxicating first sentence. It went something to the effect of: "*Congratulations on passing the polygraph exam.*" Elated, I shouted for Gail to come quickly.

"What's the matter?" she asked in a hurried voice as she rushed into the room. Then she noticed what I was holding. "You got the letter—what does it say?"

"I passed the polygraph."

"That's great!"

"No . . ." I said, reading on and suddenly feeling sucker-punched. "It's not."

I handed her the letter. I was so devastated that I couldn't find the words to say they weren't inviting me to the final interview.

"I don't get it," she said.

I slumped into a chair at the kitchen table and put my head in my hands.

"They don't want me."

"What I mean is, I don't get the end of the letter, where they wish you good luck on your future endeavors. Does that mean you can't apply again?"

"I don't know."

It was a good question, so I called Augusta and asked. "Try again," they simply told me. It was the right answer, but it wasn't reassuring. Would passing the tests again yield a different result? Was I just wasting my time? After all, I couldn't change my past.

"Maybe this isn't what the Lord wants for us," Gail said.

"What else is there?"

No disrespect to the men and women who make good for themselves with careers as corrections officers, but I was born to be outside. Working at Thomaston suited me fine as a temporary gig when I could daydream of becoming a game warden. Take that away, and I was no better off than an inmate committed to the prison for life thanks to my previous sins. It was game warden or bust, and I felt busted.

"You know," Gail said, "Maine isn't the only state with game wardens."

She was right. In 1988, I tested for the New Hampshire Warden Service and scored high enough to earn an interview with the Major and the Colonel. My oldest daughter, Amanda, was born by that point, so there was some extra pressure as I took a seat in the conference room. It was a big room for just three people, and it felt like I was stranded alone on my side of the long mahogany table. That said, the Major and the Colonel quickly put me at ease. I'd scored within the top five of their candidates, and it was clear from their expressions that they were excited to talk. The beginning of the discussion seemed more like a recruitment pitch than an interview, but then they asked about drug use, and I told them the truth. Their approving smiles melted into disappointment.

I thought of my father on the drive home from Concord, New Hampshire. He must have been terribly conflicted on that fateful day when he tearfully apologized for everything he'd done over a game of pool with my sister. Even if he was genuinely remorseful for his crimes and the way he'd fractured our family, he also had to know there was no going back. He was trapped long before the police surrounded the apartment building.

While I came to my senses much sooner than he did—all of my transgressions occurred when I was a minor—I still couldn't escape my past. That seed of doubt originally lingering in the back of my mind matured into full bloom, fear of wasting my time now possessing a stranglehold on my thoughts. But like all addictions, quitting my dream of becoming a warden wasn't easy. Throughout my attempts to get hired and my daughter's birth, I continued doing ride-alongs with John and other local wardens. I was gaining knowledge and experience, so I figured that I might as well try again. When I took the entrance exam for a third time in 1989, competing with over two thousand applicants, I scored in the ninety-sixth percentile. Once again, I submitted to the marathon polygraph test, but this time I was invited back for the final interview.

It was another large conference room in a nondescript concrete government building. This time, interviewers outnumbered me four-to-one. Colonel Larry Cummings and Major Bill Vernon were there, along with a lieutenant and a civilian. I was so nervous that I forgot their names as soon as I shook their hands. "Terrified" doesn't even begin to describe my mental state. In a matter of minutes, I completely sweated through my three-piece navy suit as they fired scenarios at me. From the ride-alongs, I had a strong sense of what the Warden Service's policies and procedures were *supposed* to be, and I gained confidence as the interview went along. As our scheduled hour came to a close, Colonel Cummings cleared his throat to ask the final question.

"You've done well in the application process," he said, but I'd come to expect disappointment, so I sensed the "but" coming. "*But*, you have a checkered past, and we're interviewing twenty-five qualified people for ten open positions. Why should we take a chance on you over the other twenty-four candidates?"

I hid my hands under the table so they couldn't see them shaking. "Sir," I said with the frightening realization that the entire interview and everything I'd done to get into the Warden Service came down to this one make-or-break question. "This is my third time applying to the

Warden Service over the past four years. During this time, I've gone on countless ride-alongs, many times staying out all night before having to go to school or work in the morning. I've loved every minute of it, and I can't imagine a career doing anything else. If you give me a chance, I promise I'll be one of the best wardens in the state."

Three weeks later, I received a call from Sergeant Bill Allen. Not only did Bill have a starring role in many of John's stories, but he also instructed one of my classes at Unity, and I'd gotten to know him personally. The fact that he was responsible for training new Warden Service recruits put a baseball-sized lump in my throat as we exchanged pleasantries.

"Congratulations," he told me. "You're hired."

Sergeant Allen went on to explain when I'd report to the police academy for training, but honestly, everything else he said on that call was a complete blur. I couldn't wait to tell Gail the good news.

3

A PROMISE TO KEEP

"You're gonna catch some *real* poachers tonight," Warden Brian Worth told me. "Unlike your classmates—all of them are out writing ATV tickets!"

I was a rookie warden fresh out of the academy, temporarily working as a floater in a large area ranging from Unity to Skowhegan until I received my permanent district assignment. As is the case for all new wardens, I was also on probation for the first year on the job. Brian was a seasoned warden, and during my training, he'd played the role of a drunk smelter yelling obscenities and looking to fight. I quickly learned that his gruff personality and penchant for colorful language wasn't an act. For what he actually said to me that night, simply add several words you wouldn't say in front of your mother to his speech above.

"Yes, sir," I said as if we were still at the academy. He was intimidating, and if I could have physically turtled my head into a shell, I would have.

We were in Augusta in mid-summer. The Kennebec River was low, causing Atlantic salmon to stack up like cordwood in a spring pool as they tried to obtain what little cold water and oxygen they could to survive. It was easy snagging for poachers who were sneaking down to the river at night and using large treble hooks with extra weights to foul hook the helpless salmon. According to the information we'd received, one poacher had already caught twenty-five fish that he was trying to sell to local stores and restaurants. Our plan was for Brian and Warden Lloyd Perkins to set up surveillance across the river from the spring pool while

Sergeant Lowell Thomas and I waited in a parking lot in the middle of the city to get called into action.

"This shouldn't take long," Sergeant Thomas told me as we pulled into an empty parking lot behind a large brick building. It was a humid night, and our clothes stuck to our bodies as if they were vacuum-sealed. Staring into the yellow glow of a nearby streetlight, wishing there was a breeze as we watched cars drive by, it felt more like a police stakeout than a Warden Service operation. Fortunately, Sergeant Thomas was right about the anticipated timeline. It wasn't even a half-hour before the radio crackled with news that our suspects had arrived at the pool. Minutes later, they'd already snagged and bagged a salmon, signaling it was time for us to move in.

Sergeant Thomas drove us to a side street near the river. We were in the midst of a long dry spell, making it impossible to sneak quietly down the riverbank. In addition to the sticks and dried undergrowth that crunched with each step, there were tons of bottles, trash, and broken glass to help sound the alarm.

"They're bound to hear us coming," Sergeant Thomas whispered to me. "If they do, follow my lead. We'll need to close the gap between them and us in case they run."

I nodded, more concerned with containing my heavy breathing. I'd spent so much time in ride-alongs dreaming of this moment that my enthusiasm was blazing at full throttle while my nerves tried in vain to pump the brakes. If I messed up the operation in front of three experienced wardens, I'd be back to writing ATV tickets!

As we neared the river, I could hear the thwacking sound of a large salmon slapping its tail on the ground. Then one of us—maybe me, I honestly don't even know—snapped a stick.

"Hey," one of the poachers yelled, "who's out there?"

"It's just Steve," Sergeant Thomas shouted back. He began walking purposefully toward the pool. As instructed, I followed his lead.

"Steve who?" the poacher asked.

"Game warden!" we both yelled in unison, shining our flashlights on their startled faces. It was my first bust, and I was still grinning from ear to ear the next day when Warden Timothy Peabody photographed me with the seized salmon before placing them into the evidence freezer.

As the summer of 1990 came to an end, I was assigned the Lincoln District, which included Howland, Enfield, Chester, Woodville, and several unorganized townships. This posting caused many senior wardens to raise their eyebrows as they tried to provide me with a fair warning.

"Be careful," they said. "That's a mill town—those boys play hard."

They weren't kidding.

I quickly learned that the mill workers earned salaries that allowed them to buy all the toys they wanted—guns, ATVs, boats, and trucks. Their swing shift schedules also permitted playtime at all hours, day and night. In an area surrounded by wilderness further than the eye can see, the only real entertainment was outdoor recreation activities, and it wasn't uncommon for them to bring their favorite thirty-pack of beer along for the fun. Thus, they played hard. It was a tough assignment for a new warden, but I'd made a promise to the Colonel to be the best warden I could be, and I intended to fulfill that pledge.

It wasn't exactly easy sledding. Changes were afoot in the Warden Service that impacted our job performance. The most consequential was a crackdown on overtime hours. When my class was sworn in, Colonel Cummings told us directly, "If any of you are caught working more than eight hours in a day, you will be fired." It was an odd thing to get told when we were pledging fealty to the warden creed, a portion of which states: *I will wage unceasing war against violation of the fish and game law in every form and will consider no sacrifice too great in the performance of my duty.*

From an administrative standpoint, the eight-hour-a-day rule made sense. Limiting overtime enabled warden leadership to preserve the budget for critical search and rescue situations. For district wardens such as myself, most of us didn't care too much about getting paid overtime—we were more than happy to work extra hours without additional pay to catch bad guys, but this wasn't permitted either for our safety.

Like any great team, the Maine Warden Service is comprised of men and women with various talents. Some wardens are exceptional woodsmen, while others excel at communicating with the public, reading a suspect's body language, or leading a K-9 search. We all bring something to the team. But the one trait all wardens must possess when catching bad guys, especially night hunters, is a do-whatever-it-takes, bulldog mentality. Quite often, being in the right place at the right time is a matter of sitting out all night, every night. So while the eight-hour rule may sound like common sense, for the older generation of wardens who were accustomed to making their own schedules, the change was earth-shattering. It propelled many senior wardens, such as my mentor, John Ford, into retirement.

For me, I'd become addicted to the cat-and-mouse game of nabbing poachers under John's tutelage. I knew what "the good ol' days" were like, but I was required to march to a different drumbeat. It's as if I finally made the football team, only to have the coach announce that we were playing two-hand touch from now on. That said, I was a new warden on probation. I couldn't afford to even think about breaking the rules— especially since I had a healthy fear of my lieutenant.

I first met Lieutenant Langdon Chandler upon my assignment to the Lincoln district. When I walked into his Bangor office, my initial reaction was that he looked like an administrator. He was short (we called him Smally) with a receding hairline graying on the side and a small paunch that came with the territory of working a desk job.

"You're late," he snapped without the slightest inclination to shake my hand. I looked at my watch—*I'm five minutes early*. He must have known what I was thinking. "In my division, if you aren't at least fifteen minutes early, you're late. Got it?"

"Yes, sir."

"Good. Now," Chandler said without inviting me to sit down, "I don't like to do this because new wardens are notoriously hard on their vehicles, but trucks are assigned to districts, not wardens, so you'll be getting a brand new GMC."

Nervous, I couldn't help but smile.

"I don't know what you're smiling about. You're gone if you so much as put a scratch on that truck."

He went on to warn me about the eight-hour rule and detail all of the other ways I could get fired before coming off probation. It was a long, rough conversation, but over time I learned that there was a method to his madness and the hardline introduction was for my own good. Once I proved myself as a worker bee, the gruff facade melted away, and Lieutenant Chandler was a fair leader who went to bat for me on many occasions. Getting to this point, however, took some time.

While following the eight-hour rule, my first year in the Lincoln district started slowly with few night-hunting arrests. Then I realized that if I couldn't outwork the poachers, I had to get crafty. Literally. I made a decoy partridge out of burdock and dried flowers. When using a decoy, my rule was that it had to look real enough for me to shoot it. The brown, clingy, round burdock burrs held together nicely in the shape of a plump bird, and the flowers added the right accents for the lighter-colored feathers on the chest and wings. From fifteen yards away, the burdock bird was spot-on. I deployed it on a woods road where I suspected people were hunting illegally, and—I kid you not—every vehicle that noticed the bird had someone dangerously fire a shotgun out the window.

The best part about the burdock bird is that shotgun pellets mostly passed through it. All I had to do was some light remodeling after each shot, and the bird was ready for action. I was barely able to write the tickets fast enough. It was unbelievable. The only sad part was that I rarely had someone get out of their vehicle to take a legal shot. I continued to rack up citations with the burdock bird, and news of my success traveled fast through the warden ranks. Lieutenant Chandler was even allegedly boasting about it to the other division leaders. If he was starting to like me, it wasn't long before I tested his confidence.

District wardens typically collaborate and work together, especially during hunting season when we develop "fall partnerships" to catch night hunters. One day early in my Lincoln tenure, I was riding with David Crocker, a senior warden I had an immense amount of respect for because he was a genuinely nice guy, and he'd apprehended countless poachers over the years. He worked the district to the northeast of Lincoln that included small communities such as Winn, Prentiss, and Springfield, and he was showing me around his area in mid-day to familiarize me with it. It struck me how loaded his district was with farms—and where there are farms, there are night hunters working the fields.

"The boys over here don't stop night hunting until there's snow on the ground," David said in response to my observation. "Hunting season doesn't matter to them when they're hunting illegally to begin with, but snow ends their fun because it's too easy for us to collect evidence."

This realization got my gears grinding. It was a week after the season, and we still didn't have any snow. A full moon was coming on Friday, and the forecast called for a bitter cold but clear evening. The local boys knew we worked hard throughout the hunting season, and they were probably expecting us to take a much-needed break. Add the natural light from the moon, and from a poacher's perspective, you couldn't imagine a better scenario.

"I bet we can catch some guys by surprise if we work the fields in your district Friday night," I said.

"I'd love to, but I'm off."

Sadly, David's wife had succumbed to cancer at a young age, making him a single parent with two teenage daughters, so I didn't push because I knew how valuable his time off was.

"You're welcome to work my district without me," he offered. "I bet the poachers will be out, especially if they drive by my house and see that I'm home, which I know they do."

Excited to nail some bad guys, I later called my sergeant, Mike Marshall, to see if he'd work David's district with me. Mike was responsible for ensuring we were doing our best to catch poachers. Bragging rights were also on the line—it's putting it lightly to say that conviction tallies are competitive between wardens and divisions. But Mike was also in the unenviable position of keeping us from working too hard by enforcing the eight-hour rule. It was counterproductive, but his response wasn't a surprise.

"Yes, but we have to clock out by midnight."

"Don't worry, Sergeant, we won't break curfew."

After John Ford retired, I inherited one of his masterpiece deer decoys under the stipulation that I had to make him proud by catching night hunters with it. I gladly accepted, realizing that I was developing a list of promises to keep.

We brought the decoy with us that night to a cut clover hayfield in Webster Plantation. The field was glazed white with frost, so I walked around the woods and approached it from the back to avoid leaving visible tracks while setting up the decoy. The tricky thing with using a one-dimensional decoy is placement. Too close to the road and it's easy to tell that it's a fake deer through a scope. Too far away and it's hard to spot with the naked eye when someone drives past. Then there's the moon's rotation to contend with to make sure the natural light is shining on it *just right*. I kept running out to reposition the decoy throughout the night as Mike directed me with hand signals from the road.

I was the wheelman, which is to say I was driving. I'd backed my new truck into the woods, careful not to scratch it on any trees, Lieutenant Chandler's threat still fresh in my mind. We covered the truck with a forest green parachute so light wouldn't reflect off its chrome, and Mike and I stood beside it, playing the waiting game. As the twinkling constellations floated across the sky, I started to lose conviction in my plan. Nights that we work fields and come away empty-handed far outweigh those where we catch poachers, so there's always a point where we have to call it quits. The temperatures were in the single digits on this evening, and like batteries in the cold, our enthusiasm depleted faster because of it.

We climbed back into the truck to warm up, and I noticed on the dashboard clock that it was almost midnight. *This is it*, I thought, *Mike's going to call it*. But we got to talking. While Mike and I have very different backgrounds, we're both Christian, and we found that we had more in common than we knew as we delved into deep conversations about faith and family. Even so, I kept stealing glances at the clock, waiting for him to say something. To my surprise, midnight came and went without a word.

Around twelve-thirty, the sound of an approaching vehicle ended our conversation. I shut off the truck, and we both climbed out to watch. The vehicle was approaching from the far side of the road, but the trees blocked our view of it. All we saw were beams of light bouncing off the branches above our heads. A bright spotlight was then cast upon the decoy as if it took center stage in a school play. It was dead quiet, and the subsequent rifle shot rang out so loud it sounded like a cannon. We sprang into action, tearing the parachute off the truck and leaving it in the woods to retrieve later.

"Let's go!" Mike barked as we climbed into the truck. An all-around great guy and a Scout leader who obtained the Eagle rank as a teenager, Mike is typically soft-spoken and mild-mannered. To see his eyes burn with intensity and hear the sudden agitation in his voice caught me by surprise and added to the pressure in the heat of the moment.

"I'm trying," I said, struggling to get the keys out of my pocket.

"Why didn't you leave the keys in the ignition?"

"I don't know!" It was a rookie mistake, and I instantly felt stupid, realizing that every second wasted was time for the poachers to escape. It seemed like I fumbled with the keys for an eternity.

"C'mon, c'mon!"

One thing was for certain—I'd never make this mistake again. Fortunately, it didn't end our pursuit. I finally got the truck started and drove out of the field onto Tucker Ridge Road without turning on my headlights.

"There they are," Mike said as soon as we hit the pavement.

Even though their headlights were on, I was able to drive up nose-to-nose with their three-quarter-ton Ford F-250 without them realizing we'd arrived. It was almost comical watching three guys sitting in a row on a bench seat in their cab break the law from up close. They didn't notice us because the driver was busy aiming a rifle out of his window while the right-side passenger shined a spotlight over the roof. It felt like we were at a drive-in theater—only missing a bag of popcorn—as the men became even more animated when the decoy didn't budge from the second shot. They must have thought it was the dumbest deer on this side of Bangor!

All three poachers jumped in a synchronized freak-out when I turned on my headlights and the blue law-enforcement strobe light. The driver swore as he pulled the rifle in and handed it to the middle passenger. Mike launched out of my truck, and I quickly followed. The shooter put his vehicle in reverse and started to back away as Mike pounded on the driver-side door, yelling at him to stop. I threw my Maglite at their windshield to mark the truck. It smashed off the glass with a loud crack as they sped away from us.

"Looks like we're going for a ride!" I yelled to Mike.

We ran back to my truck as the poachers turned their vehicle around. Siren blaring and blue lights flashing—my first high-speed chase was on, kicking my adrenaline into overdrive. It was amazing how we'd gone from hours of boredom to instant chaos!

"Dispatch, this is twenty-two, nineteen," I practically shouted into the radio microphone while holding the steering wheel with one hand. "We're engaged in a high-speed chase, headed north on the Tucker Ridge Road in Webster Plantation." Accelerator to the floor, we'd quickly gotten up over seventy miles per hour and were closing in on eighty. It was dangerously fast for a narrow country road that thread like a needle around winding curves walled with trees flashing past in a blur and across stretches of farmhouse fields. "The vehicle is a newer model Ford two-fifty, dark blue with a crack in the windshield." I went on to provide the license plate number.

There was no response from the Orono dispatch. I repeated my message and again didn't hear back. After reciting the plate number for the third time, Lincoln Police Officer Michael Knights came on and asked dispatch if they received my radio traffic. Orono finally acknowledged the chase, and they started informing area troopers.

"I got a good look at the driver," Mike said to me. "That's Danny Cabot from Lee. He's well known to law enforcement as a convicted felon and suspected drug dealer."

"Then he just committed another felony by possessing and shooting a firearm," I said.

"You got it."

"We can't let him get away," I said, more to myself than anything, realizing that the ante on our chase had just gone up.

At the end of the Tucker Ridge Road, Cabot turned north onto Route 170, but not long afterward, he put his blinker on and pulled over to the side of the road along an open field. Surprised that he was giving up, I breathed a sigh of relief and parked behind him, maintaining a vehicle-and-a-half length between us as was protocol. Mike reported that we'd stopped to dispatch, and I could see Cabot watching us in his rearview mirror as we climbed out of my truck.

Cabot's reverse lights suddenly glowed white and the back tires started spinning, kicking dirt toward the front of his truck. I beat Mike back to our truck, and I put it into reverse, thinking that Cabot was trying to ram his larger vehicle into my radiator to disable it. But Cabot had worse intentions. Before I could back away, he turned his truck and sliced it down the passenger side of mine, trying to take Mike out. Everything was happening so fast, but it also seemed to be in slow motion. I felt paralyzed amid the smashing sound of his truck grinding down mine, concaving the passenger door like a beer can.

Mike was in the truck, but I didn't know if he was hurt. I jammed the gear shift into drive and floored it. We sat in stunned silence for well over a minute as our truck excelled to over ninety miles per hour, maintaining a close distance to Cabot.

"Did he get you?" I yelled over the siren, fearing his leg was pinned against the door.

"I'm okay," he said in a sobering tone that lacked emotion. Mike picked the radio mic off the floor and informed dispatch that the chase was back on, heading north on 170 toward Kingman.

Cabot turned right onto a side road when we reached Kingman, followed by another right-hand turn that had us heading back toward 170. As he slowed to make the left onto 170, I seized the opportunity to perform a pit maneuver, a technique where the front of the pursuing vehicle hits the back corner of the lead vehicle to spin it sideways in the road. I'd observed this technique at the academy, but I'd never done one myself, so I didn't know how it would go with full-sized trucks. Cabot's tires screeched across the pavement, and his vehicle went sideways as I rammed into it. He over-corrected, and his truck started going sideways in the other direction, sliding toward a trailer house near the road. I hit the brakes and backed off to keep from hitting him again and pushing his truck into the trailer. Cabot regained control and, realizing we'd nearly gotten him, increased his speed to over a hundred miles per hour.

Mike updated Orono to let them know we were now traveling south on 170. "We just bumped them," he tactfully explained.

"Bumped them?" I yelled. "We rammed them!"

As much as my adrenaline was filling me with spit and vinegar, I was also incredibly nervous that one of us was going to crash at these speeds. Route 170 crosses the Mattawamkeag River twice where we were and has its fair share of corners. Cabot had a distinct home-field advantage. He knew the area like the back of his hand, but I was a fish out of water in an unfamiliar district, traveling many of these roads for the first time. I prayed that we didn't encounter a high school kid driving home late at night.

When Cabot turned left onto the Osgood Road in Prentiss, he further pressed his advantage by shutting off his lights and using the moonlight to navigate. Osgood was a gravel road, making matters worse by creating a dust plume that trailed his truck like a comet tail. I tried to maintain a three-second difference between our vehicles per my training, but this safety precaution wasn't created with dirt roads in mind. The distance caused my headlights to reflect off the dust as if I was driving in a dense fog. At the speed we were going, it was suicidal. The next thing I knew, the road before me disappeared. Late on a turn, I cut the wheel sharply, and for a split second, I felt helpless as we fishtailed around the corner. I winced, expecting the back end of the truck to crack into a tree. Miraculously, it didn't. I spun the wheel back, regaining control.

"That was close!" I shouted.

"Yep," Mike said, deadpan.

We came to the end of Osgood Road, where Cabot's dust trail swept left onto Route 171 toward the township of Drew. He'd turned his lights back on, but he was far enough ahead of us by this point that we only caught fleeting glimpses of his taillights on long stretches.

"Can this thing go any faster?" Mike asked.

Is he crazy, I thought, *every corner is a near-death experience!* The speedometer on my truck only went up to ninety-five miles per hour, but the needle was pinned as far as it would go.

"I have it floored," I told him.

The intense adrenaline rush of the chase started to wear on me. I was sweating like crazy, and I could feel myself overheating as if I was running a fever. Wiping my palms on my pants to dry them, I took several deep breaths to calm my engines. Out of the corner of my eye, I thought I saw a plume of dust on a side road as we shot past.

"Did you see that?" I asked.

"See what?"

"A dust cloud on that road?"

Mike hesitated, which drove my internal thermometer back toward its boiling point. We were flying down Route 171 at over a hundred miles an hour. If Cabot turned, every second that passed significantly increased the distance between us. On the other hand, if the dust cloud was a figment of my imagination and we went back for nothing, Cabot was home free.

"I didn't," Mike finally answered, "but there's no sign of them in front of us anymore, either. You better turn around."

I shut my siren and blue strobe lights off and turned around. The dirt road was at least a mile away, and when we got back to it, there was no sign of dust in the air. I doubted myself—*maybe it was mist*—but we were committed at this point. There was no choice but to take the road. I felt sick to my stomach at the idea of the poachers getting away. Even though we had a plate number and the vehicle was damaged, it would be hard to prove who was in the truck if we didn't apprehend them. The thought also occurred to me that this might be the last ride of my warden career. I was still on probation, the passenger-side door of my new truck was smashed shut, and there was no telling how much damage the front sustained when I rammed Cabot's vehicle. So much for not getting a scratch!

After driving for about five minutes down the side road, we came around a bend and found Cabot's truck idling in the middle of the road. His elbow was hanging out the driver's window, and I realized they were listening for my siren. *Good thing I shut it off!* All of a sudden, we were off to the races again. Mike updated Orono on our status, letting them know that we were on a woods road somewhere in the township of T4R8.

This time I kept to Cabot's bumper to avoid getting lost in his dust cloud again. Cabot tried shutting his lights off, but I was on him like flies on stink. He then turned onto a rutted, two-track woods road, its deep grooves loaded with rocks and frozen-over pits of mud. Again, his knowledge of the area came into play as he took advantage of having the bigger truck by trying to get me stuck. I feared it was going to work. Our high-speed chase considerably lost speed, but forty on this skidder road had our heads knocking into the ceiling. Ahead of us, the passengers in Cabot's truck were also bouncing around like crickets in a jar.

Cabot spun through a washed-out section of the road, raining clumps of mud onto our windshield. I turned on the wipers and wash, and for a moment, I couldn't see anything through the cloudy smudge. Then a streak cleared, and I saw his truck turn slightly sideways. Recognizing an opportunity to wedge him in the narrow road, I floored it.

"Don't hit him again!" Mike yelled.

It was too late.

The hood of my truck folded up on impact. My body shot forward like a slingshot and was whipped back by the seat belt. Everything in the cab—from my Delorme map to our empty coffee cups—went airborne. Tethered by its coiled wire, the radio mic smacked the windshield and swung back against the dash.

But my strategy worked. Cabot's truck was turned sideways in the road, stuck. The doors opened, and the passengers clambered out to make a run for it. My head spinning, I tried to follow suit, but I'd thrown my Maglite at Cabot's truck before, and it took me a moment to dig through the flotsam to find my backup. I finally located it and took off at a dead sprint into the woods. After a beat, I stopped to catch my breath and listen for the poachers. My truck's blue strobe light was flashing through the trees like some twisted fair funhouse, and the siren was still blaring, making it near impossible to hear any stealth movements. Further muddling the situation, the police radio in my truck kept crackling with dispatch asking for "twenty-two, nineteen," my call number, and sirens blared in the distance from troopers trying to find our location.

Someone was running through the woods to my right. While it was hard to hear in general, the leaves underfoot were dry and frozen, making anyone hightailing it stand out like a black bear crashing through the woods.

"Hold it," I yelled, quickly closing the gap between us, "game warden!"

These guys were bad news. They'd taken us on a dangerous high-speed chase, and in trying to take Mike out with a truck, they were willing to go to any length to escape. Knowing they were likely armed, I wasn't about to allow them to do me harm. I cocked my arm to club the man with my Maglite, but I caught myself before following through, stopped by a badge on the man's shirt shining in the flashing blue light.

"It's me!" Mike shouted.

Before I could apologize for nearly cold-clocking him, another man was running. I gave chase, pursuing him to a fir thicket. We were beyond the flashing blue lights at this point, and while it was bright from the moonlight where I stood outside the thicket, it was pitch black inside. My badge and the other brass on my uniform sparkled like sequins in the light. Knowing I was an easy target, I drew my .357 revolver and pointed it into the darkness.

"Drop your weapon and come out," I yelled, my voice crackling from a mixture of nerves and adrenaline, "or I'll shoot." There was no response. I slowly circled the thicket, trying to spot the man. "C'mon now."

Mike gave up on the man he was pursuing, and he came running toward my location, slowing to a walk as he got closer.

"He's right here in this thicket," I told Mike.

"No," Mike calmly said from ten feet away, "I don't see anything."

I lowered my weapon, questioning myself. As any hunter knows, even a squirrel can sound like a big game animal in these conditions. I might have only heard what I was expecting to hear.

Then Mike dove onto the ground.

"Hold it," he shouted, "you're under arrest!"

I jumped on the pile, realizing that Mike saw the man the whole time and was bluffing—he even fooled me!

"I won't fight," the man at the bottom of the pile acquiesced. As we cuffed him, someone else took off behind us through the woods. I gave chase, but the troopers were closing in, and their sirens masked the commotion of the man fleeing. He eluded me—at least for that night. The man we caught was the ringleader, Danny Cabot. Through him and the evidence collected, we were able to identify and apprehend the other two poachers—one of whom was also a convicted felon. The guy who escaped at the end had laid on the floor of Cabot's truck when the foot chase began, waiting for us to clear the area before making his getaway.

I was on pins and needles for a couple of weeks after the chase. Given the damage to my new GMC, I was expecting Lieutenant Chandler to chew me out at the very least. Oddly, I never heard a word from him directly about it. Through back-channels, I did learn that he reported it to the other division leaders and the colonel as exemplary warden work.

While I like to think that my burdock bird helped earn me some benefit of the doubt with the lieutenant, I can say with certainty that it led to my closest fall partnership. David Georgia, a senior warden, impressed by the high volume of success I was having with the bird, wanted in on the action. He shared my addiction to catching poachers, and we became fast friends. Dave and I were inseparable during hunting season, spending more time together trying to catch poachers than we did with our families. That's one of the sad truths to being a game warden. Fortunately for me, Gail understood the commitment of my warden oath. Not all wardens are so lucky.

The 1991 hunting season was a turning point for Dave and me. My probationary period was over, and, seeing that nobody got fired from violating the eight-hour rule the previous year, wardens began pushing the limits. Before long, an unsaid, don't-ask, don't-tell policy was in place between district wardens and their sergeants. With the shackles off, Dave and I soared to the top of the night-hunting apprehension leaderboard. We caught and convicted over a hundred individuals in five years. One year, we nabbed thirty-two, a state record dating back to 1988 when the mandatory minimum sentence went from a five-hundred-dollar fine and two days in jail to a thousand dollars and three days in the slammer. As I write this, our record still stands.

There was no doubt in my mind that I was keeping my promises as a warden, but I still had a hard lesson to learn—there's a price for success.

4
RUFFLED FEATHERS

It was late September. A heavy frost was in the air, creating that "itch" for hard-core poachers. Likewise, I had the bug to bust them, but it was my night off, and despite Dave Georgia's best efforts to coerce me into sneaking out for a stakeout—something I was prone to do on my rest days—I had a commitment to keep. My two oldest, elementary school-aged daughters *loved* contemporary Christian music, and I promised to take them to a concert in Bangor. After full sets from two bands, several encores, endless shrieks and cheers from my girls, and a great memory of daddy-daughter time, it was well past midnight when we drove back into Lincoln.

My ears were still ringing from the concert, and my girls were fast asleep in the middle row of our family minivan when a silver Ford Ranger with a white cap on the bed pulled out in front of us. It proceeded to swerve like a snake down the road. Wardens have the same authority as police officers to apprehend traffic violations, and operating under the influence (OUI) convictions were a focus when I came into the service. After completing the police academy and warden school, they told us that we were more trained in OUI enforcement than any prior class.

"You will enforce OUIs, *or else*," our instructor said, point-blank.

We all knew what *or else* meant. I soon learned that the hard-nose directive was due to OUI enforcement being another new methodology that displeased the old-school wardens. For them, the standard procedure was to give intoxicated sportsmen a ride home. They saw the system-atic process for prosecuting OUI apprehensions and the voluminous paperwork that came with it as a time suck from their preferred work of enforcing fish and game laws. Many of them would tell you that they didn't become a game warden to be a police officer. However, their push-back was mostly because appreciative passengers often spilled the beans on poachers, so it was a win-win scenario for everyone. As a younger warden, I didn't see that I had a choice in the matter—enforce the law, *or else.*

It didn't take a trained eye to see that the guy driving the Ford Ranger was drunk off his keister. I had to do something before he caused an accident, but this was prior to cell phones, so there was no way to call it in. Driving the family minivan, I also lacked police lights or a siren. Even if I could get the truck to pull over by flashing my headlights, I was in plain clothes without my badge or service weapon. That's a situation that can go sideways quickly, and I wasn't willing to risk it with my girls in the back.

When the truck turned onto Transalpine Road, which I lived on, a plan formed. I pulled into my driveway and ran into the house, yelling to Gail (who, I'm obligated to point out, was fast asleep in bed) to retrieve the girls from the van because I had to catch a drunk who was going to get someone killed. Grabbing my badge and service weapon, I jumped into my truck and took off without putting my uniform on.

After several miles of high-speed driving down the road, there was no sign of the Ford Ranger. A pair of red taillights emerged in the distance, but I realized it was a full-size Chevy without a cab as I drew closer. This vehicle wasn't operating as erratically as the Ford, but it occasionally drifted over the centerline and onto the soft shoulder. *Is everyone drunk tonight*, I wondered, realizing it was thirsty Thursday at the bars in town. There was probable cause to conduct a law enforcement stop, but I wasn't sure it was worth risking a situation while I was in plain clothes. It appeared this guy was going to get home safely, and it was so late that the state troopers were likely off their shifts, so I was on my own.

The Chevy's left blinker came to life, and the truck turned into a driveway. I suddenly realized it was Frederick Hazard behind the wheel. Freddie was a big drinker and notorious poacher that I'd been after ever since getting the Lincoln district, but he was a wily old-timer who always seemed to slip through the cracks while others took the fall for deer that he shot. I stopped my truck just past the trailer house where he lived, which I knew was his daughter's place, to think through the situation. The opportunity to put some pressure on him seemed too good to be true, but Freddie had a reputation for being a nasty drunk. In the times we'd crossed paths, he was obstinate and argumentative. Now fueled with liquid muscle, he'd likely want a fight.

Here we go again, I thought as I backed my truck up, *another big mess I'm getting myself into*. I called my position into the State Police, catching the dispatcher by surprise because I wasn't signed in, and stepped out of my truck to confront Freddie.

"Game Warden Bill Livezey," I shouted to announce my presence. Freddie was walking up the ramp to his daughter's trailer, and while we were a good twenty feet apart, I could already smell the alcohol on his breath. "How much have you had to drink tonight, Freddie? Why don't you come back over here."

To my surprise, he dropped his head in defeat and shuffled toward me. This behavior was way out of character for Freddie. At the very least, I expected him to shout at me to get off the property.

How much had he been drinking?

Freddie took a circuitous route across the lawn to get to me, conspicuously staying away from his truck. Instinctively, I shined my flashlight into the bed and gasped at what I saw. The entire bed was wet with fresh blood, and a buck knife covered in blood, tallow, and deer hair was stuck in the tailgate. There was also an open white cooler with streaks of blood on the outside and what appeared to be a deer heart inside, along with two white trash bags dripping with blood that were filled with regular household waste.

"What's all this blood about?" I asked.

"Hmm," Freddie shrugged, standing nonchalantly before me with his hands in his Carhartt coat pocket. Average in height and build, he was in his early fifties with that tough, leathery complexion earned through decades of woodsmanship. His dark hair was greasy and slicked back as if he'd been wiping sweat from his forehead. "I dunno. Someone musta stole my truck while I was in the bar."

"Freddie, do you expect me to believe that someone stole your truck, shot a deer, left the heart in a cooler, and then returned the truck to you? All without you knowing?"

He took his time answering me, carefully concocting his story.

"I was in the bar for a few hours, and I had some beers, so how would I know if someone took my truck?"

"Where were the keys?"

"Above the visor."

Freddie had the shifty dark eyes of someone who knew his lie was weak.

"Show me your hands."

He'd washed them, but I noticed deer hair on his jeans.

"Don't move," I said as I went to search the cab. Fresh blood was smeared all over a new flashlight and the plastic packaging it came in, as well as on a single-shot, twelve-gauge shotgun laid across the passenger seat. Several rounds of slugs and buckshot were loose on the seat and dashboard.

"Is this your gun, ammo, and flashlight?" I asked.

"Yes."

"They're covered in blood—did the people who stole your truck also borrow your gun and flashlight?"

"Gee, I guess so." His answer was dripping with sarcasm.

"Who helped you with this?"

"I don't know whodunnit."

It was pointless to press him any further. He'd never tell me what happened or who was involved. That's how it worked with the older generation of poachers. While you could count on their kids, hopped up on drugs and who-knows-what to point fingers, guys like Freddie knew what comes around eventually goes around, and his lips were airtight. It's the reason he'd eluded getting arrested for game violations to this point. But this time, I had *him*. Even without the deer's body, it was a rock-solid case because there wasn't a defense attorney around who could argue that the deer survived without a heart.

I ran Freddie through some field sobriety tests, which he failed fantastically, and told him to put his hands behind his back. "You're under arrest for possession of a deer in closed season and operating under the influence." After reading him his Miranda rights, he had nothing to say, so I handcuffed Freddie and loaded him into my truck.

Warden Durward Humphrey from the Newport district, who happened to be up North visiting his father in the hospital and heard the radio chatter on his way home, offered to help me collect evidence. Together, we seized the cooler, flashlight, gun, and ammo. Noticing bloody paper towels in the trash, we took the bags, too. Freddie was processed at the Lincoln Police Department while Durward and I dug through the trash bags in an evidence room and found several pieces of mail containing the same woman's name but with different addresses. I knew Freddie didn't have a girlfriend, so there was a great chance that this woman was connected to his accomplices.

We found her in the system. According to her license, Mary Winnet was in her mid-forties, six-foot-two and close to two hundred and forty pounds, with brown hair and hazel eyes. There was just one problem—none of her addresses checked out.

"The story on her is that she has trouble making rent, so she bounces from one place to another," said a young Lincoln police officer who, at three in the morning, was happy for the entertainment. "Anyway, I wanted to let you know that Fred Hazard posted bail, and his daughter just picked him up."

"We might be out of luck," I said to Durward.

"Yep, they'll be two steps ahead of us now. No doubt Freddie has already called his buddies."

I rubbed my stinging eyes. "Let's regroup in the morning. Maybe there's something we're missing."

Durward came to my house the next morning, and we dug through the trash again. We weren't finding anything new, but then I got a call from Mike Knights, a friend of mine in the Lincoln Police department.

"Your adventure last night is the talk of the station this morning," Mike told me. "The woman you're looking for, I remember her getting kicked out of the Clay Trailer Park not too long ago. At the time, she was driving a red, two-door Mazda coupe."

It was a long shot, but Durward and I decided to take a drive through the trailer park as a last-ditch effort. To our surprise, we found a red Mazda coupe parked at a trailer. I got out to examine the car while Durward ran the plate.

"What are you doing?" a man in jeans and a Guns N' Roses T-shirt yelled at me from the doorframe of his trailer.

"Looking for the owner of this car."

"That's my car," he said in a heated tone. "What about it?"

"We're trying to find a tall woman who drives a car just like this."

"I'm obviously not her, and I live here alone."

"We understand. Sorry to bother you."

As we climbed back into the truck, the man came toward us, waving a hand in the air to get our attention.

"Wait a minute," he said, his demeanor completely changed. "Come to think of it, I've seen a woman driving a car like this around here. I think she's on lot fourteen."

"Okay," I said, taken aback by his sudden cooperation, "thanks for the help." After the man retreated to his trailer, I turned to Durward. "What are the odds there are two people here driving a red Mazda coupe?"

"Beats me. I'd be surprised if there's more than two in the county."

The driveway at lot fourteen was empty. At the front door, I smelled the lingering odor of recently smoked pot. There was no response when I knocked, but the locked padlock outside the door indicated nobody was home. Next to the trailer was a small white shed, and from the stoop, I could see a crimson smudge on the edge of the door.

"Does that look like a bloody handprint to you?" I asked Durward.

"Could be."

I walked over, and it was indeed a bloody smear with deer hair stuck to it.

"Bingo, we've got the right place." I knocked on the shed door and called out to anyone who might be inside, but there was no response.

"Well," Durward said, "let's go write a search warrant affidavit."

No sooner did he say this than a red Mazda coupe came into the driveway. A large woman in jeans and a pink shirt matching Mary Winnet's description scrambled out of the car and hastily strode toward us, a wild look in her eyes.

"Take it!" She exclaimed, gesticulating frantically with her hands. "Just take it! I want it out of my house."

"Mam," Durward tried to say, "Please calm—"

"My boyfriend Ronnie was out tying one on with Freddie Hazard last night, and those nitwits shot that poor deer and brought it here. I told them I didn't want it here, but would they listen to me? Noooooooooo!"

Eventually, after several more incriminating statements, we calmed her down. We explained that she had the right to make us get a search warrant, or she could consent to let us inside the trailer.

"You don't need no warrant," she said with a huff. "I told you I don't want the deer here—I want nothing to do with it—and I meant it. Follow me." She unlatched the padlock and led us inside to the refrigerator, where she swung both doors open. "It's all in here. Take it. I want it out."

Save for a half-empty gallon of milk, some condiment jars, and a few items wrapped in tinfoil, the fridge was filled with the quarters and bulk pieces of deer meat piled onto cookie sheets and plates. The freezer was also stuffed with deer meat packaged in white paper. Durward and I exchanged a knowing glance. There was too much meat for it to have been from one deer.

"Mary," I said, "the freezer meat is frozen solid, that couldn't have been from the same deer shot last night."

Her face flushed red, and she let out a big sigh. "Oh, that deer was from a couple of weeks ago. I told them fools I didn't want that one here either, but they don't listen to me."

"Okay, thank you for your honesty," I said. "This does mean that you're in possession of illegal deer meat, but since you're cooperating, we prefer to deal with your boyfriend and Freddie Hazard."

"I understand. Thank you."

"One other thing, though. We can smell marijuana. How much of it do you have in the house?"

She exhaled another sigh. "I'm sorry, Warden," she said while handing me a baggie of marijuana from her purse. "It helps with the nerves, you know?"

"Actually, I was referring to the green marijuana that I smell."

This news produced the biggest sigh yet. "Follow me." Her large frame nearly filled the dimly lit hallway as she led me to a closet door. Inside were several harvested plants hanging to dry. "I really am sorry. Go ahead and take 'em. We won't break the law no more. I promise."

Sometimes, that's how it goes. I'd spent years planting decoys and sitting out all night trying to catch Freddie Hazard in the act. Then, on my night off, when I least expect it, I nab him red-handed! And it was all because I was trying to stop a drunk driver that wasn't even him. On top of the game violations and the OUI, we got drug possession on his accomplice to boot. Maybe I got lucky. Maybe Freddie's luck ran out. I like to see it as divine intervention. Lord knows I needed an assist on that one.

While the older wardens bristled at enforcing OUIs, I had a knack for it. The police training we received was good, but my upbringing was my real advantage. When it came to drugs and alcohol, there wasn't anything I hadn't experienced first-hand at my parents' bar or out dealing with Dad. I inherently knew all the tricks, all the tells, and all the hiding places. They couldn't fool me because I'd lived in their shoes.

The trouble I had was being on the first wave of wardens required to enforce OUIs. The good folks of the Lincoln district were accustomed to my predecessor handing out warnings and free rides home. Nothing against him—that's how it was done in his day—but I ruffled many feathers by enforcing the law. My strategy was to treat everyone the same, figuring they'd eventually see me as strict but fair.

I couldn't have been more wrong.

Working in the Lincoln district, it wasn't long before I truly learned what it meant when people told me that mill towns play hard. Everywhere I went, I was arresting outdoor folk for enjoying too much libation during their recreation. Hunting, boating, snowmobiling, there wasn't a season of the year where I wasn't enforcing OUIs. The trouble really came when I arrested well-to-do businessmen who believed they were above the law. They had the money to hire defense attorneys, and time after time, I took a beating on the stand as their lawyers tried every weaselly trick in the book.

As for personal confrontations, there were many. One I'll never forget, a marina owner went on a rage, getting right in my face and calling me every name in the book for pinching one of his customers. When he finally tired himself out, I calmly explained that his friend was racing a speed boat around Mattanawcook lake at night, nearly crushing a young family in a canoe. It was by the grace of God that he didn't because this very scenario has put our dive team to work on countless body retrievals. This situation and myriad others earned me a national boating enforcement award along with a citizen's petition to have me removed from the Lincoln district. To this day, I still catch wind of people bragging that they were the reason I eventually transferred to Sherman. While they are welcome to have their fun, the truth is that their pushback didn't bother me too much because I was doing my job, and if that saved a single life, it was worth it.

Besides, the petition was child's play compared to the response I received from ruffling feathers in the drug community. Forget playing hard—those guys did retribution hard.

"Take a seat," Lieutenant Chandler told me. By this time, I'd earned my way into his good graces, so I no longer feared getting called into his office; however, the nature of my visit was causing apprehension. Sergeant Marshall had told me over the phone that "Some drug guys are out to get you. Go see the Lieutenant."

That's all I knew.

On the drive to Bangor, I mentally ran through the list of people who could be *out to get* me—whatever that meant. It was a long list. I had a nose for marijuana (thanks again to Dad), able to smell a green crop in the woods from a considerable distance. Many growers had taken significant financial losses because I'd turned the Maine Drug Enforcement Agency (MDEA) onto their secret gardens. I could even smell pot in a car days after it was smoked. The scent was probable cause to search a vehicle, which more times than not turned up other drugs or evidence. I also had the first hunting while under the influence of drugs conviction reviewed and upheld by the Maine Supreme Court. To top it all off, the guys we pinched for night hunting were often the same ones hustling drugs.

Who could be out to get me? Pretty much, everyone.

"A concern has come up," the Lieutenant said in the same business-like tone he'd use to discuss our retirement plan. "In exchange for a lesser sentence, a convicted child molester has relayed credible information on a threat to a law enforcement officer."

"What's the threat?"

The Lieutenant looked me in the eyes. "Bill, there's a ten-thousand-dollar price on your head."

"That's crazy," I laughed, looking around to see if there were any hidden wardens in on the joke. "How do we know this guy isn't just saying stuff to help his case?"

"We don't, yet, but you and I both know that he doesn't get a reduced sentence unless we can prove what he's saying is true." He folded his hands on the desk and leaned toward me. "I think it's real. He gave specifics."

"Such as?"

"He named you as the target, along with three growers and dealers in the area that have put up the money. Does the name Jean Grossman ring a bell to you?"

"Oh yeah, I've uncovered several of his gardens."

"Well, he's the alleged ringleader. According to the informant, the plan is to place a homemade bomb with a tripwire into the trunk of a junk car in your district and make an anonymous call that there's a poached deer in there."

"And then when I show up to check it out . . ."

"Boom."

It was late in the summer of 1992, just before the September marijuana harvest season. It was conceivable that the area's biggest growers didn't want me further interfering with their cash crops. Still, it's hard to describe how I felt at that moment. *Surreal* doesn't quite cut it. A ten-thousand-dollar-murder-for-hire plot was something you'd see in the movies or hear about in the major cities. But in the woods of northern Maine? It seemed unfathomable.

"What's being done about it?" I asked.

"MDEA is getting search warrants as we speak. As for what we're going to do, you'll be partnering up with Crocker or Georgia for a while. We don't want you doing any work alone. Not even a routine traffic stop."

"I understand."

"And you're going to wear a bullet-proof vest while on duty."

"A vest, seriously?" At that time, wardens never wore bullet-proof vests. These days, vests are form-fitting and worn every day, so it's like a seatbelt in that you feel naked without it. But back then, they were cumbersome, heavy, and hot, so while I wanted to be safe, the idea of actually wearing one while boating or camping in a field wasn't exciting. Little did I know that this situation set in motion the policy for all wardens to wear vests, which came to pass in less than a year. "So, I have to wear it when working hunters?"

"No, Bill, you have to wear it anytime you're on duty."

"As in, everywhere?"

"Yes. From now on, whenever you're in uniform, you're wearing the vest."

It's in my nature to make light of situations such as this. "What if they shoot me in the head?"

He didn't miss a beat. "That's a risk we're willing to take."

The MDEA brought the ringleaders in for questioning and searched their residences, seizing a considerable amount of drugs. They also found detailed instructions on making homemade explosive devices at Jean Grossman's house. The murder-for-hire plot was real, but because no one admitted to it and there wasn't any evidence proving they'd put a price on my head, Grossman and his accomplices were only charged with drug crimes.

A few months later, a team of wardens canvassed the town of Winn for poachers. Dave Georgia and I worked a field on Phillips Road that routinely attracted foot jackers, and David Crocker and Jason Bouchard were backing us up from nearby Route 168. Crocker and Bouchard set up outside a seasonal residence, a short distance through the woods from our location, in a perfect position to cut off any fleeing poachers that Dave and I encountered at the end of Phillips Road. Everyone in Winn knew the house wasn't occupied, so we put decoys in both locations to double our efforts.

Dave and I overlooked a deer simulator we'd constructed with our own money that had a lazy Susan built into the neck of a fully mounted buck. Via remote control, we could turn the deer's head, wag its tail, and set off a rat trap that knocked it over when someone took a shot. We started the night out on the ground in sleeping bags at the edge of the field, but after several hours, half-frozen, we migrated to the truck. Unable to start the engine because a foot jacker would hear it idling, we stayed bundled in the sleeping bags. After a while, we heard a vehicle slow down near the house on Route 168.

"Those guys might be in business," I said to Dave.

Sure enough, a rifle shot pierced the night, followed by the poacher's vehicle taking off. As we scrambled out of our sleeping bags, I listened for Crocker and Bouchard's response. It took a few long seconds for their truck to get going, which gave the poachers a big lead—the main ingredient for a chase.

I started my truck to assist in the pursuit, but our breath had formed a thick frost on the windshield. We didn't have time to wait for the defroster to work its magic, so I blasted down the road with my head out the window like a dog. The frigid air slapped my face and stung my eyes. Barely able to see, it wasn't long before my cheeks and ears were also begging for mercy. Fortunately, the chase only lasted about five miles, quickly extinguished when Mike Marshall, who was staking out another location in Winn, blocked the end of Route 168 with his truck.

When we arrived on the scene, the wardens ahead of us were already apprehending the poachers, one of whom was none other than Jean Grossman, the man who'd put a price on my head. Jean was an old-school drug dealer who ruled the roost through fear and intimidation. Average in height and build, with long, dirty-blond hair roped into a ponytail and a squirrelly beard, he was a scrapper who didn't shy away from a fight. Grossman was known for settling differences through threats and retaliation against property, and we believed that he was responsible for a rash of camp break-ins. His night-hunting exploits were also well documented with us wardens.

Needless to say, he looked good in handcuffs.

But this isn't where the Jean Grossman saga ends. A week after the poaching arrests, Dave and I were once again camped out on the edge of a field watching our four-legged, remote-controlled supermodel. We bagged a poacher in his seventies late that night, and when we called it in, the police radio was exploding with conversation about a fatal shooting at Grossman's residence.

"You wanna PR this guy and go check that out?" Dave asked.

I already had the personal recognizance form in hand, which allowed us to arrest and release the poacher without bail on the promise that he'd later appear in court.

It was after four in the morning when we arrived at Grossman's house. All of the detectives had left for the night, and the only one there was Trooper Brian Strout. Assigned to protect the crime scene, Brian gave us a tour and explained what happened. We'd naturally assumed that Grossman was the shooter, but he was the victim. The medical examiner had already removed Grossman's body from the house, but a large, dark pool of coagulated blood was still on the white linoleum kitchen floor. Inside the sink, there was a deer tenderloin that Grossman was in the process of cleaning.

"It's fresh," Dave said. "Probably from last night."

"Yep. Losing his rifle in our bust last week didn't even slow him down."

"He's got plenty of weapons," Brian said. "Come check this out." We followed him through the house to a bedroom. Along the way, there were stashes of deer and moose antlers everywhere—mounted on the walls, piled on side tables, and stacked in corners of rooms.

"There's no way he shot all of these himself," I said.

"This is nothing," Brian told us. "There's an old bus out back in his junkyard completely stuffed with deer heads and antlers?"

"From the camp break-ins?" I speculated.

"Likely," Dave said. "He probably also bartered antlers for drugs. This guy was sick."

"Speaking of which," Brian said, making a grand, sweeping gesture of the bedroom. Piled on top of the bed were at least twenty rifles and shotguns they'd found throughout the house, and the top drawers of a double-wide dresser were pulled open and packed with handguns. "We believe he was also trading drugs for guns. There's over a hundred in here."

"A lot of good it did him," I said.

The State Police apprehended the shooter, a man from Texas living with Grossman, who confessed to killing him over an unpaid debt. After all the terror Grossman caused, threatening people and poaching, he died on his knees, begging for his life. Since he put a price on my head, most people assumed I was relieved by his death. Not the case. I would have preferred that he saw his day in court for the poaching violation. I know that it's naive to think the thousand dollar fine and a slap on the wrist would have reformed him, but we were close in age, and I couldn't help but see the parallels in our lives. Had my life not been transformed by God, and if I hadn't met Gail, would I have succumbed to a similar fate?

Unbeknownst to me, I was still being watched.

Throughout my dogged determination to catch poachers, my nose for drug and alcohol violations, and my willingness to continue performing my duties under the stress of a price on my head, a small faction within the Maine Warden Service was taking note. This secret was revealed to me in 1995 when game warden investigator Terrance Hunter approached me.

"Are you familiar with the RPU?" Hunter asked me.

The nomenclature has changed over the years, but at the time, RPU stood for Resource Protection Unit, a specialized team within the Warden Service responsible for covert operations.

"Yes," I said, my mind already racing ahead in eager anticipation of where this conversation was going. "I'm always amazed at the amount of evidence you guys get in such a short time."

"Great, then you should know that we're currently accepting applications for a couple of part-time operatives to expand our unit and take on more cases. The thing is," Hunter quickly continued before I could say anything, "most of the guys who apply will fail at undercover work. It's not that they aren't good wardens or that they don't try hard—because they do. But we're not playing around with your run-of-the-mill, mom-

and-pop poachers. We're after the worst of the worst. Real scumbags. Our success lives and dies on whether or not we can integrate ourselves into their social groups, and most wardens—"

"Smell like a cop."

"Exactly!" Hunter's face lit up. "But you don't. No offense, but you've lived their lives. You know how to behave naturally around them, which is something we just can't teach. I'm also betting that from your time as a prison guard, you've picked up some good experience at making friends with some unruly characters."

"I think so." I immediately thought of one guy who would yell and swear at me in front of the other prisoners but then slip me info on the sly.

"Look, I know you love being a warden, and there's nothing more exciting than undercover work, but I don't want to sugarcoat this either because I also know you're a man of faith and family. Undercover work is the most dangerous thing you can do as a warden, and it involves being isolated from family and friends—sometimes for weeks at a time." Hunter stopped himself, likely realizing he wanted to give me a fair warning without scaring me away. "But it's also rewarding work."

A silence fell between us for a moment as I thought through the implications.

"So," Hunter said, "what do you think?"

5

ONE STEP AHEAD

My first undercover case was working a pirate rafting guide named Keith Penny. Whether they're licensed and behaving nefariously or guiding illegally, guides are easier to contact than straight poaching suspects because they're looking for business. You can't randomly call a poacher and say, "Hey, some guy gave me your number," but that scenario is common with guides. As my first foray into becoming Bill Freed, the rafting case was deemed safer than working hunters, but let me tell you, I got more than my feet wet.

Coinciding with his pirate rafting service, Penny operated a bed and breakfast on the Kennebec River. It was an ideal situation for under-the-table guiding that enabled him to scout and recruit potential rafting clients through the B&B. If a warden ever stopped them on the river—and we had—Penny trained his rafters to say they were friends of his staying at the inn and that the rafting was just for fun. As long as they didn't admit to specifically paying for rafting, we couldn't nab him. The only way to catch him was through an undercover operation—and he knew it.

However, the B&B also provided me with an alibi. Posing as an out-of-state fisherman who needed a place to stay, I booked the reservation from a Pennsylvania phone number and spent my first day there fishing near Penny's B&B, where he would surely see me. That night as I was plowing through a burger in the dining room, Penny told me that one of his rafting buddies was coming over for drinks, and I was welcome to join them. My warden antenna went up—things were about to get interesting.

While guides are easier than poachers to contact, it's harder to gain their trust because they view everyone as a potential law enforcement agent. Maine is one big small town, and the guiding communities are as tight-knit as they get. Undercover wardens had worked guides for years before I came on the scene, so word had gotten around that we were on to them. As a young male staying at the B&B, I was a prime candidate for a rafting trip, but Penny also knew that I was likely too good to be true. Sure enough, as soon as Dave Frost arrived, Penny's buddy and a fellow pirate rafting guide, the large bottle of Jameson came out.

"Have a shot," Penny said as he poured three glasses and slid one over to me.

"I don't know." I leaned back and patted my belly. "I've got to let this beast settle."

"You're a big boy—you'll be fine," Penny said in his whiny, high-pitched voice that filled the house like nails on a chalkboard. He was broad-chested with a round face, a mop of shiny black hair he kept swiping from his forehead, and from his time on the river, narrow slits for eyes and such a deep tan that he could pass for Hispanic. "C'mon now, it's on the house!"

Penny was testing me. If he'd passed me the bottle, I could pretend to take a swig while plugging the end with my tongue, but there was no evading the shot. It sat on the table before me like a haunted doorway into a past life. I'd barely escaped the first time; I had no interest in going back. But I also wanted to prove to Terrance Hunter—and myself—that I could be a covert agent. Several highly successful undercover wardens had preceded me, and they'd often used the excuse of being alcoholics as a reason to avoid drinking. There was no doubt in my mind that Penny was aware of that tactic, and that's why he was pushing the shots on me.

Many new undercover agents fail to make the grade because they're from different worlds, and they aren't able to meld, connect, and gain the trust of their targets. That shot was more than a test for me, it was my final exam, and it burned going down. I did my best to conceal the pucker face.

Penny quickly refilled the glasses.

After the second round, he excused himself to go to the bathroom. That's when Dave, a skinny, blond-haired, blue-eyed adventurist living the lifestyle of a winter ski instructor and summer rafting guide, started in with the questions. It's funny how close the bad-guy behavior is to police procedures in these situations. Penny had deliberately left me alone with Dave so he could double-check my story for inconsistencies. I was prepared for this, so when Dave asked me why I was in Maine, I told him that I'd gone to college here (I didn't say Unity!) and that I was in the area looking for places to live because I was moving back soon. My story needed to include a plausible reason to come back so they'd invite me to go rafting.

When Penny returned to the room, he and Dave exchanged a furtive glance. Something was said between them without either of them saying a word.

Penny poured another round of shots.

"Have you ever been whitewater rafting?" he asked me.

I'd passed the test.

"No," I told him, already feeling flush from the whiskey.

Penny launched into his sales pitch, promising I'd have the time of my life. As the shots continued and his trust grew (funny how that happens), he went from saying that he'd guide my buddies and me for only two hundred dollars into a full-on diatribe against the Maine Warden Service.

"They're trying to get me with undercover wardens," he told me with some other choice language mixed in. "But they won't because I'm too smart for those bureaucratic idiots. The way they get you is by exchanging money, but I'm careful. I only take cash, and I collect it here at the inn where they can't prove it was for rafting. I'm untouchable."

Two months later, I returned for a rafting trip with three "friends"— Doug Kulis, Irene Mottram, and Jim Fahey—who were all part-time undercover wardens. Penny was always mindful and on the lookout for law enforcement, so Irene was an essential part of the rafting team to keep suspicions low because there were so few women in the Maine Warden Service at this time.

We paid Penny his two hundred dollars in cash, plus tip, at the B&B before going to the river. To a casual observer, his operation looked legit. He had a giant yellow raft, personal flotation devices (PFDs), paddles—everything you'd expect except for helmets. Penny also looked the part, wearing a bright yellow windbreaker beneath his large blue PFD, a gray ball cap, black swim trunks, and Teva sandals. While the legitimate rafting outfitters were outraged by his lowball price, the real issue with illegal guides from the State's perspective is safety. When pirate guides don't attain the proper certifications, there's no way to regulate whether they are appropriately skilled and taking the necessary precautions.

Penny did give us a basic tutorial on paddle techniques, guide commands, and safety measures before shoving off. "If someone falls out, grab their PFD by the shoulders to pull them in. If you end up a swimmer, keep your feet pointed downriver and your toes up—you don't want to go head-first into a rock." The run-through was quick because it was secondary to his most important message: "If we get checked by a warden, tell him we're friends, and this is a free trip. Everyone cool with that?"

We laughed and agreed.

The river was flowing strong, pulling us toward the rapids like a swift-moving conveyor belt. While it was August and most of the state was enjoying an eighty-degree day, it was overcast with a slight breeze and temps in the mid-sixties on the river that morning, so we dug our paddles into the dark water with enthusiasm to stay warm. I'd never been rafting before, and butterflies started to form in my stomach as we approached our first series of rapids. I'd always sunk like a rock in the water, and I couldn't help but perseverate over the thought of falling out.

"Here comes Taster," Penny yelled from his perch on the back of the raft. "These are class three rapids. Then we'll hit some class fours. Whatever happens, don't drop your paddles—they cost me a hundred bucks each!"

Was he serious?

We ripped through the first series of rapids in a blur. Water splashed all over us, and that feeling of a lump forming in my throat followed by air suddenly being sucked out of my lungs as we crashed over a wave was exhilarating. We hooted and hollered and heckled each other as if we were college buddies. It was a blast, the best two hundred bucks the department could spend under the table.

And then we hit Magic Hole.

Sitting in the front of the raft alongside Jim, I remember looking straight down the nose at the crashing water swirling back as we went over the falls. It's that distinct moment, seemingly frozen in time, where your brain says, *this ain't good.* The next thing I know, I'm underwater, getting thrashed about like an ant in a washing machine. I gasped for air and my lungs filled with water. The paddle was long gone, and I frantically swung my arms around, trying to grasp anything. Logically, the PFD should bring me to the surface, but I had no idea which way was up. The force of the water was pinning me under, trapping me in place. As a warden, I knew far too well how often people drowned in this type of situation.

Something bumped my head, and when I reached up, I realized it was the raft. I pulled myself to the edge, and Doug hauled me back in. He later laughed and told me that my eyes were bugging out of my head. No joke—I was coughing up water for two weeks after that adventure.

There are some undercover cases where I sympathize with the targets because they're good people doing bad things. This operation wasn't one of them. Between the drinking and the hydraulic bath, I couldn't wait to get to shore and don my Philadelphia Phillies ball cap, the signal to several awaiting warden investigators that the transaction was complete and they could apprehend Penny after we left.

Waking up in the B&B with a raging hangover nearly caused me to quit the Resource Protection Unit before my undercover career really started. By passing Penny's test, I'd failed another. The Lord had provided me with salvation from the dark spiral of alcohol and drugs that tore my family apart growing up, and now I'd failed Him by accepting temptation. The nausea that morning was an unsympathetic reminder of how the bible describes a fool: "As a dog returneth to his vomit, so a fool returneth to his folly." And I'd done it for what? To bust a pirate rafter—was *that* worth it?

Keith Penny was crude, but he was child's play compared to the circumstances I'd encounter with more intense undercover cases. With a family of my own to think about—did I really want to put myself in those situations? I was seriously conflicted, my conscious battling it out in a full-fledge tug-of-war. While I shared my father's name, the last thing in the world I wanted to become was him. At the same time, I saw the difference that I could make working undercover, and it was lightyears ahead of the impact I had as a uniformed warden. I'd taken an oath to do whatever it took to protect Maine's people and wildlife resources, and I'd worked incredibly hard to earn this opportunity.

Was I willing to give it up so quickly?

I finally realized that it was possible to work within the world of alcohol and drugs without getting sucked in. Many undercover wardens before me succeeded at catching bad guys without getting intoxicated. Yes, they'd worn out the excuse of being an alcoholic to avoid drinking, but that just meant that I needed to develop my own story and strategies. I had to become a better actor.

Avoiding drugs was easy. All I had to do was say my workplace tested, and I could talk the talk without walking the walk because I had a treasure chest of stories to tell. Alcohol was the real trick. The problem with the Penny case was that I'd unwittingly put myself into a predicament where I had no choice but to take the shot. If I supplied my own alcohol, I could better control the situation. Penny just wanted to see me drinking to "prove" I wasn't a warden—what I was drinking didn't matter. As long as the beer was in a can, they couldn't see how much I drank, and I could dump it out at bathroom breaks. Or, I could bring mixers such as rum and Coke where I controlled the ratio. All I had to do was "mix" drinks at the sink, dump some of the rum down the drain, and no one would be the wiser.

Armed with my new game plan, I was willing to give undercover work another shot. My next case brought me to Big Machias Lake, where Wink Gallagher, a resident of New Jersey who owned a camp on the lake, was illegally guiding hunts to pay for his travel and hunting expenses. My Pennsylvania cover story was a perfect fit, and I quickly learned that Wink was one of several New Jersey camp owners on Big Machias Lake who were guiding illegally. With the case's scope suddenly expanded, I intro-duced my "uncle" to the crew, undercover investigator Albert St. Savior. Together, we spent two hunting seasons working the New Jersey camps.

Wink's place was a dump. Mold and moss covered the rotting roof, the inside reeked of mouse urine, and I'll spare you the gory details of the outhouse. We packed a bunch of guys like a minivan on a family camp-ing trip into this little place, and at night, if the snoring wasn't too bad, we could hear the mice in the walls. But they didn't stay there. The camp was littered with everyone's trash—empty chip bags and such—sending mice dashing across my sleeping bag or even my head searching for food. Needless to say, it wasn't the type of place where anyone was paying close attention to whether I was drinking my beer or dumping it out. And while Wink and the other guiding camp owners were the primary targets, I quickly learned that their clientele wasn't exactly on the up-and-up either.

One of Wink's guests, Gene Salvatore, was a hunter safety instruc-tor in his early seventies from New Jersey who'd been coming to Maine with Wink for years. One night over "drinks," Gene confided in me that he'd killed and mounted some birds of prey—notably, federally protected hawks and owls. We shared this information with the New Jersey Department of Environmental Protection (NJDEP). Since I had an established relationship with Gene and he believed that I lived close to him, everyone agreed that I'd pay him a visit.

"I've got something to show you," I told Gene as we exchanged pleasantries in his driveway. I pulled a dead sharp-shinned hawk that I'd gotten from our department freezer out of a garbage bag, thinking it was going to impress him.

"Put that away," he scolded me. "Do you have any idea how much trouble you'll get in if anyone sees you with that?"

His reaction took me aback. Was he jerking my chain when he told me about the owls and hawks he'd killed? Had I pulled NJDEP into the case for nothing? If so, I was going to have some explaining to do.

My fear was short-lived. Gene led me into his house, and the first thing I saw was seven racks of antlers on a table.

"You can only shoot one buck a season in New Jersey," Gene tells me with a sly smile, "but these are all of the racks I've gotten so far this year."

Holy cow, I thought, *this guy is a killer.* And he was a hunter safety instructor! But I hadn't seen anything yet. His basement was a mausoleum of mounted birds—all types of hawks, falcons, owls, song-birds, even blue jays—most of which are federally protected under the Migratory Bird Treaty Act. I couldn't believe the sheer volume of it all.

"Come see this," he tells me, and we go into his bathroom, where the window overlooks a pigeon village consisting of two ten-by-twelve-foot pens and an adjacent working shed. Propped on two poles at least twelve feet high above the pens was a cage made of chicken wire with a single pigeon inside. Atop the cage was a rusty old muskrat jump trap.

"I raise homing pigeons," Gene explained, "which are great for attracting birds of prey. It's ingenious how I've set this up. From above, the lone pigeon looks like it's separated from the flock and is easy picking. Wouldn't you know that the hawks land on the trap every single time."

"Wow." Jump traps are spring-loaded with two metal jaws that clamp onto their prey's leg and don't let go. It's illegal to use foothold traps like this in New Jersey to catch muskrats or raccoons—let alone federally protected raptors!

Gene mistook my astonishment for admiration. "Let's go outside—you gotta see how this works."

More than fifty pigeons pecked at grains on the ground or roosted on platforms within the pens. They weren't the least bit interested in us. What caught my eye was a rope that ran from the trap to the top corner of one of the pens.

"That rope—along with the raised cage—is the genius part if I do say so myself," Gene bragged. "When a bird lands, they end up knocking the trap off the cage. But the trap is too heavy for them to fly, so they hang upside down between the pens until I get to them. It's completely out of sight from my neighbors. I caught a Cooper's hawk this morning, and nobody around here has the faintest clue."

"Can I see it?"

"What's left of it." Gene went into the shed and returned with a wicker basket filled with over thirty tails of all shapes and sizes from different raptor species. "I catch so many that I don't bother mounting them. I just keep the tails."

I was floored. I'd never seen anything like this. Gene was trapping birds purely for the sake of killing, single-handedly altering the raptor population in the region. New Jersey threw the book at him for it, and rightly so. Typically lax on their penalties for wildlife crimes, they pinned him with a twenty-five-thousand-dollar fine and jail time. The sentence for trapping hawks was so harsh that the district attorney didn't bother holding him accountable for the seven deer.

Gene also impacted me by erasing any lingering doubts about working undercover. I'd taken an oath to preserve and protect by any means necessary. Though I didn't particularly enjoy the situations that undercover work put me in, I had the background and the social skills to fit in with the bad guys. It was my duty to put unrestrained poachers like Gene out of business.

Most of Wink's clientele were regulars with the desire to exceed the legal game limits. Wink was also an interesting character in his guiding strategies. He'd keep them out for an hour or two after sunset, or they'd start an hour before sunrise, but to him, as long as they were hunting the edges and not staying out late, they weren't night hunting. Let's just say that the State of Maine has a different definition.

One guy in Wink's camp, Big Steve, was more hardcore. He was dead set on shooting a deer to be the envy of the other guys, driving around at all hours, night after night. But he wasn't having any luck. For whatever reason, the deer weren't out. It became clear that we needed to intervene.

"I have to call my wife," I told the guys one afternoon when we stopped at the Ashland 1 Stop for grub. While they went inside, I jumped on the payphone and called Warden David Milligan. "You guys need to set up some equipment," I told him. "We're driving all over God's creation, and we haven't seen a single deer. We'll be hunting beyond mile sixty-five on the Realty Road tonight. You guys can set up anywhere between there and mile thirty." I gave him a wide area to ensure they could get a location that fostered the right illusion.

"Okay," Dave said. "We'll set up shop."

"Perfect." As I was talking, Big Steve exited the store and came toward me. True to his nickname, he was a tall, beefy guy that looked like a bear with his shirt off. He also had a short fuse when things weren't going his way, and I envisioned getting picked up by the throat and throttled for calling Dave. Visibly, I kept my calm, but internally I was freaking out as Big Steve got close. "Honey, I gotta go," I told Dave. "I love you too, bye." I could only imagine the confused look on Dave's face as I hung up, and I *really* hoped he didn't have me on speakerphone.

"You want anything?" Big Steve asked.

"Yeah," I said, a tidal wave of relief washing over me, "I'll grab a hoagie." Whenever possible, I used Pennsylvania language to preserve my cover. In this case, "hoagie" replaced "sub."

That night, when Big Steve asked who wanted to go for a ride, I volunteered to drive. It was just the two of us, and sure enough, we spotted a buck in the woods around mile fifty. Steve was so gung-ho to shoot it that he jumped out of the truck with his rifle loaded before we came to a complete stop. As soon as he fired, several flashlights suddenly illuminated us, followed by uniformed wardens running toward us yelling, "Maine Warden Service!" I gotta tell you, being on the other end of the bum-rush, even my heart skipped a beat—and I knew what was coming!

Because our call was cut short, I hadn't told Dave to preserve my cover, so I jumped out of the truck and ran down the road as if I was trying to escape. Dave gave chase, and when we got far enough away, I jumped into the bushes and told him to treat me like Big Steve. He handcuffed me and led me back to the scene. I was arrested, charged, processed, and bailed alongside Steve. Upon our release, everyone was standing in a group outside—good guys and bad—and I realized my boots matched those of the wardens. It was another situation where I was sweating bullets for a few moments, but thankfully Steve didn't notice. That was the last time I wore anything department-issued while undercover.

Those two seasons at Wink's camp helped me better understand the profile of serious poachers. Wink's guys didn't have a history of being convicted felons like many hardcore poachers, nor were they into heavy drugs, have any severe behavioral issues, or display a penchant for domestic violence. Their normalcy likely kept their game violations under the radar, and the only reason we caught them was their association with Wink. However, there's one trait that ties all habitual poachers together—ego.

While any nitwit can shine a spotlight into a field and shoot a blinded deer, the real ego boost is getting away with it. The more success they have, the more they think they're the Tom Brady of poaching. Despite a considerably stacked deck in their favor—Maine's wilderness is vast, and wardens are few—habitual poachers genuinely believe they have special skills to deceptively kill animals and outsmart law enforcement. No one else is on their level.

Ego is also their Achilles heel. You see, egos require feeding, and often, all it takes is a few well-timed comments—"Man, how did you spot that deer? I would never have seen it!"—to assimilate myself. Egos also love an audience. "That's a smasher buck. Want a picture with it?" (Thanks for the evidence, by the way.)

Wink was a scrawny guy in his mid-fifties, but he appeared closer to seventy, literally baked from constant heat and sun exposure through his roofing business. He looked like a question mark from his side profile the way he stood with his back arched and his head hung forward. Wink's ego was massive, having ballooned from illegally guiding and poaching for decades. His big thing was that he'd shoot a bear and then get someone else to tag it so he could get another. Most of the hunters at his camp were there for deer, so there was always someone willing.

One day I went out with him searching for a bear he'd shot in the wee hours of the morning. The bear had escaped into the darkness, and he'd lost track of it. If we found the bear, the plan was to have his camp cook tag it. We slowly worked our way through the thick regrowth of an old clearcut, thin whips scraping against our arms and legs, when Wink held up his fist as if he was a platoon leader signaling for me to stop. He crouched low and started inching his way toward a logging road in front of us. I followed his lead, and Wink looked back at me with a proud smile as if he was teaching me a great lesson.

"This is why the wardens can't catch me," he whispered. "I'm always one step ahead."

I couldn't argue with the guy. When I glanced down, he was precisely one step ahead of me.

6

THE POACHER KING

"Take the shot," my guide, Levi Prince, instructed in a strict tone that intimated it wasn't optional. "Take it now."

The .338 Winchester Magnum rifle kicked into my shoulder from the explosion. A split second later, the meaty black bear lost its grip on the pine tree and plummeted to the ground with a crashing thud, setting off a cacophony of barking from the Plott Hounds. The bear landed in a mess of blowdowns, hidden from our view. Then, one of the dogs broke free.

"Back!" Prince yelled, but the dog ignored his command, jumping over the initial blowdown to attack the bear.

That dog's dead, I thought. There are few things in the Maine woods more dangerous than a wounded bear.

Prince unholstered his .454 Magnum revolver and charged the brush. He scrambled over the blowdown and jumped into the fray. Two blasts from his handgun erased *that* danger. Almost as quickly as he'd attacked the bear, Prince marched back to us and turned his sudden venom onto his friend and hunting partner, Jack (Bubba) Heath. Bubba was responsible for the dog's lead.

"You idiot!" Prince yelled. "Are you trying to get my dog killed?"

Make no mistake, in this prolific hunting and poaching ring, Prince was king. The case file painted him as a recovering alcoholic who occasionally fell off the wagon. He was an emotionally unstable, fifty-five-year-old licensed guide with a hair-trigger temper feared throughout the community. Given his reputation for intimidating other hunters and even punching landowners, it was amazing he hadn't been arrested before this case. Average in height and build, Prince wore camo pants, a green wool jacket, and an Indiana Jones–style brown leather fisherman's hat that cast a shadow over his brooding face. His salt-and-pepper beard was perpetually stained with chew spit on his chin—he had a wad stuffed in his right cheek at this very moment—and there was a serious, unwavering, predatory glare in his dark eyes that kept everyone on notice.

The sudden look of unbridled fear on Bubba's face told me everything I needed to know about the case file's accuracy. As is typical with poaching ringleaders, Bubba was Prince's sidekick. He copied everything Prince did, right down to his trick to mix Red Man chew with Wrigley's gum to keep the wad together, because Bubba wanted to be Prince. And now he was cowering like a beaten dog in front of his master.

"It was an accident," Bubba cried. "The leash slipped."

"The leash slipped?" Prince snarled. "An accident? I know all about accidents." He raised his cocked revolver and waved it in Bubba's face. "How 'bout I have an accident right now and blow your head off? That dog's worth ten times more than you!"

All I could think was, *I'm witnessing a homicide.* The .454 is practically a handheld cannon, the caliber made for big game—specifically, bears, and not just the type we have in Maine. A close-range shot to the head would be like hitting a dandelion with a baseball bat.

Fully emasculated, Bubba collapsed to his knees, sobbing into his hands.

Prince continued to berate him at gunpoint for at least ten minutes, calling Bubba every foul name in the book. I kept thinking, *What if the gun goes off?*

Twenty minutes later, they got to work dressing the bear for me as if nothing had happened. It was the first day of a week-long guided hunt and everything, with the minor exception of using more dogs than the allowable limit, was by the book. What was I going to do now? The local game warden was adamant that Prince and his cronies were filthy, but I no longer had a legitimate reason to hang around them.

Getting Prince to take me on as a client had been a trick unto itself. I initially called him and spun a story about going to the Fryeburg Fair the year before and talking to an older man at the gate who told me Prince was the guy for guided bear hunts.

"That's Frank," Prince said. "Good guy."

I had to keep from laughing. It's incredible how many times I've pushed a made-up story in my career, and the bad guys found truth in it. But when I asked Prince if he'd guide me, I hit a dead end.

"Sorry," he said, "I'm full this fall. But I can give you some names."

Now I was really stuck. Lacking a clear course of action, I started calling the people he referenced. I figured Prince wouldn't send business to rivals he disliked, so maybe the guys on the list would somehow connect me back to him. The first number returned an answering machine, and I left a message. On the second call, a guy answered, and we got into talking about availability and rates, but we didn't book a hunt.

A week later, I was still spinning my wheels on what to do when lo and behold, Prince called me. One of his clients allegedly canceled, and he now had an open week. The cancelation story was an obvious ruse—he was using his buddies to screen whether I legitimately wanted to go hunting.

Prince was no dummy.

I didn't expect to bag a bear on the first day, and once again, I wasn't sure what to do.

"Shoot," I said. "I took the week off to go hunting, and it's over already?"

Prince gave me a sideways glance from the gut pile. He then looked to Bubba and Rick Blanchette, another licensed guide, who were both secondary targets on the case. The men returned silent expressions that seemed to say: *It's your call.*

"Why don't you stick around and hunt with us for the week?" Prince said.

I was in.

During my time with Prince, I stayed in what he called the hunter's cabin, an old trailer home on his property adjacent to the dog pens. There was a minefield of feces around the place, making it nearly impossible to get into the cabin without stepping in a pile. The dogs also kept me awake, barking throughout the night. From time to time, Prince opened his bedroom window and yelled at them, and if they kept barking, he'd come out, drag a dog out of its cage, and beat it senseless.

He was brutal.

In the evenings, Prince hung out with me in the cabin or invited me into his house, where his live-in girlfriend, Trisha, cooked us dinner. More often than not, I found myself in an uncomfortable situation where they got into an argument that came precariously close to knock-down, drag-out. I stayed out of Prince's personal business as best as possible, and we formed a friendship to the point that he invited me back time and again to go hunting as a buddy, not a client. While he welcomed having me around, Prince remained guarded about doing anything illegal in front of me. I knew he was up to no good because he'd openly talk about going night hunting and other shady stuff, but Prince didn't like witnesses when he committed the significant, class D crimes.

Still, there were times when his impulses got the best of him. One day we were driving along a woods road when Prince exclaimed, "Bobcat!" He jumped out of the truck and took a shot. A savvy poacher that was extremely woods-wise from years of experience, Prince was losing his fastball on marksmanship. He clipped the bobcat in the rear, and it scampered away. Realizing he'd shot a bobcat out of season, Prince quickly explained it away as, "Oh, it was just a fox, so I missed it on purpose."

On another occasion, Rick shot a buck while road hunting. As we retrieved it, a doe in heat came within twenty yards of us. Prince grabbed Rick's rifle and fired a round, missing. Snapping out of it, he turned to us and said, "I thought I saw antlers," even though we'd all seen that the deer was as bald as a bowling ball. The guys and I exchanged glances—*who is he kidding?*

While Prince remained guarded in his illegal activity, the fact that the king accepted me made it open season for poaching from the rest of his crew. They had no qualms about breaking every possible game law in front of me. One weekend I went hunting with Bubba while Prince was out of town. This trip created a whole brouhaha that nearly ended the case because I was *Prince's* client and hunting buddy. Seriously, poachers sometimes get more territorial over who hunts with who than they do girlfriends and wives. And in this case, it was Trisha that got nasty over Bubba stealing Prince's client. Poor Bubba was just eager to prove that he could guide. I stayed with him in North Conway, New Hampshire, where he shot everything in sight, day and night. When the case was over, Bubba got the worst punishment, as the North Conway district attorney threw the book at him.

Rick wasn't much better. After shooting that buck from his vehicle, he laughed and said to me, "Here I am, a master licensed guide, tagged out and shooting a trophy buck out the window of my truck." He knelt and picked up his .280 rifle casing. "I always pick up my shells, even when I shoot a legal deer. This way, they can't prove nothin'."

Except when they see you do it, Rick.

Most undercover cases take two seasons to gain trust and get the full breadth of activity documented, but the Fryeburg poacher king and his knuckleheads of the picnic table were so prolific that we shut them down after one fall. It was necessary to close the case because everything snowballed during Thanksgiving week. Facing the end of hunting season, they started organizing illegal deer drives, bringing more friends and family members into the fold. My list of perpetrators quickly ballooned to twenty.

Deer drives work by posting a bunch of people along a perimeter. Then a few hunters fan out and walk into the zone from the opposite end, trapping the deer with nowhere to escape. As a result, it's illegal to conduct deer drives in Maine with more than three people. These guys would have a dozen folks involved, and because deer often hang out in areas together, many of the drives resulted in multiple kills. Half of the shooters were already tagged out for the year (meaning they'd already shot and reported the one deer permitted with their big game hunting license), so they'd have their wife, girlfriend, or kid tag their next deer. If it was a doe, they either knew someone with a permit willing to claim it, or they concealed it.

They'd conduct a drive in the morning, followed by another in a new location in the afternoon. The next day it was the same routine, continuing all week long.

"We nailed that deer," Rick boasted to the crew after one of the drives landed a nice, eight-point buck. He slapped me on the back and added, "The only way we're screwed is if Bill here is an undercover warden."

Everyone stopped talking. All eyes were on me.

Rick said it in jest, but a joke like that comes from somewhere. Whether he believed it or not, the thought crossed his mind. And now, everyone else in the group was thinking it, too.

"Not to worry," Rick continued, "if he is, we'll just take him duck hunting and stuff him in the beaver flowage."

A weaselly old guy named Ed grabbed my arm with a surprisingly firm grip and added, "Nah, that's a lot of work. We'll just leave him in the woods for the coyotes."

I tried not to look like a deer in headlights, but I knew I did. I was sweating bullets. This episode was still early in my covert career, but I'd already encountered several threats against wardens. Most of the time, it was simply guys peacocking for their buddies, and we took it with a grain of salt. But not always. I'd already worked a covert case where the target made credible threats to violate and slay a female warden. There was also the murder-for-hire plot to take me out. But this was the first time I encountered it in a face-to-face confrontation.

"Yeah," I said, returning serve by playfully slapping Rick on the back, "and if you're an undercover warden, we'll stuff you in the beaver flowage."

Keep in mind that we were out in the middle of the woods with a close group of friends and family. I was the outsider, and they were all armed. The worst poachers among them had already proven they were addicted to killing, and with guys like that, you just never know how far they'll take it. Especially if they think their backs are against the wall. We were "joking" around in this situation, but for all I knew, it was premeditated.

Fortunately, everyone laughed at my retort.

And that's how I received on-the-job training at responding to accusations.

Rick invited the whole crew to his house for Thanksgiving dinner, me included. It didn't take long before it became a raucous party with everyone except Prince and Bubba (and me, of course) hitting the sauce pretty hard. Prince and Bubba were both recovering alcoholics, and while I never got the specifics, they were each on medications that didn't dance with alcohol. Even though Prince was abstaining, Trisha went right to town with Jackman Martinis (Allen's Coffee Flavored Brandy and milk). I'd been around them enough to know that the situation was a ticking time bomb, and sure enough, they erupted into a full-blown shouting match in front of everyone.

"I'm going for a drive," Prince announced as he bulled his way toward the door. We all knew what that meant, and I sat at the table with a half-dumped Miller Lite in my hand, hoping he'd invite me. No invitation was forthcoming.

Prince was out solo night hunting until after midnight. Around three-thirty in the morning, the dogs went off like a fireworks grand finale. The kitchen lights were on, and J.D., Trisha's daughter's fiancé, made a trip from the house to Prince's truck and back. Something was brewing.

"What's going on?" I asked, inviting myself into the kitchen. Prince and J.D. were both securing lids to their travel coffee mugs. "You boys going huntin' without me?"

Prince looked conflicted. He obviously wasn't planning on inviting me, but now that I was there and asking to go, how could he say no without telling his new friend that he didn't trust me? If he had any lingering doubts about which side of the fence I was on, he had to make a final decision at that moment.

"Get your stuff," he told me. "We're going for a ride."

Prince insisted that he drive, perhaps to hedge his bets, and I rode shotgun while J.D. sat in back behind me.

"Get your rifles ready," he told us as he started his truck. It was more of a command than a recommendation, and I pretended that I didn't know what he meant, readying my .243 across my lap. Prince's 7mm Remington Magnum was next to my leg, still in the truck from his solo night hunting earlier, and behind me, J.D. locked his clip into place. Of course, it's illegal to have loaded firearms in the vehicle, and at three-thirty in the morning, it's probable cause for a night hunting charge. That said, it didn't take long to erase the probable designation. We weren't even to the end of Prince's dirt road when a doe froze in our headlights.

"Shoot it!" Prince shouted. "Hurry up, shoot it now!"

I fumbled with loading my rifle, trying to buy time so that J.D. was the shooter.

Prince swore at me. "What are you doing? I told you to have it ready!"

J.D. was trying to open his door, but the truck was still in drive, and the automatic door locks were on. I reached over and moved the gear shifter into park so J.D. could get out. He dropped the doe with a single shot.

Getting the deer did little to satiate Prince's rage.

"We're night hunting," he yelled, the veins in his forehead bulging from his inflamed face, "what difference does it make if you get out of the truck or not? Shoot it out the damned window!"

Prince cursed up a storm for a good hour. It's one thing to witness him berate other people, but having him bore into me with his dark eyes and feral anger was deeply troubling. I felt myself recoiling, the vision of Prince putting the .454 to Bubba's head fresh in my mind. When unhinged, Prince seemed capable of the worst crimes imaginable. He yelled at us the entire time we loaded the deer into the truck, but in the moment, I didn't realize how deep his menacing tongue-lashing cut into my psyche.

All but one of the twenty defendants in the Operation Fryeburg case pled guilty to over two hundred documented Class E and D crimes in Maine and New Hampshire. All of which resulted in jail time and multi-thousand-dollar fines for several individuals. Rick pled to $14,000, and Bubba received six months in jail.

The lone holdout?

Levi Prince.

The poaching king of Fryeburg took his case to the State Supreme Court and the U.S. Courts of Appeals after that. The funny part is that the charges against him were less than what many of the other guys faced because he'd been so careful to do his poaching when there weren't any witnesses around. But he was an accomplice to a lot of wrongdoing; the most significant charge was possessing an illegal deer from the doe J.D. shot night hunting.

His lawyers argued that my conduct was outrageous by drinking and coercing Prince into committing acts he wouldn't have done if I wasn't there. The evidence is so cut and dried in these cases that this is the only card they can attempt to play, so they played it. It's hard to keep a straight face in court when they're arguing that the guy who spent an hour cursing me out because my rifle wasn't loaded in the truck was only doing so because I put him up to it. Not quite.

Prince and his lawyer succeeded at getting a few minor violations dropped, such as hunting without blaze orange. Still, most of his charges were upheld. He took a $4,690 hit to the wallet and lost his guide's license for the mandatory three years.

I moved on without meeting the inside of a beaver flowage.

7

THANKSGIVING OATH

Tires squawked as the cherry red Ford Mustang swerved into the middle of the road to block the oncoming car from passing us. I was riding shotgun in the lead vehicle, a front-row seat to the Stoner Grand Prix. The reprobate behind the wheel stomped on the gas, and we tore into a sharp corner at over eighty miles an hour. Suddenly, the car was drifting sideways, the headlights shooting through a blur of woods. White-knuckling the handlebar above the window, I stomped on the imaginary brake in front of me as the rear tires skidded onto the soft shoulder, pulling us toward the trees. The driver cut the wheel, and, miraculously, we fishtailed out of it.

"River!" I shouted at the driver, no longer content to play it cool. "How are we gonna shoot deer if we're killed in a crash?"

He thought that was the funniest thing in the world. "You should've been with us when we hit that tree on purpose."

"You crashed into a tree on purpose?"

River took his glassy eyes off the road—the absolute last thing I wanted him to do—and looked at me with a broad, high-as-a-kite smile that lasted four beats too long.

"Yup."

"Why?"

"To get the insurance money," he said matter-of-factly as if this should have been obvious. "Three of us were in on it. We agreed to sue each other and split the payouts evenly, but that no-good bastard, Dean, cheated us."

The irony was too rich—I couldn't help but laugh.

"Oh, man, how fast were you going?"

"About forty. We had to make it look legit."

"Were you wearing seat belts?"

"Nope. Figured that might give it away. Nearly killed us, though. Dean Supermanned through the windshield, and I broke several ribs on the steering wheel. They still hurt!"

That's when it hit me—*these guys are crazier than I thought.*

Gail never loved the idea of me working undercover. She knew how important it was to me, and she supported me unconditionally, but not knowing the dangers I was getting into kept her awake at night. I was always honest with her, but there were times when I waited to tell her the full truth. This entire case was one that sat on the back burner to cool off.

River Adams was a piece of work. A twenty-seven-year-old convicted felon, he lived in Damariscotta, where he grew up, with his wife. His family all resided in the area, and his two younger half-brothers, twenty-year-old Brandon Gross and twenty-four-year-old Jacob Gross, along with their close-knit circle of friends and hangers-on, were as crooked as River. Brandon was addicted to snorting prescription narcotics. Half of their crowd had lengthy rap sheets. And to the local warden's chagrin, we disqualified two crewmembers from this investigation because they already claimed residence in the slammer.

Poaching was a family pastime, but it was a fraction of their misdoings. The Adams-Gross family were local marijuana growers and drug dealers. This case was in 2004, twelve years before recreational legalization in Maine. Frequent time in the woods also familiarized them with other growers' plot locations, and come harvest time, they stole their competitors' stashes. Theft was second nature, as automatic as eating and sleeping. They swiped anything they could get their hands on and were continually in trouble with the law because of it.

Speaking of which, I was confronted by a local police officer early in the case. I'd gone to the house where Brandon and Jacob lived with their father, pretending to be a lost hunter, and was sitting in my van afterward, looking at my DeLorme and plotting my next move. Parking roadside less than a mile from the Gross household was probable cause enough for the officer to roll up on me. We typically don't inform local law enforcement of our undercover operations—all it takes is for one of their kids to repeat something they overheard their parents talking about at school to spoil our efforts—so I went through the routine of answering his questions and having my Pennsylvania info run through the system.

Getting checked by the officer became a blessing in disguise because he wasn't the only one who noticed me sitting in my van. Shockingly, Brandon knocked on my window.

"Oh good, it's you," I said. "I thought you were the pigs again."

"They stopped you?"

"No!" I turned hot. "I was just sitting here minding my own business, and they got all up in my grill."

"I hear you, man. Damned pigs are always bothering us, too." He glanced at my map. "You wanna come hunt and party with us tonight? We can show you around."

Did I?

Each of the brothers and most of their friends were clean-cut, average-looking guys. River himself was a little over six feet tall with a slender build, closely shaved goatee, and thick, dark hair casually combed to the side. They ran around in athletic-brand hoodies with jeans or basketball shorts—even when hunting, so high that they were unphased by the cold. Of course, this was all part of their ruse. They'd run afoul of the law enough times to have learned from their mistakes. Maintaining a trust-worthy appearance was one of their tricks, helping them gain access to homes as carpenters or handymen, which they'd set up to later burglarize by leaving windows or doors unlocked. River was the mastermind, always scheming new ways to make a quick buck.

As a forty-year-old undercover agent, this maniacal group of twenty-somethings ran me ragged. I rented a hotel room when I visited, but they'd party and go night hunting until three or four in the morning, so half the time, I crashed on one of their couches. An hour or two later, they'd be up and ready to hunt again. It was dizzying. And there were plenty of hijinks. One morning, we returned to the house after a successful deer drive landed a good-sized doe. When we got out of the truck, the tailgate was down, and the deer was missing.

"Guys," I said. "The deer's gone."

"Where'd it go?" Brandon asked.

Even I wanted to cuff him. We all jumped back into the truck and tore down the street. The doe was five miles away in the middle of a busy intersection. It had slid across the plastic bed liner when River accelerated too fast, and the guys were so stoned that they'd left the tailgate down. Cars swerved around the doe as we scurried to get it back into the truck. These guys didn't have a single doe permit among them, and it was amazing that none of the witnesses reported the incident.

Despite that faux pas, River and his gang were calculated poachers. A couple of years before, Brandon was busted for night hunting when he returned to the scene an hour after a drive-by shooting. The landowner heard the shots and called the local game warden, who caught Brandon at the pickup. As a result, they no longer bothered looking for a deer if it didn't drop where it was shot. Night hunters typically don't chase deer into the woods, but there were so many wounded deer that these guys simply left to rot, it was disgusting. Sometimes, they did return to the area the following day to see if they could find the deer, but more times than not, they came up empty-handed.

River often poached with night-vision goggles and a bow and arrow to prevent detection. As a felon, he was also prohibited from possessing a firearm. When spotlighting, they frequently used two vehicles. The lead car handled spotlight duties and didn't contain any weapons. If they lit up a deer without getting caught (spotlighting is illegal, but the penalty is a slap on the wrist compared to night hunting), then the second vehicle came along and made the kill. The local district warden would have eventually nabbed them for something, but these guys were a prime example of how undercover operations are necessary to bring the hammer down on the full breadth of their illegal and dangerous behavior. And we had to put them out of business because their other preventative tactic was to shoot deer in dooryards where wardens wouldn't be lurking in the bushes. Drugs, vehicles, firearms, and houses in the crosshairs are a recipe for disaster.

It was an overcast night, preventing us from seeing much past the head-lights' glow. Knowing they were looking to shoot deer near houses, I called dibs on driving to maintain some control over the situation. That was fine by them. They liked having me drive because they could keep the party going in my light blue, 1998 GMC Safari minivan. And because they were stoned out of their minds, we only took one vehicle.

When the Damariscotta case started, the van stunk from a deer that bled out on the carpet during the Fryeburg operation. These guys didn't mind. They were lighting up everywhere we went. There was so much pot smoke in the van that it felt like a scene from a Cheech and Chong movie. It's amazing they could see out the windows at all. They were using high-grade marijuana, and I feared the constant exposure to second-hand smoke might prevent me from passing a drug test.

"Deer!" Chris Hammond exclaimed, pointing to an eight-point buck feeding under an apple tree next to a white, cape-style house. Chris was Brandon's best friend from high school, a big, goofy-looking guy with a baby face, short dark hair, and a mischievous smile. Riding shotgun, he started unrolling his window. A shot from the passenger side would have been right at the house where there was a row of windows glowing from a television's flickering blue light. Despite the fact that he was holding a 12-gauge shotgun loaded with buckshot, Chris had no qualms about firing. All his bloodshot eyes saw was the deer.

"Hold on," I said, making a wide turn in the road, parking the van at a head-on angle that put the woods as a backdrop to the deer. The buck was statuesque, staring back into our headlights. My adrenaline was pumping—I wanted to get out of there before getting discovered. I just hoped the television volume was loud! These guys were so off their rock-ers, there was no telling what would happen in a confrontation.

I rolled my window down and held the spotlight on the deer to track its movement.

Chris pulled himself out of the window and sat on the frame, aiming. His first shot hit the buck. It jumped and bound toward the woods as Chris pumped another shell into the chamber and fired a wild second shot.

Out of the corner of my left eye, I saw a bright muzzle flash. My hand was instantly burning from the fireball, nearly causing me to drop the spotlight, and there was a loud ringing in my ear. A house light came on, spurring an eruption of guys yelling for us to get out of there. Disoriented, it took me a moment to realize that Brandon fired a .270 rifle out the driver's window from behind me. It's a wonder he didn't shoot my hand off. Or worse. The muzzle compression and the gases emitted from the end of a rifle can be deadly when fired too close to someone's head. I'm lucky that I only lost hearing for a couple of days.

"Let's go! Let's go!" the shouting continued.

"Don't do that!" I yelled at Brandon as I put the van in drive and stomped on the gas. Barely able to hold onto the steering wheel with my left hand, the van was swerving all over the road. "You scared the crap out of me. Do you have any idea how dangerous it is to fire that close to someone's head? I can't hear anything out of my ear!"

"What were you thinking?" Chris joined me in yelling at Brandon. "How could you be so stupid?" He waited for a response that didn't come. Or maybe there was an answer, and I just couldn't hear it. "That's it," Chris declared, "no more smoking the good weed before we hunt!"

If only the ban on good weed had stuck. On my next Damariscotta trip, we emerged from an unsuccessful deer drive onto railroad tracks. The guys lit a fat joint as we walked the tracks to set up for another push. They'd already smoked one before the first drive, and we were going to be the pushers on the second go around, so I knew I had to be extra vigilant about the shooters' locations.

"Hey man," one of their stoner friends, who everyone called Guy, said to me. "Can I try your rifle?"

While savvy poachers want to use my gun so it gets confiscated if they're caught, Guy asked out of pure inebriated curiosity. I usually say yes without hesitation to further goodwill with the group, but I had reservations about Guy. My .270 has a sensitive trigger, and he didn't strike me as a serious hunter. He was in it for the weed.

"Yeah, sure," I relented. "Just be careful. It's got a hair-trigger."

"Cool, man. Don't worry. I'm always super careful."

Famous last words.

I double-checked that the safety was on before handing him my rifle. He traded back an old .30-30 Winchester, probably handed down to him from his grandfather, so it was no wonder he wanted my rifle.

As we walked single-file down the tracks, I got an uneasy feeling. Guy was giggling like a schoolgirl behind me from something one of the guys further back in the line said. I turned around to discover the .270, safety off, pointed at my midsection. And his finger was on the trigger!

I quickly snatched the rifle from his grasp.

"What are you doing?" I snapped. Before I could say anything more, River verbally attacked Guy. Since we were walking single file, Guy would have taken out three of us—River included—if the gun went off. It was already apparent that this was another one-season operation because this crew was raking the local deer population. At one point, Brandon nailed the heads of five does he'd shot to a spruce, insisting that I take a picture of him peering out from behind the tree. But it was also clear that I had to hurry up and put a bow on the case before someone got killed. We just had to get through Thanksgiving weekend—easier said than done.

I'd grown up around alcohol and drugs, but I'd never experienced a Thanksgiving like this. As a warden, I always worked the holiday, but missing the whole week entirely for two years in a row wasn't exactly popular on the home front. That said, Thanksgiving coincides with the final days of rifle season when trigger fingers develop a voracious itch, so my absence was begrudgingly understood. If I haven't said it already, Gail is a saint for keeping the family together while I was gone, and on this Thanksgiving, I was thankful she couldn't see the predicament I'd gotten into.

River lived in a large apartment complex where he rented out the multi-use community center for his family's celebration. They filled the banquet room with close to forty people, kids running all over the place. Serving tables lined the wall, covered with multiple turkeys and all of the traditional side dishes. An entire table was dedicated to hard alcohol and mixers, underneath which two large coolers were packed with Budweiser.

The brothers openly dealt bags of marijuana to their family, and a ghastly blend of cigarette and pot smog filled the room.

After the main meal, I sat at a round table playing poker with the brothers. They were smoking their dessert, and everyone had at least one alcoholic drink in front of them. I was putting on a good show with Captain Morgan's and Coke, which barely contained any rum, but I'd spilled some on the outside of the red Solo cup so that it smelled the part. I was the only one in the game with his wits about him, and somehow I was hemorrhaging money. River and his wife, April, were having some sort of spat, so she sat next to me at the table smoking a cigarette. Their three-year-old son, Mathew, was at our feet playing with Matchbox cars.

The room's volume rose proportionally with the intoxication level as if the adults were competing with the kids to make noise. The winner, hands down, was Diane Gross, mother to the three half-brothers. She was the alpha talker, and her obnoxious voice and cackling laugh exploded throughout the crowd like a firecracker. Diane cursed her husband, her siblings, her grandchildren—anyone and everyone who crossed her line of sight. It was all fun and games until she aimed her vitriol at me.

"I don't know who you are!" Pointing a stubby finger in my direction, Diane stood up, knocking over her metal folding chair with a clatter as if she were challenging me to a fight. Slightly overweight and a chain-smoker in her mid-fifties, Diane looked like something the cat dragged in with her leathery complexion and short-cut hair dyed unnaturally black. The room went quiet. All eyes were on me as she continued her profanity-laced tirade. "I don't know if you're MDEA, a game warden, or what, but no one—and I mean *no one*—has ever hunted with my boys like you have!"

In retrospect, this was another hard-learned lesson—I had to be more careful around women. Simply put, they're more observant than their not-so better halves. The guys bought my cover story that I was sent to the area for work and had extended the trip to go hunting. They knew I had kids, and I'd told them that my wife wasn't happy about me missing Thanksgiving, which was true, but she'd get over it (hopefully, also true!). They didn't think much about the significance of this, but to their family's matriarch, who was on her second marriage, it didn't pass the sniff test.

Suddenly at a loss for words, I could feel myself sweating as I fumbled with the cards in my hands. It's a tricky thing to feel engulfed in panic while knowing I couldn't show an ounce of fear—or else it was my goose that was cooked. Willing myself to appear calm, there was only one thing I knew to do in this situation.

"You think?" I said, laughing.

"I do. I think you're a damned—"

At that instant, all three brothers tore into their mother in a profanity firefight. They slung every colorful metaphor imaginable at her, repeatedly calling her a whore to get her to sit down and shut up.

I was beyond words. But I wasn't out of the woods.

"You know," April said to me, "I've noticed that whenever anyone brings up game wardens or MDEA that you laugh."

Cast from a Barbie doll mold, April had long blonde hair, crystal blue eyes, the full complement of an hour's worth of makeup application, and the type of magnetic proportions that attracted stares from every man and woman (albeit for different reasons) in the room. She invited the attention. Her jeans appeared ironed on, and she wore a tight-fitting, gray, V-neck cashmere sweater. As it was, April already made me nervous because she wasn't one to respect personal space, always a little too friendly. When everyone was partying, she was quick to invite me to stay at their place. After River passed out and I settled onto the couch half-asleep, she made a show out of going to the fridge and standing in front of the open door for several minutes wearing—well, let's just say less than one should with a house guest.

After the second late-night show, I started crashing at Brandon and Jacob's house to avoid the situation altogether. The funny thing is that her flirtations didn't appear to phase River. I'm no psychologist, but I suspect his lax attitude toward her behavior, coupled with River constantly being out of the house hunting and partying with his brothers, fueled her drive for attention.

"Really?" I said to April, taking a sip of my infinitesimal rum and Coke to reinforce that I was on their team.

April leaned in so close that I could smell the cigarette smoke on her breath, fixing me in an intense stare.

"Swear to me on Mathew's life that you're not a cop."

It didn't soothe the situation, but I couldn't help but laugh at this.

"I'm serious," she said, "swear to me on Mathew's life."

"Shouldn't I swear on the life of my own children?"

"No. Swear to me on *Mathew's* life."

There's a common misconception that undercover agents are required to admit they are law enforcement personnel when asked, which is hogwash. I think it stems from off-duty officers who are out of uniform having to show identification when addressing a crime. As a covert operative, I used this misinformed belief to my benefit. I'd also heard April and River swear on Mathew's life so many times to each other when I knew every word out of their mouth was a blatant lie that doing so didn't give me the slightest pause.

"I swear on Mathew's life that I'm not a cop, MDEA agent, or game warden," I told her.

April leaned back in her chair and took a drag of her cigarette, studying me.

"Good," she said, exhaling. "Let's play cards."

The brothers laughed and cracked jokes at the scene that played out before them, but their tune changed the next morning. Their minds temporarily free from alcohol and drugs, they realized their mother might be onto something. An awkward tension was in the air, and I could tell they were whispering among themselves because they started asking questions we'd already been through—where I was from, why I was in the area? They cooked up an excuse for me to go with Jacob to the store, and when we returned, I noticed the items in my overnight bag were askew. It was the second time they'd searched my bag; thank God they didn't find the small notebook hidden at the bottom.

At the beginning of the case, I'd learned that the family was aware of our covert operations. They'd paid close attention to the recent media coverage of the Fryeburg case. Brandon and Jacob's father was also friends with a man from Waldoboro who was the subject of an Albert St. Savior investigation, so they'd heard stories about an undercover warden passing himself off as a hunter who took a lot of pictures and didn't shoot anything. Once they spouted off about that, I put my camera away.

While I'd won the brothers over, the suspicion lingered somewhere in the back of their minds because it manifested in a joke. One night when we stopped at a convenience store, and Brandon went in to get munchies, Jacob talked me into pretending that I was an undercover cop. I walked up to Brandon while he was standing at the counter, pointed a finger into his back, and said, "FBI, don't move." The tell wasn't so much that Jacob put me up to the prank as it was the sudden fear on Brandon's blanched face.

Now, I know what you're thinking—*how could these guys not realize that I was an undercover agent?* What you have to understand is that unlike the Fryeburg situation where I contacted the guides, the Adams-Gross brothers invited me into their social circle. The Warden Service works hard at profiling the targets to find a personality match with the right agent. We don't always get it right, but in this case, I quickly connected with the family and their screwball friends despite our age difference. When hanging out, I was another one of their buds, never pushing them to do anything illegal and always letting them dictate when we went for a ride. They didn't see me as someone trying to get them into trouble.

And my cover story was rock solid. I told them that I worked for Hatfield Quality Meats in Hatfield, Pennsylvania. I'd actually worked at Hatfield for a year before I went to college, so I could describe the pork processing procedures in great detail. I don't want to divulge all of our undercover trade secrets, but since this was specific to my cover story, I'd also ask the targets if they'd ever tried scrapple, a pan-fried Pennsylvania Dutch breakfast food made of pork scraps and trimmings. Most people in Maine haven't had it, so I'd make a show of cooking some for them. My mother often sent me regional items like scrapple and Yuengling beer to help with my cases, and whenever I visited her, I stocked up.

I also told them that I was in Maine because there was a lab near wherever the targets lived that tested Hatfield's chemicals. Because the company didn't want people to know there are chemicals in the meat products, they'd send someone like me with an unmarked vehicle to make the deliveries. This part was all made up, of course, but my intimate knowledge of Hatfield's business made it believable. Whenever the guys urged me to get another free trip on the company to go hunting, I told them it wasn't likely to happen.

"I work the floor," I'd say. "The chemical deliveries go to the drivers first, it's all overtime for them, so they love doing it. They only offer it to me when none of those guys want to go." Then I'd call the targets up a couple of weeks later and say, "You're not going to believe it, but I got another delivery." Saying that the other drivers didn't want to miss Thanksgiving with their families also made it believable as to why I was in Maine during the holiday. Just don't try telling that to their mother.

The fact that the brothers weren't smoking pot or snorting crushed prescription pills Friday morning after Thanksgiving was the strongest indicator of how seriously they questioned my allegiance. I don't think I ever saw these guys go hunting sober at any other time. I knew I had to do something to turn the tide, so I put down the first deer I saw on the drive that morning. It worked. They were whispering that I hadn't shot anything, so killing that deer instantly put them at ease and preserved the case. Within minutes the joints were out.

Deer season, and the case, ended without any further incidents. Appalled by the volume of their poaching violations—I documented over thirty deer illegally killed or wounded—and the public safety concerns over these guys handling firearms while under the influence of drugs, the DA didn't hold back. Eight guys pleaded guilty to numerous class D misdemeanors (the highest misdemeanor in Maine) with mandatory thousand-dollar fines and jail time. River Adams took the cake with six class C felony counts of possessing a firearm by a prohibited person and twenty-five other charges for game violations and drug possession. It amounted to five years in prison before the suspensions kicked in and close to $12,000 in fines.

Through the grapevine, I've heard that Chris Hammond straightened out, now with a family of his own. I wish I could say the same for River and his brothers. Several years after this case, River was arrested and convicted for illegally harvesting and selling elvers (baby eels). Considered a delicacy and an aphrodisiac in Asia, elvers sold for over three thousand dollars a pound on the black market when River was caught.

The undercover federal warden who worked the case is a friend of mine, and he told me that River was apprehensive when negotiating the sale. River explained to him that he'd been busted by an undercover warden before.

"Well," the federal warden told him, "you have to trust someone at some point if you're gonna make money."

8

LONG SHOT

THE MIDDAY SUN WAS BLINDING AS IT REFLECTED OFF THE WINDSHIELD of my undercover truck, a blue Chevy Colorado. Squinting, I opened my DeLorme on the hood to map eleven for Turner and pretended to study the location. The contour lines showed widely spaced intervals, indicating a somewhat flat region that I knew was filled with cut cornfields and rolling wooded hills fertile for hunting. Underneath the map, the truck's engine ticked as it cooled. It was a hot day for late September, archery season, and my head-to-toe camo hunting clothes were sticking to me. I already wasn't looking forward to an uncomfortable drive home.

The map was a ruse. I knew exactly where I was, a half-mile from the home of my target, Tucker Leroux. His Maine hunting license was revoked for poaching, but the local game warden was confident that Tucker was still up to his old tricks. Tucker was described as a perfect case match for me, an outgoing, talkative guy who liked to hunt in Maine and Pennsylvania. "Once he learns that you're from Pennsylvania, he'll suck you right in," they told me.

When it was supposed to be easy, I'd learned to be suspicious.

I already had two active cases going at the time, and I was only planning on being in Turner for the day. Hopefully, a few people would ask me what I was doing, and I'd give them the line that my grandfather used to take me hunting in the area, and I was trying to figure out where. Making contact with a target is a long game, and the goal that day was to be seen and get people talking, greasing the wheels for when I returned the following fall to work the case.

As a blue, full-size truck approached, I looked up from the map and cast a confused expression. The truck slowed down and turned around. It had a cap on the back with tinted windows so nobody could see inside the bed, which always raises suspicions with game wardens. I smiled to myself as it pulled up on the road behind me and the passenger window went down—the first local to take the bait.

"Hey," a man in his early thirties wearing a camo Realtree ball cap shouted as he leaned across the passenger seat, "you from Pennsylvania?"

"Yeah," I said in a friendly tone. You never know how people will react to an out-of-state hunter casing their territory.

"Follow me."

Before I could respond, he drove away. I quickly gathered up the map and jumped in my truck, thinking, *Was that Tucker Leroux?* It looked like the guy I'd seen in pictures from the case file and his Facebook profile—long forehead, rectangular eyeglasses, and a dark, closely shaved goatee with a white patch on the right side of his chin. He led me to an old farmhouse on a hill where I knew Tucker lived. *This was the guy.* By the time I'd parked my truck and gotten out, he'd already run into the house and returned with an armful of antlers like a kid showing off his little league trophy.

"Check these out," he said, proceeding to describe each deer and how it was shot. I'm a talker, and I couldn't get a word in edgewise.

"I'm impressed," I said when he finally took a breath. "You must really know where to find 'em around here."

"You bet," he said with a proud smile. "You wanna come in and grab a beer?"

"Sure."

"If you want to see where the deer are at, we can go hunting tonight," he said as we walked toward the front door.

"Tonight?" I said with an honest-to-goodness laugh. I couldn't believe how fast he was moving, cheating me of the opportunity to feed him my go-to lines.

He stopped walking. "Do you not do that?"

"No, it's cool. I don't care how I fill my fridge. I'll just need to call my wife—that's all."

"Believe me," he said, "I get it."

And just like that, he sucked me in. It *was* too easy.

"There," Tucker said, shining his spotlight over the top of his truck and into the field. The doe picked her head out of the long grass and was momentarily mesmerized by the light. Stalling, I fumbled with the bolt action on my Ruger M77. "Gimme that," Tucker said, ripping the rifle out of my hands. He slid out the driver's window and sat on the frame. A single shot to the chest felled the deer.

"What did you do that for?" I complained when he returned to his seat. "It was *my* turn."

"You're too damned slow. It would have gotten away."

That was Tucker Leroux to a tee. He was the most compulsive killer I've ever worked. Deer. Turkey. Whatever. Possessed by an urge to kill, there were several instances like this where he pulled the rifle away from me or Chet Eaton, his hunting buddy, purely to be the one pulling the trigger.

Tucker's single-mindedness nearly cost me an eye on another occasion. We were road hunting during the archery-only season when he shot a trophy ten-point buck with his muzzleloader out the driver-side window of my truck. Eager to get it out of there as fast as we could, he grabbed a broadhead arrow from Chet's quiver. I bent down to get a look at the deer as Tucker hastily jammed the arrow into the bullet hole. The razor-sharp head rocketed out of the exit wound and nicked my eyelashes. A quarter of an inch further, and I'd be known as one-eyed Bill!

While many serial poachers steer clear of game wardens in public situations to avoid unwanted attention, Tucker is the guy who pretends to be our best buddy. After getting confronted by a landowner who knew Tucker's hunting license was revoked, I watched as he immediately called the local district warden to sweet talk him before the landowner could inform him of the incident.

"I swear I wasn't hunting," Tucker lied. "I was just showing my buddy Bill some good places to hunt."

Another time we were out night hunting, and we stopped at a store for refreshments. I was pulling a Coke out of the cooler when I heard Tucker say, "Hey, Josh, how's it going?"

I turned around to see who he was talking to and nearly had a panic attack at the sight of Warden Josh Smith dressed in his Class A field greens.

"Meet my friend, Bill," Tucker said, introducing us. "He's up from Pennsylvania."

Josh later told me that he was afraid he'd blown my cover, but his poker face that night was perfect. He didn't so much as flinch when we shook hands and exchanged pleasantries.

After leaving the store, we weren't even a mile down the road before Tucker spotlighted a field.

"Are you crazy?" I asked. "We just saw the warden."

"Don't worry, this isn't his area. Besides, he's going home anyway."

Tucker was right. *But still.*

The brake lights to Emmit Leroux's silver GMC glowed red as the truck came to a stop on the gravel woods road. Tucker was riding shotgun with his father in the lead vehicle while Chet sat with me in my undercover truck. It was an overcast Pennsylvania afternoon in late October, the foliage had already faded from brilliant bursts of color into a sea of unremarkable raw umber, and I watched as Tucker aimed his muzzleloader out of the passenger window to finish another natural beauty.

Remarkably, the antlerless deer was unfazed by the shot. Emmit and Tucker prided themselves on being skilled long-distance shooters; it seemed inconceivable that Tucker had missed at forty yards. Through the wide-pane back window, I could see Emmit hand his loaded muzzleloader to Tucker, who stepped out of the vehicle and dropped to a knee for his second attempt.

Movement in the trees on the opposite side of the road caught my attention. "Game warden!" a man in his Pennsylvania forest green uniform yelled as he emerged from behind a tree and approached the vehicle. *Good simulator,* I thought, realizing why the deer hadn't dropped or fled. Chet saw the warden, too. Swearing, he quickly unloaded his rifle. I had an MOU—a memorandum of understanding—between Maine and Pennsylvania for me to operate there as an undercover warden, but there was no risk of this warden knowing who I was. Still, I waited a moment for him to approach the Lerouxs before crowding the scene. It seemed ill-advised that he was operating a decoy stakeout by himself.

"No, no, no," Tucker said, shaking his head when I joined them. "I was out of the vehicle for both shots."

"But you were riding with loaded rifles in the vehicle," the warden said. He was a young guy, and from his position on the opposite side of the road, there was no way he could see whether Tucker was in or out of the vehicle when he fired. I could tell by how he quickly shifted from one violation to another that the warden was conceding the point and fishing for an infraction that would stick.

"No, we weren't," Tucker lied. "I got out of the truck, dropped to a knee to quickly load the muzzleloader, and fired."

"The shots were awful close together," the warden said.

"I'm fast. I'll show you if you want to time me."

"That won't be necessary." The warden put his hands on his hips and looked us all over. "You fired from your knee next to the truck?"

"Yes."

"Then you weren't the required twenty-five yards from the road."

"Warden, I'm a retired police chief," Emmit said, which was true. He was a former Lewiston police officer before becoming the chief of police for Mechanic Falls. The patch on his brown Carhartt jacket showed that Emmit was also a licensed master guide in Maine. He'd been pounding beers since breakfast that morning, but you couldn't tell from his speech. Sixty-one years old, Emmit was the classic definition of a functional alcoholic. Built like a bull with bear-paw hands, he had wispy, paper-white hair and a thin mustache that trailed the corners of his mouth. Aside from witnessing his drinking, the spiderwebbed veins on his Rudolph-red nose were the only visible sign that he was a drunk.

"Can you show us some leniency?" Emmit continued. "In Maine, you simply have to get out of the vehicle to shoot on woods roads. We didn't realize that twenty-five yards are a thing here. It's an honest mistake.

From one LEO to another, I swear I wouldn't have knowingly let my son break the law."

I knew this was the wrong thing to say. As a warden, it's infuriating when a police officer acts like our laws aren't applicable to them. And this certainly wasn't a situation of an accidental violation. The Pennsylvania warden would have flipped if he knew everything these guys were doing. Already far exceeding the bag limit, many of their deer were killed at night or shot from a moving vehicle. They were also scamming Pennsylvania's deer tagging system by lightly filling out the tags in pencil and storing them in Ziplock bags with the meat to preserve, erase, and reuse on their next trip. On top of recycling the tags, they also went to the courthouse and claimed that their tags were lost or stolen to get an extra set. Essentially, they were tagging four deer each for the price of one. They were also killing deer in regular wildlife areas and tagging them with D-Map tags, which are extra doe tags available in special regions such as regrowth forests where deer destroy the saplings.

"They didn't know," I said to the warden to make it look good. I was also nervous that getting busted might derail the case by deterring them from committing further violations. "Can you cut them a break?"

The warden ignored me. "As an LEO," he said to Emmit, referring to a law enforcement officer, "you know that ignorance is no excuse."

After the warden took their information and informed them that charges would be coming in the mail, we left the scene and found a place a couple of miles away to pull over and regroup. "I can't believe Tucker got away with shooting from the truck," Emmit said, laughing. He then went on a rant, telling everyone to keep their mouths shut about what happened. He was more concerned with their reputation. "Now, let's load back up." And with that, we continued road hunting.

As a former police chief, Emmit Leroux was a disgrace. I don't know if he was crooked as an active cop, but when I got to know him, he was an alcoholic with pancreatic cancer who'd stopped caring. Emmit was prescribed oxycodone, an addictive opiate painkiller, but he preferred to self-medicate with the bottle. Instead of taking his prescription, he had Tucker sell the oxy for him. They were also peddling marijuana, which I assumed they stole from local growers. It was a big joke in their family that Emmit had gone from law enforcement to a drug dealer and rampant poacher; however, the issues it created weren't a laughing matter.

Not only was Tucker his dad's drug dealer, but he was also his biggest customer. His oxy addiction frequently led to loud, abusive arguments between father and son. Emmit wasn't so much concerned with Tucker's addiction as he was the money owed him. Tucker argued that his dad was being greedy, which is how he rationalized skimming off the top when brokering deals to help pay for his dependency. But it wasn't enough. On one Pennsylvania hunting trip, Tucker's tab ballooned to the point that Emmit cut him off. Tucker went into withdrawal, becoming feverish with severe shakes and excessive vomiting to the point of dry heaving. I tried to tell him that he was in no shape to go hunting, but he wouldn't relent. Instead, we road hunted to the hospital, where he was admitted for a phantom back injury. I sat in the parking lot for four hours while Tucker faked his way through an examination. The doctors weren't about to give him oxycodone, but they prescribed Vicodin to tide him over for a while.

"You see them tweakers," Tucker said, taking a sip of AMP soda (he'd stolen a case from a Pepsi truck at a convenience store). We were staying at a campground in northern Pennsylvania filled with year-round resident trailers and seasonal RV visitors who used it as a hunting home base. Tucker was referring to a young couple in their mid-twenties that we'd crossed paths with several times coming and going from the adjacent fields. It was apparent from their emaciation, hollow eyes, and zombie-like trance that they were strung out. "I'm gonna ask them about their hookup."

"I'm not sure that's a good idea," I said to no avail.

The woman, who introduced herself as Kat, agreed to make some calls. Later that evening, after we'd returned from night hunting, Kat got in my truck and directed us to a drug dealer's residence in the town of South Creek. The property was littered with trash—beer cans, soda bottles, and empty cigarette packs covered the ground like leaves; plastic grocery bags clung to bushes as if they were forgotten Halloween ghost decorations. We went around back to where a broken washing machine was rusting out next to an old garage-sized shack that looked like it was dissolving away. The roof was sinking in, only faint memories of white paint remained, and a ring of green algae was creeping up the bottom slats.

"Wait here," Kat said to us as she slipped into the shack.

"I don't like the looks of this," I whispered to Tucker.

"Me either."

A few minutes later, Kat returned and told us that drugs from New York were on the way. "You can wait inside," she said, but even Tucker recognized this as a bad idea. Instead, we went night hunting, returning an hour later, when Kat came out with two Percocet and two oxycodone pills that Tucker bought. "There's more coming if you want to come in," she said.

This time, Tucker agreed.

The half-rotten door squeaked on its hinges as a wave of stale air laced with sweat and the remnants of marijuana smoke greeted us. The floor and the walls were covered with an orange shag carpet, giving the dimly lit room a tunnel effect. We walked around a pool table, upon which was an open bench warrant for Dan Bishop, to the back of the shack where three tattered couches that looked like they'd been salvaged from roadside pickup were arranged in a horseshoe. Two guys splayed out like doilies on the center couch tracked us with their eyes as we approached.

"This is Dan," Kat said, introducing us to the guy on the right with a mop of unkempt dark hair, pockmarked complexion, an oversized hooded gray Champion sweatshirt, and black jeans. At the mention of his name, he came to life and sat up.

"Thanks for the hookup," Tucker said. "What else you got?"

"I can't get any more oxy," Dan said, "but I can score you a fentanyl patch."

"How much?"

"Forty."

"I'll take it."

Two skinny blonde-haired women entered the shack and sat on the couch to Dan's left. One of them removed a pipe from her purse and prepared to light it. From my drug-dealing days, I knew they were about to freebase cocaine.

"You guys wanna smoke?"

Kat sat down on the couch with the other two women—she was in. Tucker's obvious desperation likely put to rest any initial concerns they had about us being cops. I always benefited from looking younger than my age, but I still stood out as the oldest guy in the room. My nerves kicked in. Would they get suspicious if I was the only one not smoking? I wearily eyed Tucker with a sideways glance, wondering what he would do. There was a slight smile on his face, and for a split second, I thought he was going to accept.

"Nah," Tucker said, "I hate crack."

"I'm out too," I added. *Thank God*, I thought.

Dan shrugged his shoulders. "Suit yourselves." He took a toke of the pipe and then stood up with surprising balance. "Chill here. I'll be back soon with the patch."

Soon was a relative term in Dan's world. We sat on that fetid couch for a couple of hours. Whenever I tell people that I worked as an undercover game warden for twenty years, their eyes light up, and I can tell that exotic, movie-fueled visions of covert work are racing through their minds. Sure, there's action, but the job as a whole isn't nearly as thrilling as they think. In these moments, I remember sitting in that drug cave as time came to a standstill, watching the addicts melt away like comatose candles. As if I were a watchman in a funeral parlor for the living dead, I stared at the door, willing it to squeak open. It did a couple of times, but it was just more addicts looking for Dan, the drug man.

We'd first arrived at Dan's house around ten o'clock, and it was after one in the morning when I finally gave Tucker *the* look—*we've gotta get out of here!*

He nodded.

"What a bunch of dirtbags," Tucker said as we walked back to my truck.

That's a matter of perspective, I thought, laughing to myself.

On Tucker's insistence, we continued night hunting until nearly three-thirty.

We almost didn't see the deer grazing alongside the long white chicken barn at the DeCoster farm in Turner, Maine. A waxing crescent moon hung like a fishhook in the partially cloudy sky, scantily lighting the field. Driving without the headlights on, I was focused mostly on the road. Tucker probably wouldn't have spotted the doe either if it hadn't raised its head as we drove past.

"Stop, stop, stop!" Tucker chanted. "Back up, back up!"

I followed his commands.

"Get the spotlight. C'mon, quick!"

Roughly a hundred yards of open field separated us from the doe. Spooked by the commotion of us backing up and getting into position, the deer took off as I hit it with the spotlight.

"I see you," Tucker whispered in a childish voice as he tracked the doe through his scope. The deer was at top speed in a full-on sprint. Tucker and his father got their kicks off long-range shooting. They often drove around specifically looking for deer to shoot at four hundred yards or more. Don't get me wrong, they could make these shots, but the extreme difficulty also caused them to fatally wound far too many deer that got away. For this very reason, no conscientious hunter would even attempt this shot during the day. But Tucker didn't have a conscience. He only saw red.

Clear of the chicken barn, the doe had nearly escaped to the woods when the rifle crack rang across the field. Tucker had intentionally waited until the last possible moment to pull the trigger. The doe instantly disappeared from the spotlight as if he waved a magic wand at it.

"Right in the crease," Tucker boasted as he pulled my .22 Hornet rifle back into the cab. By *crease*, he was talking about the fold behind the deer's front shoulder. It's the ideal spot to shoot a deer because it preserves the best meat and punctures both the lungs and the heart, knocking the animal down.

"No way," I said in complete disbelief. At the speed the doe was running, he had to lead it by a good distance. Factor in the hundred-yard range, and a bullseye shot was unfathomable.

"I'm telling you, I got it in the boilermaker."

I was still shaking my head.

"You'll see. Tomorrow morning we'll go in through the woods and retrieve it."

Around three-thirty that morning, I sat on the toilet at his mother's house with my notebook. Sneaking into the bathroom in the wee hours of the morning was the only time I could find privacy to document the crimes taking place. This particular notebook was defective; many of the pages were glued together, creating a cracking noise as I pulled them apart. In the silent house, it felt like I was popping packaging bubbles.

Footfalls in the hallway outside of the bathroom stole my breath.

"What are you doing in there?" Tucker asked.

I looked down at the notebook filled with page after page of Tucker's wrongdoings. How could I hide it? Under the towels? Out the window? Simply walk out of the bathroom the way I came in, with it hidden under my shirt and tucked into my waistband?

"What do you think I'm doing, dummy?" I shot back.

"Don't you ever get any sleep?"

"How can I? We're chasing Bambi twenty-four-seven. This is the only time I can take care of business."

Tucker snorted. "Yeah. Right. Good night."

We crept through the woods shortly after daybreak and found the doe along the treeline behind the DeCoster farm. Sure enough, Tucker nailed it in the crease. It was despicable, but I'll say this, that's the best shot I've ever seen. Hands down.

In what was another single-season case, I documented nineteen deer—nineteen!—that Tucker personally killed that fall in Maine and Pennsylvania, along with two hundred total crimes committed by him and nine other associates. In Maine, Tucker was sentenced to nine months in jail after suspensions, two years of probation, and several thousand dollars in fines. He also earned jail time and fines in Pennsylvania.

Emmit served fifteen days in a Pennsylvania jail for drug trafficking and his wildlife crimes, but he managed to avoid jail time in Maine. During the case, his defense argued that he was only selling narcotics to his son to limit Tucker's addiction and ensure the welfare of Emmit's grandson. After witnessing their shouting matches over the drug money along with the endless jokes about Emmit being a cop-turned-criminal,

I knew the defense's argument was fallacious. They also made the case that administering Emmit's prescriptions were too complicated for the prison's medical staff. Bear in mind that these were the same drugs he'd been doing without and selling.

The judge, however, agreed with the defense.

9

YOU WOULDN'T BELIEVE
ME IF I TOLD YOU

BURIED DEEP IN THE WOODS OF PATTEN, MAINE, THE CAMP WAS NORTH of the Katahdin schools on Route 11. That's all State Police Detective Brian Sears from the Gray office in southern Maine had to go on when he contacted me. My first ten years undercover were part-time for various budgetary and resource allocation reasons, so I was still serving as the district warden for the Sherman-Patten region. Sears hoped I could help his team find the camp with my knowledge of the area.

As a slight twist of fate, I also knew the fugitive. Dustin Fisher was a long-term resident of the East Wing cell block in the Maine State Prison when I served as a corrections officer. He was a gangly beanpole of a man with a wiry mustache and full sleeves of prison tattoos, but what I remembered most about him was his dark, watchful eyes. Like a motion-sensor camera, Fisher tracked everything going on. He put up a good front, usually friendly with the corrections officers, but you could tell that behind those toiling eyes, his machinating gears were grinding.

Not surprisingly, Fisher was anything but rehabilitated upon his release. He teamed up with another former inmate and career criminal previously under my watch, Lincoln Cyr, for a series of armed home invasions. During one of the break-ins, Cyr made a name for himself by slicing an ear off a homeowner.

As my mentor John Ford used to say, both men had reservations at the crowbar motel. The district attorney was most interested in coming down hard on Cyr for the assault, and Fisher initially agreed to testify against him for a reduced twenty-year sentence. But Fisher also had a severe form of hepatitis, and his doctors had given him less than twenty years to live. Moreover, he knew his life expectancy as a rat in prison was appreciably shorter. So instead of checking in, he checked out and went on the run with his girlfriend.

Fisher was the textbook definition of armed and dangerous. He literally had nothing to lose, and according to Sears' informant, Fisher made it known that he would kill or be killed before allowing himself to get arrested again.

I didn't have the foggiest idea about the mystery camp's location, but I started connecting inmates like a bad guy family tree as I went down memory lane. Kody Bernard was another jailbird with Fisher and Cyr, incarcerated on a nine-year sentence for nearly beating a man to death with a pipe. He lived in the neighboring town of Stacyville, and I'd had several run-ins with him and his crew as they were avid poachers and drug dealers. Had Bernard hooked up his jail buddy? It seemed plausible, but his family's camp was in a township south of Staceyville—not north of the Katahdin schools in Patten as the informant had indicated.

Sears agreed that it was worth checking the camp out.

We arrived just before nightfall. An old blue Ford Ranger matching the description of Fisher's getaway vehicle was parked outside, instantly putting us on high alert. Adrenaline pumping, the small team of five State Police officers and myself fanned out around the camp, fully expecting a firefight. I didn't for a second doubt that Fisher was more likely to come out of the camp in a body bag than handcuffs.

From the outside, the camp appeared large enough for three rooms on the ground level along with sleeping quarters of some kind—probably an open loft—on the second floor. The silver chimney pipe poking through the roof looked recently replaced, and aside from where a bear clawed cedar shingles off the building's southwest corner, there were no apparent signs of decay. It was late August, and the warm daytime temperatures were already succumbing to crisp autumnal air in the evenings. No doubt Fisher and his girlfriend were planning on holing up here for the winter. It was an ideal hideout. The maze of woods roads coming in required someone to know exactly where they were going to find the place. On a couple of turns, even I questioned myself.

Twelve-gauge shotgun in hand, loaded with two rounds of buckshot followed by slugs, I positioned myself among several pine trees, facing one of the camp's short-side windows. I was sweating profusely beneath my heavy bullet-proof vest. As a law enforcement officer, we've trained for these scenarios so often that it seems surreal when the actual moment arrives. Sears gave the signal to move in, and I sprung from my hiding spot, shotgun shouldered, staring down the barrel at the window, looking for any sign of movement. It's easy in these scenarios to see things like the glint of a barrel that isn't actually there. Senses cranked to hypersensitive, I heard the crunch of pinecones underfoot and the huffs of my running breaths, as if I was outside of myself, anticipating the crack of a gunshot that would ignite chaos at any moment.

I crashed into the side of the camp like a hockey player hitting the boards. Peering through the screened open window, there was a table with a bag of Nacho Cheese Doritos and five Coors Golden bottles. The officers out front yelled "Police," and a wave of light flooded the room as they flung open the unlocked door. Several moments later, they shouted "Clear!" And just like that, the adrenaline rush came to a crashing halt.

But we weren't out of the woods yet. Sears and I looked inside the pickup while the other officers searched the camp. There was a man's black leather jacket on the driver's seat, a pack of Marlboro cigarettes on the dash, a couple of empty Sprite cans on the floor, and a woman's hairbrush, lipstick, and makeup kit in the glove compartment.

A tingling sensation washed over me.

They're here.

But where?

I scanned the treeline. This far north, the deciduous leaves were already starting to turn, adding glints of red and yellow to the landscape and making it near impossible to identify anything that didn't belong. The drive into the camp had been slow going, and the squad cars made a racket bouncing in and out of the muddy potholes, mufflers scraping gravel. No doubt they heard us coming and fled into the woods. Were Fisher's cunning eyes tracking us now? Did he have a scope fixed on any one of us?

We searched the surrounding woods until darkness without finding a single footprint, cigarette butt, or anything else to suggest they'd fled on foot.

"Someone must have picked them up," Sears said.

I nodded my head in agreement, but something in my gut said it didn't feel right.

Sears used his police radio to contact ATF—The Bureau of Alcohol, Tobacco, Firearms and Explosives—and inform them that Fisher was recently at the camp and may still be in the surrounding area. ATF requested that Sears and his team stay around for their agents from southern Maine to arrive. While we waited for the feds, Sears stationed an officer at an intersection to the camp road, and I brought the rest of his team around to Bernard's home and those of his bad guy buddies.

Our reception at each stop wasn't exactly warm and cozy.

Bernard looked from Sears to me with a sneer when the detective asked him if he'd recently had contact with Fisher.

"Haven't talked to him in years."

Bernard was lying. We knew he was lying. And he knew that we knew he was lying. That's how it worked with seasoned criminals who went through the judicial system more often than they saw a physician for check-ups. Unless we had a bargaining chip, he wasn't saying a word. The only achievement of these visits was to put the bad guys on notice that they were committing a felony if they assisted Fisher, and we'd prosecute them for it. It was a long shot, but maybe we could starve Fisher of his support system.

After midnight, we returned to the camp with the ATF agents. I led the caravan, and on the drive in, I carefully inspected each mud puddle for any sign of a vehicle coming or going since we'd left. There were several ways to get there, so someone could have circumvented the officer stationed on the main road intersection, but I didn't see any sign of activity.

Once again, we fanned out around the camp and charged it with our guns drawn, my heart pounding as I peered through the side window into the darkness, officers yelling and bursting through the front door. Once again, nobody was there.

Sears and I continued following our previous steps as we searched the truck.

"The jacket's gone," Sears noticed.

I felt nauseous. By the blanched look on Sears' face, he did, too. We simultaneously realized that Fisher was out there the whole time, likely watching us when we first searched the place. He'd had a free shot if he wanted it, and now we'd given him time to regroup and escape.

"He's long gone," one of the ATF agents said to the other. Dressed in their black tactical getup and sporting the physique of guys who lifted weights in their sleep, they had an intimidating air about them.

"Yep," the other officer agreed. "Probably made his way to the highway for a pick-up."

The highway he was referring to was Interstate 95. As the crow flies, it was only a couple of miles away.

I pulled Sears aside for a private conversation.

"He's here somewhere," I said.

"He *was* here," Sears corrected. Tall, handsome, and well put together, Sears was a prototypical State Police detective. "But now that he knows we've found his hideout, he's not going to come back here again. Like the ATF guys said, he probably hoofed it to the highway by now."

"That doesn't make sense. If Fisher was going to flee, why would he waste time and risk getting caught returning to the camp? It may only be a couple of miles from here to the highway, but that's no way out. It's all swamp—even the most experienced woodsman would struggle. I doubt he's going to drag his girlfriend through waist-deep muck. I think he came back here for supplies to camp out in the woods."

"I hear you," Sears said as he checked his watch, giving me the distinct feeling he was placating me, "but it's after two in the morning. We've searched the woods around the cabin twice now, and we haven't found a single footprint or a shred of evidence. There's nothing more we can do here tonight."

The ATF agents and the other State Police officers were already loading their gear back into the cruisers. Suggesting that we bring in a K-9 unit—at least a two-hour wait for one to arrive—would have been peeing into the wind.

"Look," Sears said, "I'm going on vacation for a week with my family tomorrow—well, today, actually, so I have to get back to Portland. Here's my card. Call my office if you hear anything about Fisher's location."

As a detective, there's never a good time to go on vacation. You're always in the middle of something big. If you don't force yourself to step away, you'll burn out quickly and quite possibly find yourself divorced. I've been in Sears' shoes many times, so I understood why he was hot to trot, but it didn't put my mind at ease. I returned home around five in the morning and went to bed. It was a fruitless attempt. I tossed and turned until eleven, fixated on the idea that Fisher was somewhere close to the camp the whole time.

There had to be something we missed.

After brunch, I paced the house, still trying to think of how Fisher evaded us. Unable to let it go, I called the area wardens and troopers to see if anyone could surveil the camp with me, but everyone was preoccupied. So I put my uniform on and gathered my gear.

"You're going after that fugitive, aren't you?" Gail asked. A mountain of clean, unfolded laundry loomed before her on the couch, and our toddler was tugging at her legs. The older kids were running wild and screaming throughout the house, playing hide-and-seek. They were having fun, but it was only a matter of time before an argument ensued. You could set your watch to it. Amid the chaos, she saw right through me. It's one of her superpowers.

"Duty calls," I said, smiling like one of the kids caught sneaking candy.

"Alone?" She phrased it as a question, but there was no mistaking this as a statement of disapproval. We both knew that going solo after an armed and dangerous fugitive contradicted all departmental safety protocols—not to mention common sense. (In fact, the Warden Service later used this situation in training to illustrate what *not* to do.)

Dustin Fisher had nothing to lose. As I called my kids in for a hug and kiss before heading out, it was painfully obvious that I was putting everything on the line.

I hid my truck off a spur road a couple of miles before the camp. Working my way in by foot, I carefully inspected the muddy road for any sign of footprints or vehicle traffic. There wasn't a single trace. No one had driven in or out of the camp since our law enforcement caravan left, and there was no sign of anyone walking it before we arrived. Getting closer to the camp, I got out my binoculars to surveil its surroundings, ultimately settling myself in a cluster of bushes with a good vantage point. The element of surprise was now in my favor. It was my only backup.

The hours ticked away. Slowly. Whoever came up with the expression of "watching paint dry" clearly never participated in a backwoods stakeout. Daylight turned to dusk like ink absorbed into a paper towel, and the only action I observed were two squirrels chasing each other through the undergrowth, reminding me of my kids playing hide-and-seek at home.

Around eight o'clock, I ran out of snacks. Why didn't I pack more? I should have known better. There was that bag of Doritos in the cabin. Was it still there? Had it been moved when we checked the place a second time or was that a figment of my imagination? Maybe. But the jacket was gone from the truck. Someone had come back for it.

My thoughts kept returning to the road. Why hadn't we seen any footprints or vehicle tracks? It had rained earlier in the week, making the road soft and muddy. There's no way someone could have walked out that way without leaving footprints, even if they were keeping to the grass in the middle of the two-track or the side banks.

It was as if they vanished into thin air.

Wherever they went, they're not coming back. Not again. We flushed them out, and Sears and the ATF muscle were right. They're long gone.

What was I thinking?

Stretching my stiff legs, I abandoned the sanctuary of my hiding spot to have one last look around. It was a clear night, and the moon was three-quarters full, making it just bright enough to see without a flashlight. Around the other side of the cabin was an old ATV trail that appeared out of use from the saplings growing in. We'd checked it out earlier, but maybe we missed something? It wouldn't take long for me to look it over—the trail only ran for about a mile along the base of a ridge before connecting with another woods road. I stashed my shotgun and binoculars and kept my service pistol and portable radio with me.

Venturing down the trail, I occasionally turned on my flashlight to spot-check the soft ground and muddy areas for footprints. The path provided a glimmer of hope that became fully diffused when I reached its conclusion at the road. The only tracks I found were from moose. It was now after ten-thirty, my stomach was growling, and, having hardly slept the previous night, I was so exhausted that it felt like my head was in a blender. It was time to go home.

Confident that Fisher wasn't in the area, I turned the flashlight on permanently to keep from tripping. About halfway back to the camp, I came to a pine blowdown in the trail and noticed a man's bootprint in the mud on the other side. At first, I assumed it was mine, but I'd gone around the tree earlier. Shining my flashlight toward the steep bank, it looked like the ferns at its base had been trampled. In the distance, there was a faint screeching sound. Moose make weird, unearthly, and unnerving mating calls at night, but this wasn't quite like that. Maybe raccoons fighting? Or trees creaking in the wind? I briefly shined my light into the branches above—they were dead still.

My boots sunk into the muck as I slowly worked my way into the ferns. Flicking my light on and off, I was onto several fresh human prints. My heart once again kicked into high gear. The weird screeching sound was also getting louder, clearly coming from the top of the ridge. I took my handgun out of the holster and began climbing toward the noise. The bank was so steep that with my gun in one hand and Maglite in the other, I had to wrap my forearms around trees to pull myself up. As I neared the top of the ridge, I suddenly realized what that eerie sound was—snoring!

As I neared the nesting fugitives, second thoughts crept in. I *should* have backup. Fisher was armed—what if he got the drop on me? But there was no way I could give anyone verbal directions to my location. I'd have to backtrack to the camp and meet them there. That would take hours. What if Fisher heard their vehicles? It's amazing how far sound from below travels up to elevated locations in the still of the night. And would anyone believe that I'd tracked Fisher down from his snoring?

I couldn't chance him getting away. If he did, we might never catch him.

Mere steps from the chainsaw snoring, I slipped and quickly hooked my flashlight arm around a small maple tree to prevent myself from falling backward down the sharp slope. Turning on my light, Fisher and his girlfriend were lying on their backs at my feet. I nearly fell on top of them! Snuggled into a small cavity beneath the top of the ridge, they were lying on an unzipped brown sleeping bag with another one draped over a branch above them. It was a great hidden location on the hill where they could watch the trail below without being seen themselves.

The handgun Fisher used in the break-ins, what appeared to be a nine millimeter (I'd later learn that it was a replica CO2 pellet pistol), was lying inches from my right boot and no more than a foot from his grasp. Still clinging to the maple, I fumbled with my flashlight and handgun for a moment in my haste to grab his gun before he awoke.

"Game warden!" I yelled upon securing Fisher's handgun, shining my light on their faces. "Roll over and put your hands on your back—you're under arrest."

Fisher awoke immediately and did a double take looking for his gun.

"Friggan Livezey," he said calmly, correctly pronouncing my last name, which nobody does. "How did you find me?"

"You wouldn't believe me if I told you."

At this point, Fisher's girlfriend woke up. She was a bigger girl with straight brown hair and blotchy red rosacea patches on her face, and she immediately began screaming obscenities at me.

"Roll over and put your hands on your back," I repeated.

The watchful man I'd known always to be scheming something merely stared back at me with a blank, lost expression on his face.

"At least let him have a cigarette!" the woman yelled.

"Don't move your hands," I told her.

She ignored me, lighting a cigarette and putting it in Fisher's mouth.

"I told you to roll over," I said again. Fisher still didn't comply, and without backup, I was running out of options. Needing two more hands, I once again fumbled with my flashlight and gun as I reached for my pepper spray. "Last chance," I warned, giving the spray a vigorous shake that was mostly for show. This act alone usually gets the bad guys to behave, especially if they've been maced before. Fisher slowly turned his back to me, and I quickly shot the pepper spray at their faces as he jumped up and ran for the top of the ridge.

Instinctually, I gave chase. *Oh no*, I thought, realizing I'd run straight through the cloud of pepper spray. I coughed, and my eyes and throat immediately started to burn. Behind me, Fisher's girlfriend was rolling around on the ground, blasting obscenities as if she were a witch cursing me with spells. My vision was impaired, but not nearly as bad as Fisher's. He was bouncing off trees, running ahead of me in an erratic pattern like a rabbit chased by hounds. Doing a quick U-turn, he ran straight into a beech tree that put him on the ground.

"My eyes, my eyes," he yelled. "I'm going to kill you!"

"Roll over and put your hands behind your back," I ordered while glancing over my shoulder to make sure his girlfriend wasn't going for a weapon. She was still on the ground with her hands on her face and hatred spewing from her mouth. "If you don't roll over, I'm going to spray you again." Neither of us wanted that. My eyes were still stinging and watery mucus was pouring from my nose, which I knew was nothing compared to the pain he was in from the direct spray.

Finally, Fisher complied. When I bent down to put the cuffs on him, I dropped my flashlight and the bulb went out. *Great*, I needed that! After securing them both, I called dispatch on my portable radio from the top of the ridge. Again, there was no way to direct assistance to my current location, so I told them I would meet the responding officers at the camp. Fortunately, Fisher had a flashlight that I used to guide us down. His girlfriend chastised me the whole way for making her walk so far as if I was the one who hid them in the middle of the woods.

But Fisher had something else on his mind.

"How did you find me?" he asked again. The cavity they'd squirreled themselves into was likely a known hunting perch among his bad guy buddies, so Fisher was convinced that someone ratted him out.

"Like I said, you wouldn't believe me if I told you."

A buck shot at night on the Stud Mill Road in the Walsh case. Don't I look like just another one of the guys?

Thumbs up was my signature pose. Bad guys thought I was excited for the kill, but to me it meant, "We got them."

Confiscated guns, ammunition, and hunting gear significantly add to the financial loss incurred by poachers.

Bear paws, gallbladders, cash, and other evidence from the Zhao case.

Deer killed in Pennsylvania and illegally tagged during the Leroux case.

A cookout with Randall Jones and friends where we feasted on illegally kept lobsters.

This photo of me posing with trout from Operation Red Meat in the Allagash was used in the *Portland Press Herald* to reveal my identity, ending my career as an undercover agent.

For many of the worst wildlife offenders, poaching is nothing more than fun and games.

There's nothing sporting about mass poaching. It's the purest definition of overkill.

Gail and me in Augusta celebrating our thirty-third anniversary and my thirty years in the Maine Warden Service.

This picture was taken by my youngest daughter Morgan in 2016 when she was just starting her photography business. It was a special time because we were together during a snowstorm on Christmas Eve in Sherman when she got the shot. One of the reasons I worked so hard as an undercover game warden was to make sure a magnificent buck like this would not be illegally hunted.

10

WILLING TO KILL

We were going for a ride, albeit in the wrong direction. What started as a night hunting excursion quickly detoured into a drug run.

"Don't worry," Todd Walsh said, eyeing me in the rearview mirror. "We'll find you a monster buck later." His beer breath reached into the back seat and cold slapped me in the face. Walsh kept his eyes on me for an uncomfortable amount of time—*Look at the road!*—as he held up a paper bag containing prescription pill bottles stolen from an elderly woman's house. Along with his protege, Andy Wayne, who was riding shotgun, the delinquent duo frequently targeted the homes of senior citizens for drugs. "I gotta make some cash first—that cool with you?"

Before I could reply, the Jeep Cherokee's meaty tires roared across the I-95 rumble strip at around ninety miles per hour. My stomach lurched as Walsh swore and jerked us back into the passing lane.

"Probably shouldn't crash a hot Jeep!"

Yep, they'd stolen the Jeep, too. These guys had a proclivity for Jeeps because the VIN on specific models was located on the wiper motor, making it easy for them to swap out the stolen VIN with a legal one obtained from junkyards. There are other hidden identification numbers on vehicles, but short of ripping a Jeep apart, Walsh's method passed the basic lookup.

"Don't worry, boys," Walsh said, reaching under his seat. This time the Jeep careened into the slow lane as he fished around and pulled out a black Sig Sauer nine-millimeter pistol. "I've got us covered if things go south."

"Better not jam this time," Andy said.

Walsh swore. "Bill, did I tell you about that?"

"Tell me what?"

"Last week, Andy and I broke into a pot house to steal their stash. The dude that lived there caught us in the act, so I pulled the pistol on him, but the damn thing jammed—it's never done that before." Walsh laughed. "You should have seen this guy's face. His eyes were as big as baseballs, and he musta had a giant load in his pants as he ran outta the house."

"It's true," Andy said, but his confirmation wasn't necessary. Walsh was tightly screwed together. He loosened up when drinking, but he still meant what he said. As a man of action, Walsh had a controlling force over anyone in his orbit. People feared what he was capable of, and most kept their distance. Except for Andy, Walsh's puppet. Andy idolized Walsh and jumped at his commands, whether night hunting or invading a home. In many ways, his man crush made Andy even more dangerous because I never knew what stupid thing he'd do to impress Walsh. Did he perceive the attempted murder as a green light to kill someone?

That was the big question.

I laughed along with the story, but my insides were twisting into knots. By all reasonable measures, I shouldn't have gotten this case in the first place. Walsh and Andy both lived and hunted around Greenfield, which was in Warden Dave Georgia's area and bordered my old territory in the Lincoln district. I'd worked the region many times with Dave as a uniformed warden, and in fact, I'd previously summoned Walsh for fishing without a license twenty years earlier when he was only eighteen. We missed this crucial detail during the case's review stage, but I wasn't tapping out now that I was in with the targets. Walsh and Andy had been making credible threats on Dave's life, and I wasn't going to wait on the sidelines while they endangered one of my closest friends in the Warden Service. The gun-jamming story confirmed my already blossoming fear—their threats against Dave weren't idle.

Walsh conducted two drug deals that night. He sold the hydrocodone pills off in a rough residential Bangor neighborhood, followed by a marijuana sale outside an apartment building that wasn't far from our

Warden Service headquarters. The newfound cash immediately burned a hole in Walsh's pocket.

"Let's hit the bars," he announced.

My heart sank. "What about hunting?" It was a Hail Mary attempt to dissuade him. Bar hopping in Bangor was the worst-case scenario for me. Like deer herding in deep winter, bad guys from my old districts congregated in Bangor to escape the doldrums of their small towns and blow off steam in the big city. It was a Friday night, so the bars were guaranteed to be packed, making the odds that no one would recognize me infinitesimal to none.

"We can go hunting anytime," Walsh said, his voice rising. "Tonight, I wanna bag a bar bunny. C'mon, Billy. I'm paying."

"Why didn't you say so?" Despite my better judgment, I followed my strategy of acquiescing to the bad guy's wishes. *This* is how cases are made. "My favorite kind of beer is free."

We wound up at Geaghan's pub across from the Hollywood Casino Hotel. A classic rock band was playing, and as anticipated, the place was packed to the gills. I pulled my green Philadelphia Eagles ball cap down over my eyes as best as I could to keep a low profile, but we weren't in there for more than five minutes before I locked eyes across the bar with someone I recognized—and not in a good way. He wasn't the only one, either. A sense of panic was boiling inside me. *What was I thinking?*

It felt like a recurring dream I often have where I'm reassigned to the Fryeburg crew, incredulous that we thought a second go-around was a good idea. *Of course, they're going to recognize me!* Huddled together, the group is scheming how to stuff me into the beaver flowage. At the center of it all, Levi Prince's stare bores into me. The brim of his leather fisherman's hat casts a shadow over his narrowing eyes as he marks his target like a bird of prey.

Somehow, I always wake before he strikes.

I tried to stay on the move in the bar, hoping that if someone approached me, they'd do so out of earshot of Walsh and Andy. Working the room also helped with the facade that I was keeping up with Walsh drink for drink. He kept feeding me beers that I'd dump in the bathroom or abandon elsewhere.

"What happened to my beer?" I'd say, looking around like a confounded drunk if I returned empty-handed.

Not that Walsh would have noticed if I'd dumped one on the floor in front of him. Pounding beers and helping himself every time one of the college-aged waitresses came by with a tray of gummy worms soaked in vodka, he was in full Elmer Fudd mode, hunting bar bunnies with reckless abandon and little tact. Nor did it matter to him whether or not a woman was there with someone. At thirty-eight years old and around six feet tall, Walsh had a rugged, thick-around-the-shoulders build, and his beer muscles were flexing with each gulp. His freshly shaven head and a black goatee added a layer of intimidation that helped deter several verbal skirmishes from escalating into fisticuffs.

The situation was out of my influence. There was no deflecting Walsh—he was a man on a mission. Each time words were exchanged, I retreated into the crowd to avoid getting caught in a brawl. Helplessness is ill-suited to undercover work, it's a bridge to disaster, but I had my own concerns to deal with, my head on a constant swivel to avoid lubed-up patrons with a bone to pick with me.

As the night wore on and the band worked their way through a setlist filled with hits from The Rolling Stones, Creedence Clearwater Revival, and The Animals, Walsh zeroed in on a pair of attractive blondes in their late twenties with tightfitting jeans, playful attitudes, and boyfriends. The latter of which didn't appreciate Walsh's wandering eyes—or hands.

"Back off," one of the boyfriends said to Walsh, hooking his arm around the woman's hips to draw her away. The territorial boyfriend had a rough look about him, shoulder-length blond hockey hair, tattered blue jeans, and a military green plaid flannel shirt with the sleeves rolled up to his elbows, revealing inked forearms. But he also had the frail appearance of a heavy user. Close to Walsh in height, he was nowhere near his weight class.

"Or what?" Walsh challenged, clearly thinking the same thing I was—this wouldn't even be a fight.

The boyfriend pulled his shirt up, revealing a long sheathed knife strapped to his belt.

Walsh laughed.

Oh, no.

I couldn't retreat on this one. If the knife came out, I had to act.

The two jousting drunks stared each other down. Walsh started to take a step forward—and then the barbell rang, signaling last call.

"I need a beer," Walsh said matter-of-factly as if the ringing triggered a conditioned response and he'd completely forgotten about throwing down. I couldn't believe it. I was literally saved by the bell!

Twenty minutes later, the bar lights came on promptly at one o'clock. I breathed a sigh of relief, foolish enough to think we were getting out of there without incident. The respite was short-lived. We found ourselves—not by accident—trailing the two blondes and their boyfriends across the parking lot.

"I can drive," I said as we reached Walsh's stolen Jeep.

"Nah." He opened the driver's door for himself.

"Watch this," Andy said to us with the giddy slur of a drunk who thinks he's struck genius. He started unzipping his fly.

Seriously, now what?

"Hey!" Andy yelled to the ladies while urinating in the parking lot.

Walsh howled his support—as if Andy needed any encouragement.

The situation could have spiraled a hundred different ways. The last thing I expected was for one of the women to walk back to us and confront Andy as he watered the pavement. It was the same girl Walsh frisked in the bar, the one with strung-out Crocodile Dundee for a boyfriend.

"Are you trying to show me your penis?" she asked, eyebrows raised, hands on her hips.

"It's not for window shopping."

"You're dreamin', honey." She walked away, visibly getting into it with her boyfriend upon returning to him.

"Jump in," Walsh told us.

Even with Walsh driving, I gladly climbed into the back seat and buckled up. We couldn't get out of that parking lot fast enough for my liking. Walsh, of course, had something else in mind. Instead of heading directly for the exit, he drove toward the other group. They noticed, and for a moment, time stood still, everyone frozen, waiting to see what would transpire.

Andy lowered his window. "Last chance," he yelled to the woman who'd challenged him. "Why settle for Vienna sausage when you can get a hundred percent certified beef?"

"Say that again!" In one swift movement, her boyfriend brandished his blade.

Andy didn't flinch. "Oh, we're having a knife fight?" He grabbed a buck knife from the glove compartment and jumped out of the Jeep. "Let's go!"

I had to do something. Preventing a murder superseded preserving my cover, but it wasn't as simple as announcing my authority. I was unarmed, without restraints, and lacking backup. There was no telling who the yahoo boyfriends were and how they would react, but Andy and Walsh were willing to kill, and they weren't operating with an ounce of rational thought—their actions a Molotov cocktail of booze and testosterone. Blowing my cover to stop the fight was quite possibly an act of suicide. But if I didn't do anything and someone was killed, it would forever weigh on my conscience. Not to mention, I'd get fried in the resulting media hell-storm.

The boyfriend squared off, but he must have seen the crazy in Andy's eyes because he quickly thought better of it and retreated around a parked car.

Andy gave chase.

The two women screamed hysterically. It was total chaos.

What could I do?

"I'll end this." Walsh reached under the front seat for his gun.

No time to hesitate—I had to make a split-second decision.

"Cops!" I yelled.

Walsh swore and jammed his gun back into hiding.

"Get in," he yelled at Andy, who quickly scampered back while the other group flocked to their vehicle.

We drove out of the parking lot as a Bangor Police cruiser came around the corner. I was bluffing when I yelled cops—I had no idea one was nearby. The officer and I locked eyes briefly as our vehicles passed each other.

You have no idea what you almost encountered.

"That was close," Walsh said. "Thanks, Bill."

It was around two in the morning when we returned to my hotel. Despite everything we'd been through, Andy still wanted to go night hunting. Here's another aspect of undercover work that lacks luster. Imagine that your boss—drunk and drugged—runs you ragged on a road trip all night, comes within a split second of stabbing someone, and then, when your eyelids feel like anvils, insists on breaking the law some more into the wee hours of the morning. And you can't really say no because that's the whole reason you're there.

"I'm out," Walsh said. "Sorry, Bill, we'll get you a buck next time— I'm spent."

"It's cool. I'm looking forward to sleeping, too." I hoped this was enough to deter Andy, but I should have realized the futility of wishful thinking.

"C'mon, Bill," Andy pleaded. "Let's go for a ride in your truck. You have your rifle in there, right?"

Once again, I acquiesced, feeling like the younger sibling, incredulous that Walsh got something I didn't—sleep. Andy did the talking as I drove us around, his idolization of Walsh in full panoramic view. He wanted me to know that Walsh had trained him well and taught him all of the best places to go. I was in good hands. There was no way we weren't getting a deer.

"If it's brown, it's down," he said, sounding like a broken record as he scanned the fields along a back road. *I hadn't heard that one before.*

"I just want a trophy buck," I reminded him. It was one of my go-to lines, a strategy to avoid excessive killing during the cases. "Does and skippers aren't worth the risk."

"Screw that. My fridge is empty—I'm shooting anything!" He adjusted his silver-framed glasses and concentrated on a field. "You're right about one thing, though."

"What's that?"

"I'm a convicted felon; I'm totally screwed if we get caught."

"Maybe we should head back then?"

"Nah, I've got a better idea. Let's check out the fields by Warden Georgia's house."

"Are you crazy? What if he catches us?"

Andy smiled to himself. "Don't worry about him." There was a drunken conviction in his voice that planted a lump in my throat. He was doing this to impress me, I realized, but to a greater extent, Walsh. I could see his gears grinding. Andy was playing it all out in his mind, how he'd tell Walsh all about shooting a deer next to the warden's house.

"Do you think you could kill someone?" he asked.

Oh no. His fantasy was far worse than I imagined. Andy was pondering following through on their threats against Dave.

"What do you mean?"

"Would it bother you to kill someone? Could you pull the trigger?"

He was dead serious. The pale moonlight shining through the windows exposed a blank expression on his face as he turned to me, his dark and hollow eyes awaiting my response. Andy wasn't someone you'd see on the street and immediately think, *this guy is trouble*—that was Walsh. Andy's buzzed brown hair and baby face with fledgling wisps of a goatee made him look like an overgrown kid and gave the impression of innocence, but that couldn't be further from the truth. The devil was hard at work within him.

"I'd need a good reason," I said. "Like if someone was attacking my family. I couldn't just kill a person for the sake of doing it. I don't know how I'd feel afterward. Probably not good."

Andy nodded as if that was an acceptable and anticipated response. "It's something I think about a lot." He stared ahead into the void cast from the headlights. I got the impression he was talking it through with himself more than me. "I can do it, and I don't think it will bother me one bit. If I'd stabbed that dirtbag tonight, I wouldn't lose any sleep over it."

I wasn't just working poachers, thieves, and drug dealers. At this moment, it sunk in that these guys were sociopathic. The bulge in my throat continued to restrict as we passed Warden Georgia's house. His department truck was in the driveway.

Dave was home.

"There are deer in the field," Andy said, pointing out a cluster of four or five deer that were over a hundred yards from the road.

"That's too far of a shot for the Hornet," I said, referring to my .22 caliber single-shot rifle that Andy was cradling in his lap.

"Let's go to my house. We have a trail that leads to the backside of the fields."

Andy rented his place from Walsh, who had moved into his parent's farmhouse when they passed. Having a game warden for a neighbor, separated by several deer-rich fields, stoked the flames of animosity for these miscreants. As for the house, you had to see it to believe it. A do-it-yourself, ranch-style home, the house was off its foundation, close to three feet higher on one end from the other. The clapboards were rotting out beneath multiple layers of peeling paint, and the deck looked like it would collapse beneath the weight of a raccoon. Most of the house, especially the bathroom, was a giant petri dish. Black mold lived a life of luxury in the tub's creases, and rainbow algae ranged from dark green on the bottom to bright orange on the walls within the basin. Likewise, the toilet was a slip-and-slide, and a shag carpet of pubic hair covered the peeling linoleum floor. If that wasn't bad enough, the couch I sometimes crashed on was a Connect Four game of bodily fluid stains.

"What do you think of my bachelor pad?" Andy said the first time I visited. "I keep it pretty clean, don't I?"

I nearly burst out laughing, the realization that he was serious the only thing holding me back. *This place should be condemned!* Whenever I stayed there, I wanted to run straight to the doctor's office afterward for shots. But from Andy's perspective, it *was* clean compared to Walsh's house. Walsh lived in an unremitting state of filth. Stacks of used dishes and rotting food monopolized all kitchen surfaces, and the living room had so much hoarded junk that there wasn't any place to sit. Outside, heaps of trash and decomposing food attracted wildlife.

Before setting out for the fields, Andy got the bright idea to make a silencer for the rifle using duct tape and an empty liter bottle of Mountain Dew. I knew it wouldn't work, but I played along in hopes that he'd sober up and lose the wind in his sails. To no surprise, the test shot was nearly as loud as without the bottle, but that didn't deter Andy.

"What if the game protector heard the shot?" I asked, using Pennsylvania terminology to conceal my friendship. "Hunting now doesn't seem like a good idea."

Andy laughed. "Walsh likes to mess with the warden. He's been firing shots at all hours of the night for years, so Georgia never knows when we're hunting or just messing around."

Despite his bravado, Andy handed me the rifle to scope out the field when we reached the treeline. "It's a mandatory five years in jail if I get caught with a gun."

The moon slipped behind thick clouds, so Andy lit the field with a powerful handheld LED flashlight while I looked through the scope. The deer were gone.

"They probably moved into the lower fields," Andy said.

A couple of hills separated us from the lower section, and by the time we snuck onto the largest mound, the moon peaked out from behind the clouds, providing visibility without the flashlight. Dave's house was in full view from this vantage point, only a hundred and fifty yards away.

"This is crazy," I said. "We're *way* too close to the game protector's house."

"Screw him. He'll never arrest me." Andy took the rifle back and aimed it at Dave's house. "I'll shoot the bastard if he comes out tonight."

I feared Dave stepping out of his house at that very moment to investigate the earlier gunshot. The timing was about right. It would have taken him a while to wake up, look out his windows, get dressed, and call dispatch. What would happen if he did? Andy was a total wild card. Most of the bad guys I worked made disparaging or threatening remarks toward wardens at some point. That was nothing new, and usually, I brushed it off as bravado. But Andy knew that words didn't impress Walsh. He had the house in his crosshairs, and there was little doubt he'd pull the trigger. We were out of range for the Hornet, but it wasn't worth the risk.

"Not with my rifle, you won't." I snatched the gun from his hands. "I'm not going down for that."

He looked at me. Hurt. I'd broken my rule of agreeing to whatever the bad guy wants, and in doing so, splintered our kinship.

We shared a long, awkward moment of silence.

"Fine," Andy finally said. "Let's go hunt some more in your truck."

It was a quarter of four in the morning. Between the nightmarish drunken joy ride to Bangor and back, the drug deal, the bar scene, the knife fight, and thwarting Andy's threat to kill Dave, I was emotionally and physically spent—not to mention freezing from lying on the hill. Even Andy's crusty couch was sounding good.

"Okay," I said.

On the surface, Walsh and Andy appeared reckless and out of control. Drinking and driving at dangerous speeds in a stolen Jeep while trafficking narcotics was merely Exhibit A. Between the hot Jeeps—they had three in their possession when my case ended, including one from a used car lot that I negotiated to buy—the home invasions, the drug dealing, and the constant poaching, it defied logic that their rap sheets were so paltry. Andy's conviction for felony burglary was nearly ten years prior, and Walsh's most recent arrest stemmed from night hunting eleven years before this case. That episode turned into a high-speed chase between Walsh and Wardens Bruce Loring and Dave Georgia; however, Walsh pled the felony eluding charge down to a failure-to-stop misdemeanor.

From a district warden's perspective, this cold hard fact was incredibly humbling. These guys often night hunted the Stud Mill Road, a major woods thoroughfare connecting a network of logging roads that encompassed thousands of paper company woodland acres from Old Town to Washington County. Unlike other serious poachers who are extremely careful about spotlighting, these guys worked the Stud Mill Road in full winter clothing with the windows down and two spotlights going the whole time on each side. The bright spotlight beams were like two giant middle fingers to the Warden Service. After they shot a buck and complained that it wasn't as big as they thought, they threw it into the back of the truck and continued hunting with the lights on.

They had no fear of getting caught.

Dave Georgia and I had worked the Stud Mill Road on many nights from dusk till dawn. How had *we* never caught them?

The answer was painfully simple. As Walsh explained when I expressed concern over the spotlights, they only hunted the Stud Mill Road from midnight until four in the morning on Sundays through Wednesdays when it was unlikely that anyone else would be out.

He was right. Dave and I had conducted many all-night Friday and Saturday stakeouts on the Stud Mill Road without seeing a single vehicle. Why would we use our allotted working time on a Monday night when the odds of catching someone decreased exponentially? There's no way to justify that to our Lieutenant, and these guys knew it. They were reckless—but calculated.

It's hard to admit, but standard law enforcement procedures are often ineffective against the worst of the worst. Sure, these guys were bound to get caught eventually for something, but how much had they gotten away with between their prior convictions and now? How much more would they get away with before getting busted again? And when a uniformed officer finally catches them, what other illegal activities will they be involved in that we simply don't know about or can't prove?

As you'll soon learn in a coming chapter, the Maine Warden Services' covert policies and practices have gotten dissected under the political microscope. To our critics, I have to ask: Are these the type of criminals to whom you want to extend a long leash?

Because the way I see it, the only way to beat 'em, is to join 'em.

We used the State Police's tactical team to execute the warrant for Walsh's arrest. This strategy has also been criticized by news media and state politicians, but when Walsh came to the doorway and the tactical squad ordered him by a loudspeaker to show his hands, he hesitated. Only after repeated warnings, and likely the realization that his house was surrounded, did Walsh lay down the loaded nine-millimeter pistol he was concealing behind his back. What would have happened if only a couple of wardens had shown up? We'll never know, and that's a good thing as far as the families of those wardens are concerned.

These guys didn't get off lightly from this operation. As part of a plea deal, Andy pled guilty to thirty-one of fifty-two charges, served a year in jail with two suspended out of a three-year sentence, and was fined seventeen thousand dollars. Walsh served three years in federal prison, racked up over fifteen thousand dollars in fines, and had over twenty firearms along with ammunition and equipment confiscated.

Justice was finally served.

11

OVER THE LINE

The razor-sharp boning knife flashed before my face.

In the blink of an eye, my greatest fear came to life. I've already written about my obsession with being *made*, of being discovered. Everywhere I went, I furtively watched the eyes of those I encountered, looking for any spark of recognition. That's when I dared go out in public, that is. More times than not, I remained home, missing out on major family events such as my son's tournament basketball games on the off chance I'd cross paths with someone I shouldn't. At night, when my restless brain finally surrendered to sleep, The Poacher King was there.

Another glimmering flourish of the boning knife.

This was no dream.

The stroke was so close I could feel the backwash of air on my face—the drunken sociopath with the blade spewing obscenities, showering me with spittle.

No offense, but I don't think you can truly understand what I'm describing without having lived this life. The fear wears on all undercover agents. Put a group of us in a room, and it's only a matter of time before the conversation goes here. We are each other's support group.

But let me try to fit you into my shoes. Imagine hyperventilating without actually breathing. It's a physiological impossibility but tell that to your heart exploding in your chest. Throat constricted. The worst hot flash imaginable, and you're begging yourself not to sweat. A touch of nausea. Your body is programmed to fight or flight, and you're doing everything you can to douse those flames with ice water. You can't so much as flinch. You have to be cool. Calm. Collected.

Everything's fine. It's a simple misunderstanding.

But that's a lie. They're on to you. They *know*.

The knife cuts the air again. More shouting. Pure belligerence.

Steady now. Don't waver. Count to ten. Put your hands up. Palms out. Nonthreatening. You don't know what they're talking about. It's crazy. You're one of them.

Another lie.

You're in too deep. Unarmed. All alone. Outnumbered six to one. At a cabin in the middle of the woods. Their home turf.

Don't lose your composure now. Your wits are your only defense.

It's a game of poker. The ante is your life.

"Are you or are you not a warden?"

Cards down. All bets are in.

I'm sorry, I have to pause this memory here. Recanting it has my stomach doing somersaults, and I'm suddenly short of breath. *This* can't be healthy. So let's take a step back, wade into the story slowly.

The high-powered beam of white light swept across the hayfield, leaving a wave of empty darkness in its wake.

"Man, no smashers," said the stoner riding shotgun in my undercover truck. Jamie D'Ambrosio wore a black hooded sweatshirt and a winter beanie decorated in multi-colored marijuana leaves that advertised the most lucrative of his chosen trades. "Not even a baldy."

Smashers was my term for a monster buck. Insisting that I only wanted to shoot a smasher helped curtail my participation. *Baldy* was an antlerless deer. Suffice to say, Jamie didn't share my prerequisites. To him, wildlife was a means of target practice.

He flicked on the truck cab's overhead light to roll a joint he didn't need.

"What now?" I asked.

"Dunno." His fingers deftly worked the joint together like a Master Guide tying on a fly.

"We're close to the camp. You wanna go help those guys out?"

Earlier in the day, we'd taken part in a deer drive with a group of Jamie's poacher friends who were now cutting up the two does shot illegally. I was hoping to further witness those complicit to the crimes in action, but I knew Jamie wouldn't like the suggestion. He wasn't a true hunter in that he didn't care about the meat. Jaime was purely in it for the kill. Once he satiated his thirst for blood, he couldn't care less about the carcass. During the case, he shot a good-looking buck that he didn't want to deal with, so he hid it in a tarp inside a bulldozer on the woods road they hunted.

Predictably, Jaime hesitated. "I s'pose. We are hunting their fields and all." He licked and sealed the rolling paper. "You mind?"

I spat a round of chew spit into a Mountain Dew bottle, another tactic I used to avoid drinking and smoking.

"Free Willy."

Jamie D'Ambrosio was go, go, go. A loose cannon, his wife encouraged his pot-smoking to keep him off oxy and presumably to slow him down, but from what I observed, it did little to diffuse his firecracker personality. At only five foot seven, he was lean, strong, and deceptively athletic. I once watched in awe as he scaled a twelve-foot wall like Spiderman to adjust a buck mount.

My favorite movie is *The Departed*, and Jamie and his brother seemed ripped from the cast with their thick South Boston accents. They were Italians from Dorchester, Massachusetts, and the conditions of their relocation to Maine were dubious at best. Always up for a scrap, Jamie told me that he was a convicted felon for beating a guy senseless with bolt cutters. We couldn't verify this until after the case concluded because Massachusetts' recordkeeping was a rat's nest at the time and we couldn't call the police station directly because Jaime was closely connected to an officer.

"The police station parking lot is the best place to deal drugs," he once bragged.

Then there was a murder. Jamie didn't do it, and his involvement, if any, was never clear to me. But he and his brother had first-hand knowledge of who did, and so their father decided it was time to relocate the entire family before his sons became too entwined in the Boston mob scene to escape.

Not that Jaime turned over a new leaf in Maine. The lawbook was his personal bucket list. While I was working him, he brokered a ninety-pound marijuana deal when it was still illegal. Ninety pounds! That's not dealing—it's distributing. On top of the drugs, he was notorious for stealing and chopping ATVs. At one point, he admitted that he and his brother were going to steal my four-wheeler. He also worked on a demolition crew with a Bath Iron Works contract, from which he stole aluminum.

From what I've shared about Jamie, you're probably thinking—*This is the guy. This has to be the guy with the boning knife.* In which case, you'd be wrong. In terms of sociopathic behavior, Jaime was an alter boy compared to Colton Harris, whose camp we were en route.

Tucked a mile into the woods behind the Harris family farmstead, the camp was ensconced in a swamp, making the old woods road to it the only real way in or out. It was around nine-thirty when we arrived. There were three other trucks parked outside, and despite the noise from the gas generator powering the cabin, the front curtain parted as someone peered out. They knew we were there, but they also expected us, so it didn't strike me as anything out of the ordinary. Jamie and I joked about something stupid—probably our hopes that they were nearly done—as we trudged from my truck to the door.

"What's going on?" Jamie said in his booming look-at-me voice as we entered the small one-room cabin. The warm air inside carried the distinctive metallic odor of fresh blood and raw meat along with a faint whiff of propane from the space heater.

They greeted us with sideways glances and awkward silence.

A couple of guys sheepishly said, "Hey."

Aside from Jamie and I, six people were already in the camp, three of whom were processing the deer on an old wooden rectangular table at the left side of the room. Colton's twenty-one-year-old nephew, Hunter, was sitting on the beer cooler next to the window, keeping watch, and two other guys were standing around drinking. The table was the only furnishing, at the head of which was Colton. He was dressed in blood-spattered blue jeans and a camo tank top, and his arms were stained with streaks of crimson from skinning the deer. He was now carving a hindquarter. Next to him, his live-in girlfriend, Brenda, was wrapping cuts in white freezer paper. Colton's cousin, a tall, beefy guy in his late twenties that everyone called Skid, manned a manual meat grinder clamped to the far end of the table.

Simply put, the camp was their illegal game chop shop.

There was also a gigantic elephant in the room at risk of becoming mincemeat.

That was me.

During the deer drive, Danny Scott, a member of their crew, accused me of letting three deer pass my location without shooting. Colton had made it clear that we were shooting all deer—including does and yearlings—making my leniency an act of questionable defiance. The irony of the accusation is that while I likely would have missed the deer intentionally, I hadn't even seen them.

Jaime had put me on babysitting duty with his ten-year-old daughter because he didn't want her jeopardizing his hunt. She was carrying a single-shot .410 shotgun loaded with a slug, and it probably goes without saying that her muzzle control wasn't exactly practiced. We were sitting in a thicket of fir trees, and I was too busy ducking and redirecting each time she swung the barrel around to notice the deer passing by us. The next thing we knew, our hearts were in our throats as gunshots exploded all around us.

This explanation sufficed at the time, but with a couple of hours to drink, smoke pot, and talk among themselves, it was clear the tide had turned. Now, you would have thought I'd shot their dog. To stay on guard for anyone coming, they didn't so much as have a radio playing, making the camp's soundtrack the gnashing of the meat grinder and the constant hiss of the space heater. To avoid eye contact, everyone appeared enthralled by Colton trimming the silverskin and fat off the hindquarter. Considering how intoxicated he was, his butchery skills were a sight to behold. He didn't waste a movement as he stabbed the silverskin in the middle of the thigh and quickly sliced away a strip.

Brenda caught my eye and abruptly looked away with a knowing smirk. A big-boned bar girl with a plain face, short and curly dirty-blonde hair, and a nasty temperament, she loved to see deer killed. Nights like this often ended with Brenda yelling at Colton that she wanted to watch porn and ride the donkey. The funny thing was she had a respectable day job as a dental hygienist. I wouldn't want her flossing my teeth because angry was her happy. On this night, Brenda knew a confrontation was brewing, and she was reveling in it.

The tension in the room was so thick that when Jamie cracked open a Bud Light can, I flinched, thinking a shot was fired.

"I'm heading out," Danny said, finally breaking the silence. "I've gotta work in the morning." He paused at the door. "Bill, you gonna come back hunting in Maine again?"

"I hope so," I told him. "It depends on work."

"Alright, see you around."

"You bet. Have a good one."

With Danny gone, the hornet's nest he'd stirred sprung to action.

"We've heard some funny things," Colton said, looking me squarely in the eyes. Like Jamie, Colton was in his early thirties and on the smaller side of average, around five-six and a hundred and seventy pounds. His size was deceptive. A woodcutter by trade, he was lean and muscular. His dark hair was shaved close, matching the length of his two-week scruff. "There's a bunch of stories going around. People are saying there's an undercover game warden that hunts and drinks with guys before busting them."

I suddenly wished I hadn't been particular about shooting a smasher. If I'd killed a doe earlier in the case, it would have put the suspicions to rest. This was where I'd usually slip in a joke to diffuse the situation, but it was obvious this wasn't a laughing matter. I kept my mouth shut, waiting to see where they were going with it—how much they knew.

"Danny has a buddy in Turner who was busted by him." Brenda eagerly jumped in as if she'd been waiting all night for this moment. "The warden hunted with them in Maine and Pennsylvania, got him and his dad for a whole bunch of stuff in both states—including drugs. Nailed them pretty good with thousands of dollars in fines and jail time."

They knew more than I was comfortable with—another case of Maine being one giant small town. I've said it before, but it's not good when the wives and girlfriends become suspicious. The women who don't hunt (some do) aren't building the same camaraderie with me as the men. As a result, they're able to assess the situation through a clear lens, and they seem to have an innate ability to detect deception.

"You're from Pennsylvania," she said to me, once again flashing that smirk. "What a coincidence."

Colton cut a slab of meat away from the hindquarter and slapped it onto a strip of unrolled freezer paper. He extended his arm and pointed the boning knife at me. "People are saying you're the undercover agent." His slate-gray eyes bore into me beneath the curtain of his thick, furrowed brow. As drunk and high as he was, his focus was unwavering. I hadn't until this moment noticed the streak of dried blood on his forehead. "People are saying we're in trouble. Are we, Bill?"

"Yo," Jamie said, coming to my defense. "Who are these people saying things? Danny? He doesn't know anything. What does Billy have to do to prove to you guys that he's cool? You never busted my balls like this."

Brenda looked like her head was going to explode. "You're a drug dealer! We *all* know it—*everyone* knows it!"

"Yeah, okay. Good point." Jamie gave me a shrug that said, *I tried.*

"We don't know where Bill came from," Brenda said, gesticulating wildly. "You say he's cool, but how do we know? He talks a good game about killing deer, but—"

"He hasn't shot anything," Colton said.

What happened next was the worst-case scenario.

"Hunter," Colton said to his nephew, "get Bill's full name and look it up. Make him spell it out for you."

"Whatever," I said, feigning annoyance. "It's Bill Freed, F-R-E-E-D."

The moppy-headed boy pulled out his iPhone to conduct a search.

"There's no reception here," Colton said. "Go back to the house and look it up on my computer. You can take my truck. The keys are in the ignition."

Eager to play investigator, Hunter hurried out.

I was sweating bullets. Long cases such as this were already stressful because it increased the chances of something going awry. These guys were slaying deer left and right, and the community was justifiably fed up. It's a tough situation for local wardens because they hear it from people frustrated that nothing is getting done. I feel for them because it looks like they aren't doing their jobs, and in this case, one of the younger wardens cracked. When asked if this group hadn't been caught because an undercover investigation was underway, he responded, "I can't confirm nor deny."

We all know what *that* means.

My mind was racing in circles like a dog chasing its tail, connecting dots that may or may not have been connectable. Had that conversation with the local warden gotten back to Danny? Or maybe Danny was the one who talked to the warden? He already knew about undercover investigations from his connection to Tucker Leroux; trying to dig for info was a logical next step.

It wasn't lost upon me that the undercover agent in *The Departed* takes a bullet to the head in the end. A shot he never saw coming. Was this whole situation a setup? Had Jamie taken me night hunting so the rest of the crew could work up the liquid courage to do what had to be done? Jamie was already connected to one murder—perhaps it was his idea? Did he have second thoughts in the truck? Is this the real reason he was reluctant to come to the camp? Had they sent Hunter to the house because they didn't want the kid to witness what came next?

I didn't have much time to make sense of it all. Colton's disposition was rapidly deteriorating.

"You better not be a warden!" he yelled at me. It was his M.O. to go off the deep end when confronted by wardens, belligerently swearing and screaming to intimidate and confuse. I knew of at least one situation where he'd successfully drawn the local district warden away from discovering a poached ten-point buck hidden under fir bows in the back of his truck.

"I'm not," I said, hoping he subscribed to the misguided belief that I had to tell the truth.

"You better not be!" He grabbed the boning knife from the table and lunged toward me, swiping the blade through the air in front of my face.

This behavior didn't feel like an act. It was alcohol-fueled rage.

"I'll do it!" He took another swipe near my midsection.

Aptly named, the boning knife cuts flesh from bone. Colton's six-inch, stainless-steel blade had a precision point to pierce meat and a black handle with a finger guard that prevented his greasy hands from slipping over the sharp edge. In the movies, they often show perpetrators grabbing a butcher knife before stabbing someone, but the boning knife is far superior for the purpose.

"I swear to God, if you're a warden, I'll cut you to pieces!"

I believed him. Colton was a different breed of deranged. He poached because he enjoyed killing. Unlike the Turner case, where the Lerouxs took pride in their marksmanship, Colton would intentionally gutshot a deer so he could torture it. Colton took personal offense at how cunning deer could be in the forest, and he'd get his revenge by holding the nostrils of a suffering deer shut while making it smoke a cigarette or drink a beer.

"You don't feel so good now, do you?" he'd taunt.

Cigarettes and beer were for when he was feeling charitable. He once dragged a wounded doe into a pond to drown it, an act he performed slowly, continuously bringing the deer's head up for air before dunking it again. Perhaps his favorite and most perverse torture method was to field dress deer while they were still alive so he could hear them bleat in agony.

Most of these stories I heard secondhand through Jamie or Colton's own drunken bragging. I didn't for a second doubt they were real. On one hunt, Colton specifically instructed me to aim for the gut so he could "Have some fun with it." Another time I was with them, we couldn't find a deer that Colton had wounded. We came upon it the following day when the carcass was half-eaten by coyotes and rotting. Colton broke down into tears. Not because the meat was spoiled, but because the coyotes ended his game.

In all of my work infiltrating Maine's worst poaching rings, I'd never met anyone more sadistic. With someone like that, you just don't know what twisted thoughts fill his head. Was all of the torturing a build-up to a darker evil?

"You may screw us for these deer," he continued to rant, spraying me with more spittle. "But I swear I'll find you. It might take the rest of my life, but I'll hunt you down, cut your bag off, and hang it from the ceiling!"

He lunged at me again, the blade flashing inches from my face. With each threat, he was getting closer. Bolder. More aggressive. I've never been so scared in my life. I couldn't just stand there and wait for him to attack me. In police training, we're taught that action beats reaction. If you wait for the bad guy to make his move, you're dead. You have to be proactive.

I imagined an invisible line on the floor, two feet in front of me. Colton had already crossed the line with his faux stabs, but if he did it again, I was going to punch him in the chin to knock him out. I'd boxed in high school, so I knew the technique. Being right-handed, I bladed my body (also known as fighter stance) by placing my left foot in front of the right, slightly wider than shoulder length, and turning to a forty-five-degree angle to Colton to get the full force of my back and hips into the punch. I kept my hands below my hips to keep from tipping him off. My weapon was the element of surprise.

Even if I did neutralize Colton, the room was filled with his next of kin. There was little doubt in my mind that all hell was about to break loose. I planned to punch Colton and nonchalantly walk toward the door, hoping everyone would be too shocked to react. If someone got in my way, I'd also hit them.

Jamie was the wildcard in this game of poker. He wouldn't pass up a fight, but whose side was he on?

"Are you or are you not a warden?"

Cards down. All bets are in.

"I already told you I'm not."

I was laser-focused on Colton's feet, prepared for him to cross the line. Inexplicably, Colton backed off. I don't know if he realized I'd called his bluff by getting into a fighter stance or if he simply lost interest, but he grabbed a beer from the cooler and returned to his station at the table.

Even Brenda looked confused.

I wanted to get out of dodge, but Jamie and I continued to hang out and help with the deer. As awkward as it was when we first arrived, the feeling became magnified tenfold. I didn't dare attempt leaving until Hunter came back, figuring it would fuel their suspicions. Which meant I still wasn't out of the woods. I had no idea what Hunter would or wouldn't find. This case took place in 2011, and Facebook had become a game-changer for covert operatives, and not in a good way. A few times in my career, targets that I was working posted their hunting photos with me. As this case had already proven, you just never know who knows who in Maine.

Hunter re-entered the camp, and I played it as cool as a deer in headlights can, pretending not to notice him go straight to Colton.

Hunter gave him a silent nod.

What did *that* mean?

Colton came over to me. Thankfully, the boning knife wasn't in his hands.

"I'm sorry." The angry contours of his face now relaxed, he hugged me, but by the way he ran his hand over my back, I could tell he was feeling for a wire. I rarely wore one because it was too dangerous in a situation like this.

"You can't be too careful," Jamie said, playing peacemaker, "game wardens will do anything to catch us." After a beat, he turned to me. "C'mon, let's go for a ride. See if we can find a smasher."

I agreed.

"I thought you were going to punch him," Jamie said once we were outside, and the generator drowned out our conversation.

"I was going to if he got any closer."

"I wish you had! I was gonna slug Skid."

I laughed. "He's got at least seventy pounds on you."

"Man, I don't care. I hate those guys. I only hang out with them to hunt on their farm."

The truth always comes out in an undercover investigation.

12

THE PRICE OF SOUP

EDDIE ZHAO CLOSED THE WOODEN, BIFOLD SLIDING DOORS SEPARATING the front room we were in, a party space with a hot tub and an adjacent bar, from the main house's den. For a forty-six-year-old Chinese man, Eddie was a known playboy, and I couldn't help but notice that the cover was off the hot tub and the temperature set to one hundred and four—ready for business. His home was a large neo-Victorian in Presque Isle with an addition in the back that served as a dormitory for a bevy of young, mostly female, Asians—most of whom worked in his restaurant, their legal status questionable. Eddie left a crook in the sliding doors and spied on the den through the elbow cracks long enough for a commercial break. Turning to me, he held a finger over his lips.

"We have to keep our voices down." He wasn't exactly whispering, but close enough. Eddie's English was fluent, but it was his second language, so he came across as blunt at times. "My son's tutor is here. I don't want her to know what we're doing."

"Seriously? I don't want her to see me at all." For my part, acting nervous wasn't entirely an act. I was collaborating with federal agents on this case, and they had me wearing a wire with a pinhole camera that looked like an ordinary black button on my buffalo plaid flannel shirt. It was typically too dangerous for me to wear a wire, but the feds loved their toys, and Eddie wasn't a violent person, so I didn't have much of a choice in the matter. Two federal agents were observing from nearby in case backup was necessary. Still, I don't like relying on technology—it's one more thing that can go wrong. Case in point, the battery pack strapped to the small of my back was heating up. Was that normal? How hot would it get?

"Don't worry, she hasn't," Eddie said with a smile, dressed down in a black polo shirt, jeans, and New Balance sneakers. I'd gotten accustomed to meeting him on his way to the Connecticut casinos. In those situations when he was reselling the bear parts I'd sold him, he looked like he was made of money, wearing a fancy leather jacket, designer dress clothes, stylish Italian leather shoes, and enough gold rings and necklaces to star in a music video. A man of average stature with a round face and dark, short-cropped hair, he had a warm, persuasive personality and an always-on-the-go motor. "Now, what have you brought me?"

"Everything I've got right now. Gallbladders are in this cooler. The bear paws, a fully intact female bear, a cub, and the fresh deer ribs you asked for are out in the truck."

I emptied the cooler's content—sixty dried bear gallbladders and twenty-nine frozen ones—onto the bartop. A shaft of late afternoon sunlight from the window illuminated the bounty. Before inspecting the merchandise, Eddie peaked through the door cracks again.

This operation began two years earlier when another Chinese restaurant owner approached Eric Holmes, a special agent in the U.S. Fish and Wildlife Service living in Maine and a friend of mine from college, complaining about Eddie illegally trafficking in bear parts. Gallbladders are highly valued on the black market, exploited for the bile used in various Asian medicines, as are the paws, the main ingredient in bear paw soup. Maine is one of only four states in the Union where it's legal to sell gallbladders with a hide dealer license. Eddie wasn't licensed, but a loophole in the law permitted the sale of legally obtained gallbladders without it. In other words, Eddie could have a hundred gallbladders and get away with selling them by simply saying they were given to him. Of course, my task was to prove that he wasn't obtaining them legally. I'm not a big fan of government regulations, but this case was eye-opening, prompting me to lead the charge on closing the loopholes. Maine's bear population is healthy, so there is currently no resource issue, but combine loose regulations with high profit margins, and it's easy to see how quickly the tide could turn.

Being one of only four states that permits trading bear parts has turned Maine into a hub for out-of-state and even Canadian bears getting smuggled in for sale. At the time of this case, the nucleus of that wheeling and dealing was Eddie Zhao. Most of his transactions went to New York City; however, he'd recently returned from a China trip, passing through customs with ten thousand dollars in cash—the maximum amount allowed—so we believed he was getting gallbladders overseas.

The interstate commerce was a federal violation of the Lacey Act banning illegal wildlife trafficking; however, the informant posed several issues for Eric working the case himself. For starters, they were neighbors. And when it comes to informants, there's always the question of motive. Was the informant appalled by Eddie's role in the illegal bear trade, or was he trying to eliminate a competitor? Or worse, what if he was playing both sides of the fence? As much as I'd love to bust Eric's chops by saying the federal agents don't like getting their hands dirty, the safe play was to ask me to work the case.

I was dubious of the plan. The idea was for me to pose as an out-of-state bear hunter, eating at Eddie's Chinese food restaurant every day until he approached me. It seemed far-fetched because Eddie's restaurant was in the Presque Isle mall, the last place you'd expect nefarious wildlife activity. What was the likelihood that a solo hunter would eat at the mall food court every day? I mean, I can only love beef teriyaki sticks and chicken fried rice so much. Shockingly, though, the plan worked. On my second day of mall dining, Wendy Zhao, Eddie's wife, approached me in the parking lot. We'd already made small talk at the counter, so she knew my story.

"What will you do with the bear if you get one," she asked.

I played dumb. "Eat it, I s'pose."

She smiled politely because I wasn't catching her drift. "What about the leftover parts?"

"Oh, I usually dump them in the woods for the coyotes."

"Don't do that," she said in mock horror. "We'll buy them from you."

"You will?"

"Yes, we can use them."

"Oh yeah, isn't there something on the inside of the bear that's used—what is it, I forget the name, the . . ." I was wearing a wire at the time, so I hung the question out there, wanting Wendy to say it explicitly. "Gallbladder!" She jumped on the answer like a gameshow contestant. "It's the gallbladder!"

Wouldn't you know it, I just happened to get my bear the following day. I sold the large and small gallbladders and all four paws to the Zhaos for a hundred and sixty dollars. "Gas money." Over time, I convinced Eddie that I realized the money-making potential. I had a taxidermist friend in Pennsylvania who was willing to supply me with gallbladders and paws and a guiding friend in Maine who wasn't opposed to chipping in. In reality, many of the bear parts were coming from out of state, including Pennsylvania, provided by conservation departments that obtained them through confiscation or vehicle collisions. With a steady product supply, I became one of Eddie's favorite dealers. Believing that I lived in Pennsylvania, he met me halfway for two separate sales in Massachusetts. The federal agents encouraged me to make the sales there because it's illegal to buy bear parts in Massachusetts, helping their case.

All told, the current transaction at Eddie's house was the fifth sale. He'd been out of the country for nearly four months, and he wanted me to bring everything I'd amassed, including dried gallbladders that he'd previously rejected. This deal was the big one. We intended on it being the final transaction, planning to conduct the takedown the following day when the illegal bear parts were still in Eddie's possession.

"I'll give you eighty for the frozen gallbladders," Eddie said.

"Wait a minute—you agreed to a hundred over the phone."

Eddie was a relentless negotiator, and no price was set in stone until I had cash in hand. Earlier in the case, I'd eagerly accepted his lowball offers to build his trust, but at this point, I had enough leverage to start pushing back.

"I know," he told me, "but they're different sizes. They're not equal value." He retreated into the house and returned with a box of gallon-size freezer bags, dividing up the twenty-four large gallbladders from the five small ones. "I'll give you a hundred for each of the large gallbladders and fifty for the small."

"Okay, that's fair." Despite my plan to play hardball, I wanted to move things along because the battery pack was getting hotter against my back, making me sweat.

He then picked through the dried gallbladders, hemming and hawing again.

I wanted to say, "Hurry up, will ya?"

Eddie separated the fifty large dried gallbladders from the ten small ones. "A hundred for each of these. I don't want the small ones."

"Deal."

"Seven thousand, six hundred and fifty dollars," he said, calculating the total on a notepad with a red pen. He once again peeked through the sliding doors to check on the tutor. "She's leaving." Then Eddie pulled a fist-sized roll of hundred-dollar bills out of his pocket and started counting out what he owed me. The drug dealers I've worked would have cried at the sight of it.

"I'm curious," I said, "how much do you get for the gallbladders?" We weren't sure how much he was making on the other end, so I wanted to get him on record.

Eddie hesitated. He didn't want to tell me, but he also didn't want to upset his cash cow.

"Two hundred."

"Get out of here." I playfully swung my hand through the air as if swatting a fly. "That's not much more than I'm making."

He ignored the inference and instead subtracted five dried gallbladders from the allotment he wanted to purchase. "I'm not sure about these. I don't want them."

I wasn't easily dissuaded. "What about the bear paws? What do you make on them?"

Again, Eddie pretended not to hear me, focusing on recounting the money. We still had to negotiate a price for the bear paws I'd brought, so he definitely didn't want to broach that subject.

I kept blabbing, filling the void. "My guiding buddy, the one who shot the bear I have for you, looked it up online, and he said a bowl of bear paw soup goes for anywhere between four hundred and a thousand dollars in New York City. That blew my mind!"

Eddie smiled. "It make you strong with wife."

"Really? What else is in it?"

"It's secret."

"Where can I get a bowl?"

"You can't. It's not for gweilo."

"What's a gweilo?"

"You. A white guy."

"Well then, good thing I don't need soup to be strong with my wife."

The sliding doors opened, and both of our heads snapped around. It was Wendy, dressed in black slacks and a white blouse from her shift at the restaurant.

"She's gone," Wendy said of the tutor. A forty-five-year-old Chinese woman with rectangular eyeglasses, she was petite and well put together. Her black, neck-length hair had that fresh-out-of-the-salon look, and her lips glistened with rose-colored gloss. "Can I get you each a beer?"

"We have to bring in the rest first," Eddie told her.

I backed my truck up to the porch at the front door while Eddie got his assistant, a younger Chinese man living in the back apartments, to move Wendy's Mercedes and help us unload the coolers and the two bears. Eddie spoke in Chinese to the helper and Wendy as they inspected the coolers, making me nervous that they would ask why some of the bear paws didn't have claws or the hides. Like gallbladders, claws and hides are legal to sell with a hide dealer license (or back then, if legally obtained). Bear meat used in soup—or the meat of any big game animal for that matter—is illegal to sell. By removing the claws or hides on some paws, they couldn't claim that they were buying them for those parts.

"What are you saying?" I asked.

"We're marveling at how big the Pennsylvania bear paws are," Eddie replied.

"Is that good?"

"Yes, the bigger, the better."

"Do you have freezer space for all of this?" In addition to the two bears, there were a hundred and seventeen paws, plus the deer meat and ribs. My truck was like a Sam's Club of big game contraband.

"Plenty. I have five small freezers in the house plus the two large ones at the restaurant." This admission was key for planning our raid as it let us know that he was storing some of the contraband at his restaurant.

Eddie inspected the bear cub, which had a large gash on its hind end. "I don't want it."

"I'm sorry," I said, making an excuse for the quality. "It's not the cub I was going to originally bring you. Unfortunately, my taxidermist buddy sold the other one without telling me to some Korean guy in Philadelphia."

Eddie furrowed his brows in a nonplussed expression. This was the first he'd heard of my operation selling to another buyer, and while he wasn't going to say as much, he clearly didn't like the idea of competition. It was a short-lived glimpse into his thought process as he quickly returned to his jovial self, laughing at how I'd wrapped the sow bear in a blue tarp.

"The FBI is going to think I have a body in my driveway."

I laughed, but not for the reasons Eddie thought. If he only knew that federal agents *were* watching and listening to him at this very moment.

We returned to the house, going into the dining room to negotiate the rest of the sale. The table was covered with a full spread of Americanized Chinese food from their restaurant—chicken fried rice, chow mein, teriyaki sticks, spare ribs, dumplings, egg rolls, and various beef and chicken dishes—no doubt intended for me.

"Please stay for dinner," Wendy said, handing Eddie and I each a cold bottle of Moosehead lager.

"Maybe another time." I was trying to act nonchalant despite the battery pack cooking my back. Completely flushed, a fountain of sweat was soaking into my Philadelphia Eagles ball cap. Could they tell something was amiss? Or did they think I was hot from carrying the coolers? I picked a teriyaki beef stick from the table and nibbled on it. "We're hoping to get some casts in tonight before it gets dark."

"How long are you in Maine to fish?" Wendy asked. It was a Monday at the end of June, and I'd previously told them I was getting in some river time with my guiding buddy on this trip.

"I head back Wednesday—back to packing meat."

"I'd love to try fly fishing," Eddie said. "Can I join you?"

"That'd be fun, but there's no way my guiding buddy will go for it. I'm sorry, but he doesn't want you to know who he is, so you can't rat him out if we ever get in trouble. He said he'd shoot me if I told you his name!"

"I thought this was legal in Maine," Wendy said.

"Oh no," I replied, quick to jump on her comment before Eddie could interject. To make a federal case, we had to prove that the Zhaos knew they were committing illegal acts, so I seized opportunities such as this to get it on record. "My guiding buddy says this is all illegal, especially the stuff I'm bringing you from out of state. Of course, the deer I shot for you is also out of season, so I'm trusting that you won't report me!"

Wendy covered her face with her hands. "I don't see anything."

We all laughed.

"Sorry, Eddie, but guiding is his livelihood. He can't risk losing his license. Maybe you can come down sometime and fish with me in Pennsylvania?"

"It's okay," Eddie said, "I understand." He was ready to go with his red pen and notepad. "I'll give you ten dollars apiece for the fresh bear paws and five for the older ones."

"When Eddie isn't here to negotiate," Wendy said, "I always ask for some free paws."

"You too?" I teased. "Eddie somehow always talks me down in price—he doesn't need any help, thank you very much."

Wendy straightened up, hands on her hips. "Well, it's only fair. What if some of them are bad?"

"Fine, you win—you can have nine of the older paws for free. I'm glad I don't have to negotiate with you every time!"

She was pleased. What Wendy didn't realize was that she implicated herself in the sale.

With the bear paw total equaling eight hundred and eighty dollars, Eddie offered twenty for the deer meat to make it an even thousand. I agreed to keep things moving along. Eddie also explained that the deer wasn't for resale; he would eat it himself and give it to friends to try. He then handed me the cash and asked how much I wanted for the sow bear?

"A hundred and forty," I said, knowing full well they were going to talk me down. "My buddy shot the bear out of season this spring and immediately put it in a freezer, so it's good quality." I lifted my hat and rubbed my forehead on my sleeve, which nearly caused me to wince in pain. The battery pack was scorching hot, each movement like searing steaks on a grill. Was I blistering? I had to get out of there, but I couldn't act rushed—it wasn't my style, and they'd know something was off. "That's a big bear. How are you gonna process it?"

"I usually cut the gallbladders out in the driveway."

I laughed at the expense of my back. "It's not tagged. Aren't you afraid of someone seeing you?"

Eddie shrugged. "I'll park a vehicle in the way so no one can see what I'm doing from the road." He and Wendy proceeded to speak to each other in Chinese for a moment. I grabbed a teriyaki stick from the table, pretending not to be perturbed, then chased it down with a dumpling.

"A hundred for the bear," Wendy said.

"There you go again," I said with a smile, "driving a hard bargain, but I'll take it."

Eddie handed me a hundred dollar bill for the bear, bringing the total amount of cash he'd paid me to eight thousand, two hundred and fifty dollars. He didn't want me to know how much he was making on the other end because his take was likely three or four times that amount. He certainly didn't have this much cash on hand from restaurant tips.

"We're pleased with how much fat is on the bear," Eddie told me, explaining their previous conversation spoken in Chinese now that the negotiating was over. "Chinese people use it to make their hair healthy and shiny."

"Are you sure you don't want to stay for dinner?" Wendy asked, no doubt noticing that I was now on my third beef teriyaki stick.

"I appreciate the offer, but I really should get going."

"That's too bad, I brought home the food for you, and we were hoping you'd have some drinks and join us in the hot tub after."

Yet another reason I didn't like wearing a wire. There was no telling what compromising scenario I'd get into with it. A vision of taking my shirt off in front of them and exposing the wire flashed through my mind's eye—*wouldn't that be cute*. Obviously, I had to avoid the hot tub at all costs. Could they tell I was sweating even worse over this proposition? It was enough to make *me* take a swig of beer!

"Sounds like fun, but I didn't bring a bathing suit."

An easy out—right?

"You don't need one," Eddie said. "We go without."

Oh boy.

Now I was sweating for an entirely different reason. Eddie was one to mix business with pleasure, constantly inviting me to the Connecticut casinos with him, floating the promise of girls as bait. I had a hard time believing that Wendy didn't know about his extracurricular activity. This conclusion is a terrible thing to think of someone, but I'd assumed they had an open relationship, and she was willing to trade his infidelity for her Mercedes and other perks of his wheeling and dealing. Perhaps I'd misjudged *how* open their relationship truly was. They were always trying to indulge me, and I'd likely just delivered their biggest score—at what lengths would they go to keep me happy?

I didn't want to answer that question.

"Tell you what," I said. "I can't stay tonight, but the next time you go to the casinos, we can plan a get-together, and I'll bring my wife. I know she'd love to meet both of you, but she doesn't know what we're doing is illegal, so please keep it on the down-low around her." I put my hand on Eddie's shoulder and playfully waggled a finger in his face. "Now, Eddie, I'm going to warn you, my wife is very pretty, so I don't want you hitting on her."

We both laughed, but Wendy didn't find it funny.

"I pretty too."

She was serious. I assumed Wendy directed the comment at me for insinuating that her husband would find my wife attractive and for refusing her hot tub enticement. What I didn't realize at the time was that she and Eddie divorced a year prior, but they kept the facade of being married for their son and the restaurant. She wasn't as forgiving of his thirst for younger women as I'd presumed, and in hindsight, this remark was probably more for him. Still, I was the one to respond.

"That you are, which is why I can't get into a hot tub in my birthday suit with you without my wife around to chaperone."

Wendy blushed and averted eye contact. "I'll pack you some food to go."

"I can't say no to that." Then to Eddie, "Hey, you promised to show me your boat." And with that, I successfully escaped the house.

Instead of conducting the search and seizure on Tuesday as originally planned, we added new information from the final sale to the affidavits, including that Eddie intended to use the freezers at his residence and the restaurant. Then we submitted new requests to execute simultaneous search warrants at both locations to the judge, who promptly reviewed and signed them. Meanwhile, the U.S. Fish and Wildlife Service agents assisting us also obtained a federal seizure for Eddie's white Cadillac Escalade because that was the vehicle he used to transport the contraband across state lines.

We were so busy putting together an operational plan to execute the warrants on Wednesday morning that I didn't notice Eddie called my undercover cell phone three times that day. He didn't leave a message, but it wasn't uncommon for him to contact me soon after a sale, and it literally could be for anything. Once, Eddie called because I forgot the doggie bag of food they'd packed me, but on other occasions, it was to plan our next sale or to invite me on one of his wild playboy adventures. Was he trying to up the ante on the hot tub offer before I left the state? It wouldn't have surprised me.

Reluctantly, I called back.

"I have a friend who wants to buy the bear cub," Eddie told me.

Great. I'd already ditched the cub in the woods behind my house.

"How much is he willing to pay?"

"Twenty?"

"I'll do it for twenty-five."

"He'll pay twenty-five, no problem."

"This makes me a little uneasy. Can I trust him?"

"Yes, it's a very good friend of mine from New Hampshire that's coming up to visit me."

"Is it a white guy or a Chinese guy?"

"He's Chinese, and he knows what I've been doing. You can trust him. I promise."

"Okay," I said, "but I'm only doing this because he's a friend of yours."

Eddie and I made a tentative plan for where I'd meet his friend on Wednesday, agreeing to touch base in the morning. After hanging up, I immediately called Captain Dan Scott, and we brought this update to the entire operation team. The informant had originally told Special Agent Holmes that Zhao was dealing bear parts to another Chinese restaurateur in Manchester, New Hampshire, but this was the first time we'd connected these dots. Everyone agreed that it was worth delaying the takedown until later in the day to learn more about the New Hampshire buyer and see if he violated the Lacey Act by transporting the bear cub across the state border.

The cub was already covered in hundreds of white house fly eggs when I retrieved it from the woods. After hosing the cub off, I stuck it in our standup freezer at home, the bottom shelf of which was reserved for temporary evidence storage (Gail *loved* this), so it would refreeze in time for the transaction.

Eddie and I played phone tag the following morning as we tried to zero in on his friend's travel itinerary and plan a location to conduct the sale.

"I talked to my buddy in Pennsylvania," I told him when we finally connected. "He gave me permission to sell the gallbladders you didn't want for twenty dollars apiece instead of a hundred. Are you interested?"

"Yes, I'll take them. Can we meet in Houlton today for the exchange?"

Believing that my undercover role in this investigation was over, I'd already shaved my face, transforming from Bill Freed to Bill Livezey. Eddie had never seen me like this—how could I explain that I'd cleaned up in the middle of a fishing trip with my buddy without raising suspicions?

"I don't know, I've got a long drive home already today. I really don't want to make it a longer trip by going further north." Eddie was under the impression that my guiding buddy's place was in Patten, Maine, roughly a forty-minute drive to Houlton. "How about I give the gallbladders to your New Hampshire friend on my way south, and you can pay me later?"

"That works. They're going to call you when they get close. My friend doesn't speak English so good—his wife She-She will do the talking."

"She-She?" I wasn't sure I heard him correctly.

"Yes, her name is Wensi, but she goes by She-She." He paused, and I sensed hesitation on his end. "Please don't tell them how much I'm paying for the gallbladders. I don't want them to know."

Bingo. Eddie *was* reselling to them.

"I won't. I promise."

I met U.S. Special Agents Eric Holmes and Robert Rothe in a secluded, wooded area in Oakfield to have them wire me up for the transaction.

"Can I get one that doesn't feel like it's melting my skin this time?"

"Very funny," Eric said. "How about I give you the electric shock model instead?"

Cell service was spotty at this location, sending She-She's incoming call straight to voicemail. "We're waiting for you at the Island Falls exit," she said in the message, "but we won't wait long. The money is in hand."

I climbed a knoll and found a spot to call her back.

"Eddie said that you have a bear cub he wants us to get from you," she said.

Something was off. She-She made it sound like she was buying the cub for Eddie, but he didn't want it—if he did, he would have bought it from me on Monday. The only possible explanation was that She-She didn't want me to know they were in Maine to buy from Eddie. After all, they weren't making a ten-hour round trip in a single day just for a bear cub.

"Yes, I have the cub."

"I don't have anything to put it in."

"I can sell you the cooler I have for twenty dollars."

"So, twenty for the cooler and twenty-five for the cub—that's all we owe you?"

"Yep. It's my gas money. I also have some gallbladders for you to bring to Eddie, but he's going to pay me for those later."

We agreed to meet at the Irving gas station in Oakfield to make the process quicker. This location made me nervous because it was close to my home in Sherman, running a high risk of seeing someone I knew. Arriving at the gas station first, I parked my undercover truck as far away from the pumps and the store as I could. Eddie's buddy, Pai Chang, and his wife She-She arrived approximately ten minutes later in a newer model, silver Chevy Suburban. Pai was in his early forties and dressed as though he was going to a fine dining restaurant in gray slacks and a pressed white shirt. She-She was only thirty-one, an attractive Asian woman in a black mini skirt and a light blue blouse. As expected, she did all the talking. Unlike her husband and the Zhaos, She-She struck me as a first-generation American. Her English had the fluidity of someone who'd grown up speaking it.

"You have a lot of coolers," she noted, seeing the assembly in the back of my truck.

"Do you need more than one?" I asked, wondering if she wanted coolers for the bear parts they might be getting from Eddie.

"No, just one for the bear."

I showed them the cub. "Is it for you?"

"No, Eddie wants it." She and Pai had a side conversation in Chinese. Then she asked me, "What's in the rest of the coolers?"

"They're empty. I needed them for everything I brought Eddie the other day. Speaking of which, I have the gallbladders that I mentioned for you to give to him."

She-She and I once again discussed what she owed me for the cub and the cooler, and she paid me in cash. I also gave her the dried gallbladders.

"There's nothing else in the coolers?" she asked again.

"No, I sold everything else to Eddie already."

She-She and Pai spoke to each other in Chinese as they inspected the dried gallbladders.

"Why aren't these fresh?" she wanted to know.

"I already sold the fresh ones to Eddie."

"How much?"

Here we go. Eddie didn't want me answering this question, but it's precisely what the federal agents wanted her talking about on the recording.

"It depends on the size and the quality," I told her.

"So, how much?"

"That's a trade secret." I lowered my voice and pointed to the bear cub to get it on record that she knew this was illegal. "I don't want to go to jail for this, so if you get pulled over, don't tell the cops you got it from me."

"Me too," she replied.

I offered to carry the cooler to their vehicle, and in the process, I asked how long they were visiting the Zhaos.

"Just a couple of hours. We're heading back tonight."

The Suburban's cargo area was lined with cardboard. It was the type of thing someone might do if they were, say, going to transport a large bear.

"Are you picking up the big bear that I sold Eddie?"

She-She and Pai again conversed in Chinese. Then to me, "I believe so."

I laughed to lighten the mood and dispel any possible concerns that I was interrogating them. "Make sure he gives you a good price—he's a tough negotiator!"

"How much did you sell the gallbladders to him for?"

She wasn't giving up on that question. Eddie would be wearing handcuffs thanks to me in a few hours, so I didn't see the harm in breaking his promise.

"As I said, it depends on the size and quality. The big ones went for a hundred, but we agreed on fifty for the small galls."

She smiled, content that she'd gotten the answer out of me. "You really don't have anything else in the truck?"

"No, sorry, I sold Eddie all of the gallbladders and a hundred and seventeen paws." I didn't see the point in explaining that I'd given him nine for free.

She stomped her foot on the ground in mock frustration. "You should have told me before selling to Eddie."

After the transaction, federal agents Holmes and Roth followed the New Hampshire couple to Eddie's house in Presque Isle. I was instructed to change clothes and vehicles, and to be on standby in case I was needed to help tail Pai and She-She back to New Hampshire (and yes, this is how you're picturing it from the movies, where we take turns following the suspects, so they don't get suspicious because there's one vehicle following them the whole time).

But it never got to this point. The federal component had required authorization through Washington, DC, to get the case started. Extending the case would have required the federal agents to submit a formal request that could take weeks in the review process. They'd also need to bring a different U.S. attorney into the fold to sign off on warrants in New Hampshire. In short, it was a lot of hassle that we didn't have time for because the contraband would be long gone by the time they cut all of the federal red tape, so we decided to proceed with the search and seizures that night.

Eddie and Wendy were sitting down for dinner with their guests, a fresh pot of bear paw soup on the stove, when Maine game wardens, U.S. Fish and Wildlife agents, and a U.S. Customs and Border Protection officer came knocking. The customs officer was there to investigate the immigration status of the young workers living in the back of Eddie's residence. All told, over a hundred thousand dollars' worth of contraband, cash, and property (including Eddie's brand-new Cadillac Escalade) were seized, by far the largest amount of my cases. The sow bear was found in the restaurant's walk-in freezer, leaning against and leaking fluids onto food for customers.

In Maine, it's a thousand-dollar fine for each count of buying and selling "legal" bear parts such as hides, claws, gallbladders, teeth, and skulls without a hide dealer license. It's also a thousand-dollar fine *and* ten days in jail for each count of buying and selling big game meat. The Zhaos were afraid that jail time would require them to return to China, so the district attorney allowed them to plead guilty for fines only. Wendy incurred four thousand dollars in state fines, and Eddie racked up sixteen thousand. He also forfeited the eight thousand, two hundred and fifty dollars paid to me in the final transaction. The federal court hit him for another five thousand dollars in fines for the Lacey Act violations; however, the real penalty was forfeiting his Escalade, valued at over seventy-five thousand dollars. His lawyer argued that Eddie's net worth had taken a hit since the arrests. It wasn't the one and a half million reported during the proceedings, and the Escalade was essential to maintaining Eddie's livelihood. While it's not uncommon for someone to crack a joke or make light of a situation in the state courts, it's all business in federal courtrooms. No one dares to step out of line. So it took me aback when the judge interrupted the lawyer as he cried poor on Eddie's behalf.

"I don't drive an Escalade," the judge said.

The forfeiture stood.

And I thought I was blown away by the price of bear paw soup!

13

THE TEMPEST

THE MOUNTAIN OF FOOD ON MY PLATE—BAKED ZITI WITH HOMEMADE venison sausage and alfredo sauce—disappeared quickly. The other eight guys crowded around the dinner table were also using their garlic bread as a Zamboni, mopping their dishes clean. I may have been a guest under false pretenses, but that didn't change the fact that Nikko Pagano, Senior, the camp's patriarch, was a tremendous cook and a welcoming soul.

A car with its radio blaring pulled up to the camp.

"That's him," Senior said in a tone of resignation. Even he had exceptions.

I honestly don't know what I expected. This operation had gotten off to an inauspicious start. My well-laid plan of connecting with Sam Gurney via the Pagano family was shot to pieces when his engagement to Bethany, Senior's granddaughter, and Nikko Pagano, Junior's daughter, ended in a nasty breakup. As a result, Gurney wasn't welcome at the camp, leaving me to observe minor game violations such as hunting over apples from the Pagano crew that first season I worked the case.

Emotions cooled by the second fall, and Gurney started coming around again. On this November night, the man I'd waited over a year to meet burst through the door like a winter tempest.

"Boys," he said curtly as if to assert his place in the food chain.

I made one last pass over my plate with garlic bread, trying to savor it while casually taking Gurney in. On paper, I knew him to be a forty-one-year-old poacher and drug dealer from Harmony, Maine, who lived with his mother. The report noted, in the familiar straight-forward style of a game warden who didn't want to be writing reports, that he "might have emotional issues." I soon learned that this was like saying a hurricane might have wind.

Despite his arrival time, Gurney wasn't a man who missed many meals. At three-hundred and forty pounds, he had lambchop cheeks, an upper body that belonged on a bulldozer, and short legs with stumps for thighs. Dressed in black jeans, a gray hooded sweatshirt with the front collar hand-cut into a V-neck, a camo Coors Light ball cap, and beige steel-toed work boots, Gurney made a beeline for the booze counter. He helped himself to a pint glass of Bacardi and Coke that was so faintly discolored from the cola it could have passed as drinking water.

"Hey," Junior said, realizing Gurney used nearly half of the fifth. "Don't drink all of my rum."

Gurney snorted. The drink disappeared in two gulps. He mixed another equally as stiff, leaving only several ounces in the bottle.

"Are you going hunting tonight?" Greg, one of Senior's nephews, asked Gurney.

"That's why I'm here." He didn't explicitly say it, but Gurney commonly sold poached deer to the guys at the camp.

"You should take Billy with you," Greg said. The whole Pagano family called me Billy, as if I was one of their sons. "'Fraid we ain't giving him much luck."

Gurney turned to me. He was clean-shaven except for a gray-streaked goatee that hung like a two-inch stalactite from the bottom of his chin. It glistened from droplets of rum that missed his mouth.

"*You* wanna go night hunting with *me*?"

It wasn't a question. It was a challenge.

"I'm game."

Gurney downed the second glass of rum like a college kid shotgunning a beer.

"We'll see."

"Hold on," Junior said. "I don't want you getting Billy into trouble."

Junior was protective of me, and at that moment, I could have kissed him for it. Hard feelings over the broken engagement had cooled enough for Gurney to come around the camp and hunt with the guys again, but not all the lingering resentment had washed under the bridge. If Gurney was apprehensive about taking me with him, Junior's opposition sealed the deal.

Gurney pointed a stubby finger at me that would have clogged an inch and a half PVC pipe. The PG-version of what he said went like this: "My rules if you're coming with me—my gun, my light. You're driving. Go clean out your truck."

I accepted his terms. What I should have done was heed Junior's concerns.

Gurney brought a black, two-cell Maglite, capable of casting a beam of light nearly the length of a football field, and a bolt-action, .22-magnum rifle with us. As I've noted previously, the .22 isn't intended for big game, but many seasoned night hunters prefer it because it's much quieter than standard deer rifles. It requires a precision shot within fifty yards to take a deer down; otherwise, the shooter is more likely to wound the deer, turning it into coyote bait. Given how much I'd seen Gurney drink, I didn't have faith in his marksmanship.

He directed me to locations that he felt safe hunting at night. We struck out on the first couple of fields, and after about twenty minutes of driving around, it became evident that the alcohol had taken hold.

"Those guys are still sore about the breakup," he told me, slurring his Ss. "I was supposed to be one of them, part of the family, but now they don't want me around anymore. They don't get that I still love Bethany. I miss her so much."

"That's tough," I said, because, really, what else do you say to that? I could chew the fat all night if he wanted to talk hunting gear, but I wasn't prepared for his emotional dumpster fire. Honestly, when I became an undercover warden, I had no idea how frequently I'd find myself playing marriage counselor. In this case, I was quickly signing up for team Bethany. *Pack those bags and don't look back!*

"Stop the truck," he told me, "I need to take a leak."

I didn't have an urgent feeling, but I went anyway so he'd think I'd been drinking. There was more stored up than I thought, and as I was finishing up, I heard Gurney running back to the truck. His hand slapped the hood as he rounded the front and jumped in the driver's seat, slamming the door.

Oh no, the keys are in the ignition! After learning the hard way early in my career as a district warden to keep the keys in for fast getaways, the lesson was now flipped.

Gurney started the truck and began to drive away without me. Zipping up, I ran after him.

"Get in," he yelled without stopping, "or I'm leaving you here. I'm in charge now!"

I yanked the passenger door open, but he accelerated, and it slipped from my grasp.

"C'mon, Bill-ly," he taunted. "Get in the truck!"

The passenger door was swinging open, and I came close to jumping in for a second time, but Gurney pulled away again. Only on the third attempt, after a good fifty-yard dash, did he let up enough so I could get in.

"What's your problem?" I yelled. "Are you hammered?"

"Stop your whining—I'm in charge now!" He stomped on the gas, the volatility of his emotions bleeding out. "We're going for a ride!"

I secured my seat belt as we raced along backcountry roads at speeds unfit for a rollercoaster. Gurney's aggressive driving was a poor bedfellow to his delayed reaction time, causing him to jerk the truck all over the road like a concussed slalom racer. After he nearly put us into a tree clipping a corner, he came out of the turn headed straight for a massive pine on the other side of the road. I grabbed the wheel and jerked it back, narrowly avoiding a collision.

"You're going to get us killed!"

"I'm in control!"

The long-haired, wiry turkey beards I kept hanging from the rearview mirror swung back and forth as if to say, *No, no you're not.*

Gurney turned onto a long driveway and accelerated toward the garage, playing chicken with the single, industrial-sized bay door.

I braced myself. "What are you doing?"

"I wanna shoot a deer outside this house!" He turned sharply, tearing through a rose garden and ripping around the two-story ranch, carving trenches in the well-manicured lawn. "You think you're better than me. You're not better than me!" He cut the wheel again and stomped on the gas, blowing donuts on the back lawn. Sod shot in all directions from the rear tires, and each time the headlights passed over the inground pool, I could see turf grenades bombing into the water. "You're not better than me!"

"I didn't say I was!"

"Not you," Gurney told me. "This is my old boss' house. He fired me two weeks ago, but the bastard isn't better than me. I'm in control now!"

Gurney drove over the mailbox in one last retaliation before the truck bounced onto the pavement. Within seconds we were traveling over seventy miles per hour on unfit roads.

"Slow down!" I yelled as we went into a sharp corner.

The truck caught in the soft shoulder and screamed toward the woods. A blur of trees flashed by my window, mere feet from my face. Instead of hitting the brakes—the natural reaction for most people— Gurney stomped on the gas, and I again grabbed the wheel to help right the ship. We launched back onto the road, nearly into the opposite ditch.

"Stop the truck!"

"I'm in control!"

"Stop the truck!"

"I'm in control!"

Terrified, I debated breaking my cover. After the knife incident in downtown Bangor, it was only the second time I'd ever given it serious consideration. As a matter of procedure, breaking cover is the absolute last resort—only acceptable to intervene in a horrific crime or a life or death scenario. This ride surely qualified for the latter. It was only a matter of time before Gurney found a tree with our names on it.

But what good would telling him do? A storm was raging inside his head; revealing myself risked magnifying it.

The situation was entirely out of my control.

And that made two of us.

"Sam," I pleaded, "please stop the truck."

Amazingly, the magic word did the trick. He hit the brakes. Hard. The seat belt dug into my chest as my outstretched hands slammed the dashboard. As soon as we skidded to a stop, I jumped out and ran around the backside of the truck. Gurney stood in front of the driver's door like a human roadblock.

He was going to fight me. There was no mistaking the fire in his eyes.

Hopping mad from having my life flash before my eyes umpteen times throughout his redneck obstacle course, I was more than willing to oblige. Second thoughts raced through my mind as I surged toward him. First and foremost, I probably couldn't take him. He had at least a hundred and sixty pounds on me. I'd have to punch him hard in the jaw and hope for the best. That was complicated, too, because when the case was over, it ran the risk of him suing the Warden Service for *me* assaulting *him*. I'd bet my house on that outcome.

I just didn't care.

"Get out of my way," I demanded, "Or I'm gonna clock you."

His flaccid face tightened. Fists clenched. This was it!

But then his broad shoulders started shuddering as tears ran down his cheeks.

Gurney wrapped me in a giant bear hug.

What the—

"I'm sorry. I'm so sorry. Please forgive me."

All of a sudden, I'm consoling him as if he's a temperamental, three-hundred-and-forty-pound four-year-old. "I'm only upset because you nearly killed us," I said softly, patting his back. "Everything will be cool, buddy, if you get in the truck and calm down."

The new-leaf Gurney did as I requested. Once he was calm, we resumed hunting. Now, I know what you're thinking—and yes, this *was* a bad idea. But here's the thing, he was going to be doing this whether I was with him or not. He'd downed the two glasses of rum before laying eyes on me, and he was likely already hopped up on something before he arrived at the camp. Taking drugs and alcohol before hunting was his version of an office worker priming the pump with coffee. It's just how he operated, and the only way for me to put an end to it was to observe him in action. Besides, I was afraid of what would happen if I said no.

At least *I* was in control now.

We came upon a field with two does feeding approximately thirty yards from the road. I parked the truck at a forty-five-degree angle on the shoulder, illuminating the deer with the headlights and giving Gurney a clean shot. He lowered the window and aimed the rifle out. A round was already chambered, but Gurney was so drunk, he worked the bolt, ejecting the bullet into the roadside grass. An empty click was the only sound when he pulled the trigger. Gurney worked the bolt again, putting a live round into the chamber, and pulled the gun, safety off, into the cab.

Then he started crying again.

"I mess everything up."

"Let's call it a night." I gently lifted the rifle from his grasp.

When we returned to the camp, Gurney was insistent on driving himself home. I ran inside to recruit some guys to help me stop him, and I probably shouldn't have been surprised by their reaction.

"Screw him," Greg said, "let him kill himself."

On my own, I found Gurney passed out in the front seat of his mother's blue Chevrolet Malibu. I took the keys from the ignition and hid them in the camp.

After the escapade that first night together, I gave it time to blow over before contacting Gurney again. In all likelihood, he was embarrassed and didn't want to see me any more than I did him. The following fall, my third year working the case, I returned to the Pagano camp and made a point of seeking Gurney out at his mother's house. I pretended that I'd had a good time with him, and he apologized for getting crazy. He said he wanted to take me night hunting again, but he never showed at the Pagano camp that week.

Meanwhile, the guys at the camp were rightly confused as to why I wanted to go hunting with Gurney.

"He's not so bad," I lied. "We had fun."

Changing my strategy, I circumvented the Paganos altogether and contacted Gurney directly a couple of weeks later, pretending I had a work opportunity in Maine. Gurney openly talked about selling me deer, and he invited me to go night hunting with him. This time, the plan went through, and I spent a week hunting with Gurney day and night.

He drank heavily and snorted crushed Vicodin pills each time we went out, often directing me to stop at various houses where he bought or sold illegal prescription drugs.

Gurney also shot vastly more than his fair share of deer. One night, we pulled out of a field at two in the morning with a dead buck in the back of my truck when a deputy sheriff's car drove past.

"If he pulls us over," Gurney said, "get out and run for it."

It took every ounce of willpower in my body to keep from exploding at the mental image of Gurney trying to outrun the deputy. Shockingly, the deputy paid us no heed. Seriously! He had to know that nothing good was happening. As infuriating as his indiscretion was for me as a law enforcement officer, it was good for my case. The last thing I wanted was for Gurney to get pinched for a singular violation when I'm trying to prove the collective whole. Sweating the close call also gave us a good laugh and further endeared me to Gurney.

On another night, Gurney and his daughter's fiancé, Bennett Tate, tossed a doe that Gurney shot into the back of my undercover truck, a blue Chevy Colorado with a cap, and we continued road hunting.

And then we got lucky. Or so we thought.

The buck stood broadside to the road, looking back at us from thirty yards away. Even a blitzed Gurney couldn't miss. Frozen in my spotlight, it was an absolute smasher, a ten-pointer that had to be at least a hundred and eighty pounds. Gurney took aim, his excited breathing, hot and heavy, filling the cab with the pungent smell of fresh garlic from the shrimp scampi he cooked us for dinner. (Before you think I ate like a king on this case, know that I also watched Gurney drop a couple of shrimp onto the kitchen floor; covered with dog hair from a black lab, he returned them to the pan.)

Gurney never got the chance to pull the trigger. The doe in the back of my truck came to life, kicking and thrashing, bleating, even getting to its feet and banging its head on the cap. Spooked by the commotion, the buck disappeared into the woods.

"Gimme that." Gurney snatched his two-cell Maglite from my hands. In a profanity-laced tirade, he stormed into the truck bed and beat the doe over the head with the flashlight. I had to look away, but the cringe-inducing cracking sound of metal on skull occurred at least thirty times.

We weren't a mile down the road when the doe regained consciousness. "Pull over!"

This time, Gurney slit its throat.

Gurney was all out of sorts. Sweating profusely, he paced his mother's small living room like a zoo animal, caged by the yellowing white wallpaper with blue and pink stripes. The tick, tick, tick of a grandfather clock on the wall served as a metronome to his restlessness. On an antique hutch in the corner of the room, a framed image of a pudgy boy in his red Little League uniform stood out among the collection of family photos. How had that innocent-looking kid grown into the monster now before me?

"Hey man, you okay?" I asked.

"Yeah. I'm good."

He was anything but good. His hands were shaking.

Unbeknownst to Gurney, I knew he'd been arrested for felony reckless conduct and arson (basically, attempted murder) just days prior. He'd threatened a rival drug dealer by putting a gun to the man's head. Gurney didn't shoot him, but he did fire a shot at the house when he left. Later that evening, he set the house on fire while the man and his female companion were sleeping inside. The couple lived, but Gurney was in all kinds of trouble. Upon learning that the State Police arrested him, we informed them that I was on the inside. In addition to closing out my investigation, my new objective was to obtain evidence to make their case a slam dunk.

"Are you sure?" I asked him. "No offense, but you don't seem like yourself today."

"Yeah, sorry. I'm a little distracted because the cops were just here."

This was news to me.

"Seriously? What for?"

"They had a warrant or whatever for my DNA. Those pricks jammed a swab into my throat."

I made a show of looking out the front window. "Man, this sounds serious. Should I get outta here?"

"No, you're cool. They don't know about the deer."

"DNA, though . . ." I let the thought trail away, hoping he'd fill the silence.

Gurney removed his Coors Light ball cap and wiped his forehead on the sleeve of his gray T-shirt as he continued pacing. This was it, the moment of truth. All he had to do was spill the beans on starting the fire, and I'd ride this case to the finish line on a triumphant white horse.

"It's cool. They're trying to pin a house fire on me because I had an argument with the dealer who lives there, but I was at Naomi's place that night. That idiot probably passed out with a joint in his mouth or something. They got nothing."

"They just took your DNA. That doesn't sound like nothing to me."

He stopped pacing and looked at me—really looked at me—for the first time since I'd entered the house that afternoon. It suddenly felt like the grandfather clock was ticking inside my head.

"Dude, I just told you it's nothing." From the bottom-line tone in his voice, it was clear I was the one getting nothing. He then changed the subject, "Did you bring the five hundred for the deer?"

"Wow. Five hundred? We agreed to a buck twenty-five on the phone."

"Yeah, well, I take a lot of risk hunting at night to get the deer."

"I know. I'm taking the risk with you half the time."

"I don't see the cops taking your DNA. Things have changed."

"Look, I get it, but I don't have that kind of cash."

"Two-fifty."

"One-fifty. That's all I've got."

"Fine. One-fifty. You'll have to go get the deer from Tate."

He trusted me. Why else would he accept my cash for the illegal deer? The real crux was that he didn't want me to know he was capable of murder. It's the Catch-22 of befriending bad guys. Sometimes, when they like you, they don't want you to know how rotten they really are.

But there was a silver lining. Since I had to pick the deer up from Tate, I could use it as an excuse to talk to Gurney's daughter, Naomi.

"Bennett's putting the baby down," Naomi said in a hushed voice. She was the only one who referred to Tate by his first name. Wearing a black tank top and jeans, Naomi led me from the living room to the kitchen, where we could talk. She must have just gotten out of the shower because her hair was wet and pulled back. We sat at a small wooden table pushed against the wall, empty except for an open pack of Newports and a clear glass ashtray stuffed with a half-dozen butts. It's all I could smell.

Gurney told me he was at Naomi's house the night of the fire, so I took a chance and cast my fishing line. "What's this I hear that your dad talked you into being his alibi?"

"Tell me about it!" Her hands jumped off the table in indignation. I was surprised her animated voice didn't wake the baby. "Believe me—I'm not happy about it, either."

It was easy to see the resemblance. Naomi had her father's heavyset build, green eyes, and brownish hair with an auburn tint. Moreover, she carried the same obstinate, don't-care-what-anyone-thinks air about her. Naomi was young, in her early twenties, and as she spoke, her silver-studded eyebrow piercing glinted in the table's overhead light.

Unlike dad, she had loose lips regarding his arrest.

"He wants me to tell the cops that he was here all night. I mean, it's not a total lie. He was here, but only for like five minutes to get my gun."

"It was your gun?"

That was a new detail. According to the police report, Gurney's current girlfriend—if you could call her that, it was more of a sex-for-drugs relationship—Lindsey, claimed the .22 handgun was hers because the police found it hidden at her house.

"Yes!" Visibly upset, Naomi exhaled a deep breath. "It was *my* gun. Let that sink in. How do you think I feel about it?"

Tate appeared in the doorframe wearing jeans and an orange Moxie T-shirt. Tall and slender, he raised his eyebrows at Naomi. His unspoken sentiment was obvious, *You're saying too much.*

"What?" she snapped at him. "You know they're gonna find my fingerprints on the gun. How's that gonna look?"

"You don't know what he did with the gun when he left here."

I have to hand it to Tate, he kept his cool, but it was a failed attempt at putting the pin back into Naomi's grenade.

"Don't be so stupid. The police found my gun hidden in the floor—cleaned! All the other guns in the house were in closets collecting dust. I think they'll figure it out. They're gonna find your fingerprints on the gun, too, you know."

Naomi turned her attention to me, dialing back the anger in her voice.

"A cop came here yesterday."

"Seriously. What did you tell him?"

"Nothing. I'd just smoked a joint, so I didn't open the door, and he eventually left." She picked up the cigarette packet and compulsively fiddled with it in her hands. "I know they'll be back. They want me to testify."

"I'm glad I'm not in your shoes. I'd be freaking out if I had to testify against my dad in court." (I didn't tell her this wasn't a far-fetched scenario for me.)

"Yeah, well . . ." She pulled a lighter from her pocket and lit a cigarette from the pack. After a long drag, she courteously exhaled like a chimney toward the ceiling. "I'm not talking. I know how to get out of these things. All I have to do is tell them that I've got something contagious like pink eye, and they'll take a written statement."

"It's that easy?"

"Oh, yeah. I'm also diagnosed with anxiety disorder, so I can play that card, too." She took another drag. Exhaled. "They can't make me talk."

That's what you think.

Faced with my documentation of this conversation, Naomi later confessed to the false alibi. Gurney received fifteen years in prison, with all but three years suspended for arson. He served his jail time for the wildlife crimes concurrently, the significant penalty coming in the form of over ten thousand dollars in fines. Tate and a few other suspects from the Pagano camp also received several thousand-dollar fines along with light jail time.

The storm was over.

14

CAUGHT SAILING

The rain was picking up. It started a couple of hours before as the light coastal drizzle that seems omnipresent in the salty air to the uninitiated. We hadn't thought much of it at first, but now the downpour sounded like horses stampeding through the canopy. Soaking wet in wool hunting clothes and cold to the bone, we were hunkered down on the outskirts of a large haying field on Roque Island. Darkness had fallen an hour before schedule, but night hunting was the pinnacle of our plan.

Lobstermen are a different breed—contradiction baked into their DNA. As a community, Maine's crustacean pirates are notorious for being fiercely territorial and threatening to each other, let alone outsiders. It took me three years to fully infiltrate the close-knit group of Jonesport and Beals Island lobstermen. In Washington County, where the unpainted shingled houses, many with old blankets covering the windows, look as weathered and depressed as the economically starved people living inside, lobstermen are kings. Their homes are as grand as those from Massachusetts money, and they own boats that cost hundreds of thousands of dollars to buy and operate. They stick together yet stab each other in the back without a second thought because the stakes are high—the alternative to their hard-earned lifestyle is literally nothing.

"Hurray for me and screw you," is how Randall Jones, a fifty-year-old lobsterman and my guide on this miserable evening, described it.

I don't want to give all lobstermen a bad name because there are plenty of good apples, but those individuals aren't at the same barbecues as Bill Freed. The guys I got to know were tireless workers and heavy drinkers bonded together by boat and bottle tighter than an anchor hitch knot. As poachers, they were true to character. Their closed circle of friends was nearly impenetrable because, unlike most poaching rings where the top dogs are social misfits craving attention, these guys kept to themselves and each other. They didn't need friends, cutting off my supply line.

The one chink in their armor was Randall Jones. He was the first to accept me into the clan, thus opening the gateway. The importance of his friendship came to light late one afternoon when I was driving around Beals Island to get the lay of the land, pretending to hunt. In the bushes, I caught a glimpse of what looked like a deer's underbelly. Stopping to investigate, what I'd spotted was a freshly killed doe. There was a sizable wound in its shoulder, likely from a twelve-gauge slug. The island was closed to taking antlerless deer, making the kill a mandatory thousand-dollar fine and three days in jail.

The doe was still warm, and it was entirely possible that whoever shot the deer heard me coming and fled. I decided to park my undercover truck out of sight down the road and hide in the bushes. In all of the times that I've sat watching a poached deer (more than I can count), this tactic rarely works. I can only sit there for so long, and the perpetrators often don't return until much later—or worse, not at all. But this time, lady luck was on my side.

Long after darkness set in, an older model Chevrolet truck with an extended cab rumbled down the road and stopped at the deer. The operator shut the vehicle and its lights off, and two men got out.

"Let's get this thing in the back and get out of here," one of them said.

While I'd seen their license plate, I couldn't get a good look at the men in the dark. I'd need to positively identify them for any charges to stick, so I made a split-second decision to come out of my hiding place.

"Hey, guys," I said, announcing my presence.

Startled by my sudden appearance, the passenger yelled and hurried back to the truck. The driver froze, unsure what to do. I quickly explained that I found their deer while hunting. It looked abandoned, so I was going to take it when I heard them coming. I hid in case they were a warden, and I thought they might be one from their jingling keychain. The driver climbed back into his truck as I was talking, and only when I said that I was staying at Randall Jones' place did he smile and give me a nod. As the story of this encounter made its rounds, doors began to open.

How I met Randall was equally as fortuitous. I was driving around, making myself visible to locals, when I came across a truck that went off the road on Great Wass Island and got stuck on some rocks. The driver, Perry Kingston, smelled like a brewery, and I could have ice skated on his glassed-over eyes.

"C'mon," he said after I offered to help, "let's take a walk to get a rope." Perry led me to Randall's camp, where a giant pot of lobsters was boiling on an outside spit, and a handful of guys were milling around drinking and smoking pot.

After we got the rope and I pulled Perry's truck out, he went into the woods to retrieve the beer he'd hidden after getting in the accident (as if the cops wouldn't have known he was hammered).

"You play cards?" he asked me.

"Sometimes. I'm not very good."

His face lit up. "Perfect. How much money you got?"

I was in. By the following morning, Randall was inviting me to stay at his place. That was the type of guy he was. He'd give you the shirt off his back, the shoes from his feet, and fill your belly with illegal lobster.

Sailing is the term the lobstermen used for hunting from their boats. The guys bragged that it was the hardest way to hunt, and I didn't have any doubt that they were correct. "This is how we separate the men from the boys," they told me. "We'll take you out—see what you're made of."

On this torrential excursion, Randall and I arrived at Roque Island before daylight. We hunted by foot throughout the day, planning to transition to sailing well after dark. Randall's poaching exploits were legendary. If you didn't already know, he'd tell you, as he did me and anyone else who would listen during an evening of exercising his liver.

"I used to be the biggest poacher around here," he boasted in his raspy smoker's voice. "My best year, I bagged nineteen deer in one fall.

Most of them shot at night. None of you can come close to touching that."

Randall wasn't a big man, probably no more than five-foot-seven, but his fisherman persona was larger than life. He might as well have been the poster boy for seafood restaurant advertising with his thick lobster claw mustache and red, weather-beaten complexion that made him look as though he was perpetually squinting at the sun. Not to mention you could smell him coming from a mile away thanks to all of the baitfish he handled.

"If I wasn't a lobsterman, I'd have been a game warden."

We all laughed. "*You?*"

"Stop, game protector!" he mocked, using *game protector* because I told him that's what we called wardens in Pennsylvania. He pointed his long index finger at me. "You're under arrest!"

"If you were a game protector," I said, turning around what my friends told me years before, "you wouldn't have any of us for friends."

He thought about that for a split second. "Screw it. So what?"

In addition to poaching deer, Randall was unthinkable as a game warden because his fishing practices weren't exactly on the up-and-up either. He'd commonly keep shorts, lobsters smaller than the legal size, and dingers, female lobsters with a notch in their tails to indicate they are protected for breeding. Conscientious lobstermen notch the tails of females with berries (eggs) to show they are off-limits before tossing them back into the sea, whereas Randall hid them in a cage tied to a buoy near his camp in Slate Island Cove. The shorts and dingers were on the menu for his lobster bakes (one night, he cooked seventeen for us to eat), and I suspect Randall also used them in his side business selling cooked lobster meat. Once the meat was out of the shell, the Marine Patrol couldn't prove the lobsters were illegal.

Randall also harvested scallops out of season. He didn't see this as a big deal because he'd personally seeded the scallops in the cove near his camp. During scallop season, Randall routinely exceeded the daily catch limit. He'd pack the majority of the excess scallops in hard-to-access areas of his boat while leaving about ten pounds in a bucket or cooler somewhere on deck as a decoy where Marine Patrol would easily find it. The penalty for being ten pounds over paled in comparison to what Randall actually had. To put this in context, he was bringing in close to eighteen hundred dollars a day and around seventy-two hundred a week (they're only allowed to scallop four days a week)—and that was only his take on the legal scallops.

He was just one of those guys that always had to push the limits. Illegal duck hunting from the boat was common, and he'd also attach trotlines to his lobster traps, which are heavy fishing lines with baited hooks, catching and illegally keeping halibut and cod. The real kicker is that Randall wasn't even the primary target in this case!

At dusk, we hid in the tree line along a field. It was Randall's go-to, secret night hunting location where he'd stashed a car battery in the brush that he used to power a spotlight. Given the rain, he stuck with his powerful LED flashlight on this night. The body heat I'd generated walking around depleted quickly, and there was no quelling the stinging pain in my fingers and toes. My quads were also going numb. The temperature hovered somewhere slightly above freezing, but the wind had strengthened from howling to I-think-a-tree-is-going-to-fall-on-our-heads. Every time I thought the rain couldn't possibly come down any harder, Mother Nature proved me wrong.

Randall pulled a fifth of Canadian Club whisky from his backpack. He took a swig and handed me the bottle.

"This will warm you up."

I wanted to tell him that he was dead wrong. The alcohol increases blood flow near the skin's surface, making him feel warmer, but it actually pulls blood away from his core, lowering his body temperature. Each swig just brought him closer to hypothermia. Of course, this would have been a warden thing to say, so instead, I simply pretended to take a pull.

The sound of an approaching vehicle caused Randall to stop casing the area with his flashlight. A truck drove into the field and lit it up.

Randall swore like a—well, lobsterman. "There's too many poachers around here," said the guy who was currently baiting deer outside of his camp. "That's why there aren't that many deer anymore."

Apparently, the pot doesn't like being out-cooked by the kettle.

Given the rapidly deteriorating conditions and our chattering teeth, we made our way back to the boat to get off the island while we still could. *If we still could.* The tide had come in since we'd arrived, but Randall was an experienced seaman with forty years of lobstering under his belt. He'd somehow set the anchor and tied the boat off on shore with a slip knot so he could pull the boat to us when we returned. Perhaps his seaworthiness led to overconfidence regarding the weather because the real problem was the gale-force winds and pounding waves batting the anchored boat around like a rubber ducky in a wave pool. What's more, his main lobster boat was in the shop for engine repairs, so we were using his smaller, twenty-four-foot boat without an enclosed cabin. There was no escaping the driving rain that stung like sleet on our faces.

Randall pulled the boat in, and we waded into the water and climbed aboard—getting wet was a moot point. His first act on the boat was to guzzle the remaining Canadian whisky from his pack and open another bottle stored on the boat. He bought the stuff by the case, and he always kept a stash aboard. When offered, I took another pseudo swig. Randall then tried calling Austin Barker to arrange a pickup if we could get into the bay.

Austin was another secondary target in the case, a twenty-one-year-old lobsterman with an affinity for booze, drugs, and boneheaded behavior. That said, it was hard not to like the kid. He had zeal. Clean-shaven around his mouth and upper chin, Austin sported a foolish-looking combed-out beard that encircled his face like a backward blond neck pillow. Merely looking at him made me laugh. But his decision-making was dubious at best, and his record included a prior poaching arrest. I'd gone night hunting with him earlier in the case, and he asked me straight-out if I was an undercover warden.

"Because I'm hosed if you are, man."

I laughed. "No, are you?"

A few minutes passed, and then out of nowhere, he yelled, "Pull over! Game warden! You're under arrest!"

I must have looked shocked—because I was.

"I got you!" He burst out laughing. "I so got you!"

It wasn't exactly comforting to think that we were placing our hopes of rescue in Austin's thickheaded hands. I could only pray that he hadn't snorted his Adderall that evening. In fairness, he'd also been lobstering since he was old enough to help on his father's boat, and when Randall finally reached him, Austin was already working the phones to organize a search party. This reaction should tell you everything you need to know about the sea that evening—lifelong fishermen were worried about us, and we hadn't even shoved off from the island yet. It also shows the contradictory nature of lobstermen. They're like siblings. Cutting and stealing each other's traps is second nature, but they don't hesitate to respond when one of their own is in danger.

Shove off, we did. Somehow.

I've been on Maine's largest lakes in storms with four-foot waves many times. That's child's play compared to what the ocean dealt us. Hunkered down in the bow of Randall's boat, I held onto anything I could, my fingers screaming in pain. Waves crashed over the side, pounding me with saltwater. The ankle-deep pool at my feet sifted to the stern like an undertow as the bow pointed skyward on the crest of each wave, then flooded forward as we rocked into the trough. Mother Nature had caught us in the act of attempting to go sailing, and the further we got from the island, the greater her wrath.

Didn't she know I was on her side?

Meanwhile, at the controls in the middle of the boat, Randall guzzled more whisky.

"Are you okay?" he yelled, barely discernible over the wind. There was an expression I didn't recognize on his face in the blue glow of the GPS navigation lights—fear. This look scared me more than the monster waves. Randall was accustomed to scalloping in the winter when the ocean weather is rarely favorable. "You've got to suck it up and put on your big-boy pants," he'd chastise Austin whenever his young mate chickened out. I couldn't tell you how big the waves were that evening. All I knew was they were big enough to strike the dagger of fear into one of the bravest men I'd ever met.

"I'm okay if you are," I shot back.

He raised the whisky bottle in the air toward me as if to intimate a toast and took another swig of liquid courage. It wasn't a comforting gesture.

"I can't see—" Randall shut the navigation off to prevent the lights from impeding his vision.

Oh, great. In the belly of the beast, my drunken captain is navigating on instinct and landmarks. Of which there were none to see. But there were oodles of small uninhabited islands barricaded with boat-crushing rocks lurking in the darkness.

"Where are the PFDs?" I yelled.

"You don't want one!"

"What?" I couldn't have heard him right.

"The water's too cold. If you go in, you're gonna die. The PFD will just make it slow."

Another comforting thought. Crazier was learning that Randall and many of the other lobstermen didn't know how to swim. They didn't see how it mattered. To them, if you went overboard in a storm, it was game over either way—might as well make it quick.

"Get the light and shine it over the bow," Randall instructed. "Watch out for lobster lines and let me know if you see any." He also told me to grab a pole he'd rigged with a knife at the end and be ready to cut us free if we got entangled. The lobster lines were a serious threat. If the boat became immobilized, we were as good as capsized. Of course, perching myself over the bow also put me in a more precarious position.

If you go in, you're gonna die.

I'd already exceeded my quota for life-or-death scenarios by this point in my warden career. The difference here was that I had time to think about it. Usually, whether it was a drunken high-speed car race or a boning knife to the throat, the events unfolded in the blink of an eye, and the realization that I could have died was spared for afterthought. Not this time. Shaking uncontrollably from the drenched clothes clinging to my body, crossing Chandler Bay in the unrelenting storm was painstakingly long. Each wave that bashed the boat was a crude reminder of the Grim sharpening his scythe.

Drowning. Hypothermia. Pancaked against a rock-studded island. *Pick a card—any card!*

"Lord," I prayed, "I don't want to go like this."

I thought of my family, safe in the warmth of our home, unaware of my plight. It was bedtime for the kids, and my absence from the round of hugs and kisses wasn't unwonted to them. On the contrary, it *was* the routine. What had I done? Was I sentencing them to repeat my family history and come of age without a father to lean on?

And Gail. She was far from blissfully ignorant of the dangers when I stepped out the door. Did she sense I was in peril? Somehow. Someway. If this was the end, how long until she finds out? Would she ever learn the truth? Bill Freed is on this boat. There isn't a soul alive who definitively knows the whereabouts of Bill Livezey. Would I simply become missing, leaving her with the anguish of an ounce of hope?

"If this is the end, please let them find my body. Please give my family closure."

The storm subsided as we passed the lee side of Beals and Great Wass islands. It was less an answer to my prayers and more like the break between boxing rounds. Ferocious wind, rain, and merciless waves greeted us at hell's bell on the other side.

"I think we're going to make it!" Randall yelled.

A wave crashed over the bow, slapping me in the face with seawater and knocking me into the bitter pool on the deck.

"You *think*," I shot back.

"Almost there. I can do this stretch with my eyes closed!"

He told me what I wanted to hear, but I took comfort in it just the same. Eyes open or closed, I didn't see the difference. Everything looked like we were swimming blindfolded in whitewater. But like a salmon returning to its spawning ground, Randall delivered us to his dock. I honestly don't know how he did it. He'd consumed so much Canadian whisky that he couldn't have walked a straight line if I spotted him a two-foot berth.

Austin received us at the dock, his eyes red and watery—and not from smoking pot. He was shaken up.

I got out of the boat and literally kissed the ground.

Please don't misconstrue what I have to say next. Because when it came to God's creatures and our fish and game resources, Randall's moral compass lacked magnetism. The law came down hard on him for it, for which he deserved every charge—as did Austin and the rest of their crew—and I was doing my duty to deliver it.

But.

Unlike other serial poachers I'd encountered, Randall wasn't driven by a sadistic or sociopathic devil inside him. He wasn't a *bad* guy. His fallibility was a cocktail of greed, loneliness, and a competitive spirit among his mates. You wouldn't know it from looking at us—he'd lived a much rougher life of drinking, smoking, and dogged labor—but we were essentially the same age. We got along, and like the Pagano family before him, he was fun to be around, showering me with goodwill and more food than I could fit in my belly (albeit, most of it illegal).

Randall thought we were friends, and for my part, it wasn't a total bluff. He'd accepted me, a veritable stranger, into their small, close-knit world with open arms—something that just doesn't happen in lobstering communities. After surviving the storm with him and coming home to the look of relief on Austin's worried face, it was hard not to feel a kinship.

Like Judas, I'd soon betray him.

15

GOOD GUYS VERSUS BAD GUYS

EARLY IN MY LAW ENFORCEMENT CAREER, I LEARNED THAT MY TEEN-age poaching buddies were right—becoming a game warden wouldn't make me many friends. There were consequences for doing my job and doing it well. The petition to have me removed from the Lincoln district for enforcing OUI regulations was annoying at the time but is laughable now in comparison to the actual murder plot planned against me by disgruntled drug dealers. I was able to grin and bear these job hazards because I was doing good, and for that, I believed it made me one of the good guys.

Until, all of a sudden, I wasn't—utterly powerless against my career assassination.

The fateful day was May 8, 2016, when the *Portland Press Herald* plastered its front page with "North Woods lawless." A feature written by award-winning journalist Colin Woodard, the article accused an undercover operative of the Maine Warden Service (me) of numerous allegations, including padding evidence, entrapping suspects, and frequently being intoxicated while working a case in the Allagash from 2012 through 2014. I'll say this about Mr. Woodard—he's a heck of a writer. By the end of the article, I was even thinking, *This guy should get fired!* It was no wonder that the article produced as big of a public and political outcry as it did, fueled by the *Portland Press Herald* continuing to pump out story after story as more victims of my abhorrent tactics came forward. Everyone wanted my head on a platter, and the Maine Warden Service held accountable for my actions.

There was just one problem: The article was a work of fiction.

At the time, I'd never heard the term "fake news." I was completely beside myself, flabbergasted that the state's largest newspaper and one of its most respected journalists could openly distort the facts to create a false narrative—and get away with it. On top of that, they repeatedly published my real and fake name (they even misspelled Freed as Fried), along with my photo, recklessly outing me as an undercover agent while I had active investigations, potentially endangering my life. For this very reason, it's illegal for the media to reveal the identity of federal undercover operatives. Unfortunately, state agents don't receive the same protection.

For a while, my family and I needed protection. Commenters on the online article made threatening remarks and wrote that they knew where I lived, posting my town and street address. We stopped answering the phone to avoid the angry callers, and our mailbox was spray-painted with obscenities. A cease of harassment notice was also issued to a poacher I'd caught who kept calling my undercover phone. While working undercover, there were many occasions where I encountered bad guys openly talking about wanting to kill game wardens. Whether it was bravado or a dark desire, you just never knew. It's no secret that killing animals is a gateway to a more heinous crime for some disturbed individuals. I thank my superiors in the Warden Service, who knew the threat was real, and for a while, posted a hidden officer outside my house.

The entire episode took a heavy psychological toll on my family. As an undercover operative, I was sadly accustomed to being a recluse in my personal life, avoiding public gatherings in case someone recognized Bill Freed. Being afraid to go out to eat, to the movies, or shopping, because there might be a confrontation was a new experience for Gail. The kids, who'd grown up with a vague understanding of why I watched their sporting events from afar, were now teenagers and young adults who were afraid to be home alone for fear of retribution. At night, any little unexplained noise got our minds racing and had me reaching for the loaded gun holstered to my bedpost. Likewise, I trained Gail to handle two shotguns we kept loaded in the house. We also fitted the windows with blinds, and everyone in the family knew to keep the shades down and the lights off if they heard a noise outside.

These aren't things I should have to teach my family over a newspaper article. Needless to say, quality sleep was lacking and we had many late-night conversations about cutting our Maine ties and moving out of state. But we didn't want this fabricated story to beat us. So we persevered.

Believe me, I wanted to fight the story—to reveal the truth. As an active warden, I wasn't permitted to speak out or conduct interviews, which I fully understood and accepted. It's necessary for the Maine Warden Service to be extremely cautious with the information it discloses. However, the *Portland Press Herald* used our tight-lipped media relations and the sometimes lengthy process for FOIA (Freedom of Information Act) requests as a way to imply guilt. The reality is that FOIA requests can take time because potentially sensitive information must go through a thorough review. There are many reasons why the Warden Service has to be careful about what it disseminates. For example, with a tragic event, we are sensitive to the impacted families. In the Allagash bust, it was partly a matter of keeping our covert tactics out of the public eye to protect agents in the field and minimize the risk of compromising future cases. Before the *Portland Press Herald* made it front-page news, many poachers didn't even know we conducted undercover operations.

Unfortunately, our reluctance to speak out also makes us an easy target. But that doesn't make it right. Determined to hold those responsible for the article accountable, I sought legal counsel for defamation. This process was a story unto itself, but I'll cut to the chase: Ironically, as a game warden who worked undercover for twenty years, I'm considered a public figure, categorized with politicians, movie stars, and professional athletes—just with a vastly different pay grade! As a regular person, I would have had a strong, slam-dunk case. But for a public figure to win a libel lawsuit, I had to prove that the *Portland Press Herald* and Colin Woodard acted with *actual malice* toward me, knowingly and recklessly disregarding the truth. In other words: mission impossible. In the end, my lawyer counseled me to save my time and money.

I've concluded that the only thing a game warden can do to clear his name is to wait until he retires and write a book. So please allow me to explain where and how Colin Woodard and the *Portland Press Herald* knowingly led readers astray, starting with the assertion that the investigation was too costly for the crimes committed. Woodard wrote:

> *Joseph L. Giacalone, a retired New York Police Department sergeant who teaches at the John Jay College for Criminal Justice in New York, says the wardens' Allagash operation was wildly out of proportion to the suspected crimes.*
>
> *"They spent two years, and this is what they find? It sounds like a whole lot of nonsense," says Giacalone, who once headed the Bronx's cold case unit. "This should not be an operation that law enforcement would be involved in for this long unless you had people smuggling drugs or sex workers across the border."*

Does it surprise anyone that a retired New York City police officer doesn't understand the role of an undercover agent in the Maine Warden Service?

Let's shed some light on the subject for officer Giacalone. Legal hunting and fishing play a vital role in Maine's ecosystems. Monitored closely by biologists who set bag limits and permit amounts, hunting and fishing help keep animal populations healthy and sustainable. Without it, overpopulation would overtax our natural resources. Animals would die of starvation or other resulting causes such as an increased rate of vehicle collisions, which endangers people. At the other end of the spectrum, poaching threatens to deplete our wildlife populations. While it may sound absurd to suggest that Maine's deer herd or trout stock could become exhausted—that's precisely what's at stake if poaching is left unchecked.

When driving into Maine on Interstate 95, a sign reads, *WELCOME TO MAINE, The Way Life Should Be.* For many residents of the great state of Maine, especially those who live in rural communities, this motto speaks directly to our outdoor recreation heritage. Generation after generation of Mainers grew up hunting and fishing. For those in this category, these sports aren't purely about killing animals to put food on the table—they're about connecting with nature and family. Yes, some people will argue that poaching is a tradition in their families, and, sadly, they're not wrong. But that isn't how life should be.

That said, using heritage as a top reason to protect Maine's wildlife is likely a hard sell for New York City folk. So, let's put this into a context that everyone can understand. In 2020, The Maine Department of Inland Fisheries and Wildlife earned over $17.89 million from the sale of hunting and fishing licenses and permits, which was forty-two percent of the agency's entire revenue. Some of this revenue goes to the general fund, but for the sake of discussion, the $17.89 million by itself would have accounted for thirty-six percent of the Warden Service's operational expenses that year. These numbers are relatively consistent year over year (during the pandemic, this revenue increased 1.5 percent from 2019 to 2020), so if revenue were to decline because wildlife populations aren't beneficial to sportsmen, it would have to be replaced elsewhere or the Warden Service would suffer cutbacks. Keep in mind that stopping night hunters is merely one of our duties. When young children and the elderly wander off into the woods, when hikers are injured, when there are ATV or boating accidents—we're the ones who come to the rescue. If we're underfunded, it's a public safety issue.

The revenue earned by Inland Fisheries and Wildlife is small potatoes compared to what hunting and fishing generate for the private sector—gear suppliers and retailers, lodging, licensed guides, gas stations, mom and pop general stores, taxidermists, meat cutters, supermarkets, restaurants, and hunters' breakfasts at the local diner. The list is practically endless. In 2013, the state commissioned studies from Southwick Associates, an agency that's described on its website as "a market research, statistics, and economics firm, specializing in the hunting, shooting, sportfishing, and outdoor recreation markets," to understand the total economic impact of hunting and fishing in Maine.

In its final reports, Southwick Associates concluded that hunters in Maine spent $231,623,247 on hunting-related activities in 2013. What's more: "Collectively, recreational hunting supports more than 3,400 full- and part-time jobs providing more than $115 million in income. The direct spending by sportsmen who hunt and the multiplier effects of that spending in Maine contribute $191 million to the state's gross state product and a total economic output of $338.7 million." And that's just hunting. For freshwater fishing, Southwick reported that anglers spent $208,808,028 with a total economic output of $319.2 million. Considering that the Southwick study was conducted nearly a decade before this publication, it's a safe bet that the total economic impact of hunting and fishing in Maine is currently around $1 billion.

Wildly out of proportion to the suspected crimes? Maine's economy begs to differ.

The assertion that the Allagash operation was overreaching because it lasted two years is misguided at best. First of all, the rifle season for deer is only one month of the year. Factor in archery, extended black powder, and time to scout hunting locations, and there's roughly a three-month window to work poachers. My cover story was that Bill Freed was a sportsman from Pennsylvania who wanted in on Maine's excellent hunting and fishing. Using vacation time from work, I'd travel to Maine a few times a year for these activities. I certainly *wasn't* embedded with these guys for two straight years. In fact, I only went to the Allagash on nine separate occasions for a total of forty days, including the early trips where I was hanging out and attempting to make contact with the intended targets.

Two years is a typical timeline for one of our undercover operations. Given the short period in which to work, the first hunting season is used to make contact and start building trust. It typically isn't until the second go-around that a suspect opens up and shows their true colors. From there, we begin to uncover other poachers who are part of the network. We want to stop the reckless killing as soon as possible, but we also can't rush a case to the district attorney without adequate evidence. That's how the bad guys earn a get-out-of-jail-free card. Of course, emphasizing the two years was another way to suggest that undercover game operations are too expensive.

"The way in which some people were treated was heavy-handed, and that's what got me really upset," says Rep. John Martin, who has represented Allagash and other parts of Aroostook County in the state Legislature for most of the past half-century. "I'd be shocked to learn, and somebody should find out, how much money was spent in that

operation. Frankly, if we spent it looking at people involved in major crimes, it would be much more productive."

This part is laughable, and not purely because it implies that the state doesn't spend money investigating major crimes. Undercover operations are our most efficient and cost-effective means of apprehending poachers. And it's not even close. Think about it: In a regular case covered by district wardens, there might be four or five officers trying to collect evidence to build a case *after* a specific crime has been committed. More times than not, their efforts are in vain because there simply isn't enough hard evidence to connect the dots.

What's more, the most egregious poachers are wise to uniformed wardens' tactics, and they have plenty of tricks up their sleeves to evade us. For example, they might send one vehicle with a spotlight past a field at night while a second vehicle with the shooter hangs back to see if we stop the first one. Yes, spotlighting a field is illegal in the fall, but it pales in severity to catching the actual shooter. Unless we're tipped off on where poachers are going, it's extremely difficult to catch them in the act. It's a big state, after all, and we only have so many uniformed wardens.

By comparison, an undercover case only has two people involved—the operative and a case manager who handles all of the paperwork. When a crime is committed, I'm there, in person, literally catching them red-handed. Gathering evidence is easy. The bad guys are typically more than willing to celebrate and commemorate their kill by posing for photos and letting me keep spent cartridges. And we're talking about crimes, plural. The targets of undercover operations are habitual offenders. Not only are they poaching as many animals as they can shoot, but they're often drinking or doing drugs while doing so, firing from moving vehicles—you name it—posing safety issues to the general public and themselves. By the end of an operation, our case folder is four to six inches thick from documenting all crimes.

The Allagash case, dubbed "Operation Red Meat" for a good reason, resulted in over three hundred documented crimes, seventeen individuals convicted or charged with multiple class D and E crimes, as well as one felony. And these are just the crimes we filed. In most undercover operations, there comes the point where we stop documenting "small" violations such as driving with a loaded weapon in the vehicle because the totality of it all becomes absurd. In Operation Red Meat, the total amount of fines assessed exceeded thirty-nine thousand dollars. To put this in perspective, the minimum penalty for a single poaching violation is a thousand dollar fine and three days of jail time; the maximum sentence, which comes into play for repeat offenders, is two thousand dollars and a year behind bars. While a significant amount of jail time for game violations ultimately gets suspended, two of the main poachers in Operation Red Meat were sentenced to a year in jail before the suspensions kicked in. Woodard described all of this as "scant results."

Scant results? Not hardly.

Keep in mind, these crimes are just what they did when I was around. How egregious were their offenses when I wasn't there or before I came into the picture? What's also important to point out here is that for the most prolific poachers, a single conviction and a thousand-dollar fine is unlikely to deter their behavior. About the only thing it hurts is their ego. The more likely outcome is that they learn from whatever mistakes got them caught. To put them out of business for good, it takes an undercover operation to bring to light the full scope of their illegal activities.

I would like to believe that Representative Martin, a Democratic state politician since 1964 and a member of the Appropriations and Financial Affairs and Inland Fisheries and Wildlife committees, understands all of this. Instead, he chose to prioritize his political agenda by accusing me of being "heavy-handed." The article would have you believe that while the top poachers in Operation Red Meat had criminal records, they'd turned over a new leaf and were now law-abiding citizens who wouldn't have committed the crimes had I not coerced them into it.

In total, Livezey would spend 40 days in Allagash, posing as Pennsylvania hunter Bill Fried and—according to his own reports—doing his best to tempt locals into violating fish, game and other laws.

I can assure you that I never wrote anything about tempting locals into violations. As you'll see in the next chapter, these guys were no

Scouts, more than willing to commit crimes of their own admission. Before we get into that, it's essential to understand how we select targets for an undercover investigation. The suspects must meet one of three criteria: commercial situations involving the illegal buying and selling of fish and wildlife or unlicensed guiding; gross and egregious poaching over limits; or a significant public safety issue due to night hunting, intoxication, or shooting near houses. More times than not, the cases we work check-off more than one box. Each investigation begins with a research period to determine if the targets meet the criteria. If they don't, we walk away, and they never know that we were watching them. It's as simple as that. Needless to say, the gentlemen in Operation Red Meat passed the initial bad-guy test.

For starters, two of the main targets had a prior 2008 conviction for killing a moose out of season—shot at night from a moving vehicle, no less. "North Woods lawless" brushed this fact aside by explaining that the men did this "because they were in dire straits and needed the food." In my experience, poachers in dire straits don't leave the moose to rot without salvaging the meat as these guys did. Both of these men were gainfully employed at that time. One of them worked for the state Department of Agriculture, Conservation and Forestry as an Allagash Wilderness Waterway ranger! When I met them, they repeatedly bragged that they were going to show me "the Allagash way." And no, they weren't talking about playing cribbage with their grandmothers.

Still, Woodard downplayed the severity of the Operation Red Meat convictions.

In reality, the operation had surprisingly scant results. Its main target, a convicted poacher named [James McBride], eventually, and reluctantly, pleaded guilty to charges related to a plate of undocumented venison and onions he cooked for the covert agent, the improper tagging of a deer possessed by his estranged girlfriend, and the shooting of a single grouse. [Connor McBride], [James'] first cousin once-removed, was convicted of minor offenses, including taking too many trout, having his girlfriend tag a deer he'd shot, and hunting while drinking.

In *actual* reality, this case included nearly all of the most serious fish and wildlife crimes that we enforce with mandatory minimum punishments. That undocumented plate of venison was described to me by James as an "early-bird special," a one-hundred-and-forty-pound doe shot out of season while his license was revoked in *a wildlife management district* closed to the taking of antlerless deer. White-tail deer are seasonal breeders producing one to two fawns annually. So, in an area where the deer population is so fragile that biologists don't issue any doe permits during the legal hunting season, James recklessly eliminated a genealogical chain. As for that single grouse, it was shot out the driver's window of my truck from the passenger's side while I was driving—he fired *across my chest* in the cab. It was also no accident that these men had their girlfriends tag their deer. This tactic was so they could shoot and tag another. And do I really have to formulate an argument for why it's seriously dangerous to hunt drunk?

Those trout became a bigger bone of contention in the article and the trials because Connor's lawyer claimed that I'd pulled additional fish out of the freezer before taking a picture used as evidence. He argued that some of the trout "had a distinctive different appearance because those fish had been caught on an earlier day at a different location . . ." Any fisherman will tell you that this proves nothing—trout have natural discoloration regardless of where or when they are caught. I know with absolute certainty that these fish were caught on the same day, from the same waterway, because *I was there.* The judge agreed with me, and Connor appealed his charges to the Maine Supreme Judicial Court, which unanimously ruled that he was guilty.

It's important to note that "North Woods lawless" was published more than two weeks *after* the Maine Supreme Judicial Court ruling. Why is this timeline consequential? Because it highlights that Woodard and the *Portland Press Herald* weren't duped. The case facts that I'm explaining here were available to them through the court records. They *chose* to write their own story. To distract readers from the crimes committed, Woodard spent considerable print real estate accusing the Warden Service of robbing Rory Casey's mother of her canned peaches.

[Rory's mother] was famous locally for her canned peaches, made with organic fruit grown in Pennsylvania and purchased from the Amish farmers who have bought up stretches of Aroostook County farmland in recent years. She had spent hours preparing the peaches and the organic fruit from her garden and packing them in clear-glass pint jars, 110 in total, she estimates. There also were 36 jars of moose meat, which was never proven to be illicit and which [Rory's mother] maintains was from animals legally shot by her siblings. Most of it was never returned, she says, despite interventions by her attorney and Rep. Martin.

"It's robbery and thievery, and to do it by force!" she says, noting that only 33 pints were returned to her. "I'm assuming they ate it all, because otherwise they would have brought it back by now."

To her surprise, [Rory's mother]—who had never laid eyes on Livezey—was charged with four counts related to possession of poached meat. Unlike most of those charged, she pleaded not guilty. The night before the trial, the district attorney dropped all charges against her.

Look, Mom Peaches was no saint in the eyes of the law. She was knowingly processing poached game meat from her son, which is unquestionably illegal. I wasn't part of the search and seizure, but it was determined that the warden in charge of evidence collection had separated the boxes of canned moose and deer meat from the canned vegetables, and another warden accidentally carried out the box of vegetables. It was an honest mistake, and when it was brought to our attention, we returned the thirty-three cans of vegetables and Mom Peaches signed a statement confirming receipt. In this mixup, *not a single jar of peaches was confiscated*—that was a complete fabrication. The statement that thirty-six cans of moose meat weren't proven as illegal is also categorically false. It was sixty cans of moose meat along with the partially cut-up quarters of a moose and a doe deer that was hanging outside her bedroom window on the night of the raid. How do I know the moose meat was illegally obtained? I was there when it was shot at night from a vehicle, and I helped bring it to her house.

Ultimately, the charges against Mom Peaches were dropped. Not because she wasn't guilty (she was) or there wasn't sufficient evidence (there was plenty), but because her son was the primary offender. If it weren't for him illegally killing the animals and bringing them to her house, she never would have been involved. This doesn't excuse her behavior, but her son was a thousand percent guilty, and it would have been a waste of taxpayer money and everyone's time if his case went to trial. So the district attorney struck a deal. Plead guilty, and we drop the charges against mom. Ironically, this agreement opened the window for the *Portland Press Herald* to accuse us of overreaching. They admitted the dirty trickery in a follow-up article defending themselves against the Warden Service's press release that outlined the errors in "North Woods lawless."

> **Warden Service statement:** *[Mom Peaches'] canned meats were "erroneously described by the author as 'meat never proven to be illicit.'"*
> **Press Herald response:** *The wardens dropped all charges against [Mom Peaches] the night before her trial was to begin, so their claims that her canned meat was illicit were never proven.*

Technically, they are correct. But—seriously? I may not have known what fake news was before "North Woods lawless" was published, but it put me through a crash course, and I haven't even gotten to the worst mincing of words yet. The article and each subsequent rendition were a nightmare I couldn't escape. I found it deeply troubling that the *Portland Press Herald* accused me of entrapment and on-the-job debauchery, and yet they kept steering readers back to . . . phantom canned peaches.

So let's clear the air on the entrapment allegation.

On Halloween night in 2013, Livezey showed up at [Rory's] dilapidated trailer and hung out while the 36-year-old smoked joints. Four hours later, [Rory] was drinking beer and blasting away at a deer from the agent's truck using the agent's guns, ammo and spotlight. The two repeated this ritual eight more times that fall, Livezey reported.

During these illegal night-hunting expeditions, Livezey was the first to kill a deer, and [Rory] subsequently shot a deer and a moose, the agent's reports show.

"I wouldn't have been going out and doing this if he hadn't wanted to," says [Rory], who later pleaded guilty to 39 charges. He spent 90 days in jail and owes $27,240 in fines.

[Rory's] mother, [Mom Peaches], says her son was an easy mark for the agent. "The relationship they developed was that [Rory] just wanted him to like him as a person," she says.

Rep. Martin, who wrote a letter requesting leniency to [Rory's] sentencing judge, concurs. "[Rory] is as nice a guy as you can find, always wanting to help people," he says. "To me, it was entrapment."

First of all, the evidence is so overwhelming in an undercover case that the only argument defendants and their lawyers can try to make is entrapment and misconduct. We know this going into each operation, so we take every precaution to ensure these allegations don't have legs. Neither the district attorneys nor the judges involved in the Operation Red Meat cases had any issues with how I conducted the investigation. In twenty years of covert work, I haven't had a single judge rule in favor of the defendant on an entrapment defense. That's a list of over thirty-five District, Superior, and Supreme Court Justices in the state of Maine, Pennsylvania, and New Jersey, as well as Federal U.S. Justices in Maine and Massachusetts, who have reviewed, examined, heard, and presided over my investigations in a court of law. Nor would these cases have ever gotten in front of the judges if the district attorneys believed I entrapped the bad guys.

Secondly, even if I had been the one to suggest that we go night hunting and had shot the first deer, it *is* legal for me to do so if the suspect has shown a predisposition to commit these crimes. Rory Casey is the same guy previously convicted of poaching a moose at night while employed as a ranger by the Department of Agriculture, Conservation and Forestry. Drinking, smoking pot (it was illegal then), and night hunting were par for the course whether or not I was in attendance. In

Rory's own words, it was his view of "the Allagash way." Suffice it to say, predisposition was established.

As a personal rule to ensure an extra layer of protection in an entrapment defense, I never suggest that the suspects commit an illegal act. Nor have I ever had to. If the suspects required coercion, they wouldn't have passed the initial research phase of the investigation. All I've ever had to do was hang out, joke around, and tell hunting stories while they drink, smoke pot, and do whatever other drugs. Sooner or later, someone is going to say, "Let's go for a ride."

We all knew what that meant.

The article would have you believe that the Allagash poachers weren't equipped for night hunting and I was their personal Dick's Sporting Goods. That couldn't be further from the truth. Yes, I drove if they let me. They were usually drunk and high when we went out, so I wanted to drive from a safety standpoint. Another reason I like to drive is to control the situation. As you've seen in earlier chapters, the suspects of these investigations are more than willing to shoot at deer in dooryards. If I'm behind the wheel, I can force them out of this or, at the very least, angle the vehicle in a way that they aren't firing toward the house. Unfortunately, the worst poachers all seem to possess the control-freak gene, so I often only get to drive when they tell me that I'm driving.

Rory did tell me to do some of the driving. If we were in my truck, we sometimes used my spotlight, but he had a special one for night hunting that he preferred. Using my spotlight in this scenario wasn't entrapment. It's just being a good hunting buddy, which Bill Freed was. When asked, I also usually let suspects use my rifle. Wily poachers prefer to do this because if they are caught, it's my rifle that gets confiscated and not theirs—lost in the reporting of fines throughout this book is the hefty financial loss incurred by convicted poachers due to seized firearms and hunting equipment. Again, letting them use my gun isn't entrapment. I'm trying to ingrain myself into their trust and friendly gestures like this go a long way.

Of course, it's *how* the article reveals that I shot a deer that put the nail in my coffin on the entrapment defense in the court of public opinion. It's true, I did shoot a deer, but as with everything else in "North

Woods lawless," there's a lot more to the story. What you have to understand is that in just about every undercover case, there comes the point where the bad guys realize that they've been doing all these illegal things in my presence, but I don't have any blood on my hands. That's when they put me on the spot. It's a test, and if I fail, it will compromise the investigation and possibly my safety. This circumstance is why it is legal under Maine statute for covert agents to violate the laws we're trying to enforce.

An equally condemning accusation was Woodard's portrayal of my drinking throughout Operation Red Meat.

Many of those who encountered Livezey in Allagash say he often drank and provided drinks to others, although the agent claimed in his reports that he poured most of his beers out or nursed his drinks during multiple three- and four-hour visits to the Moose Shack to gather intelligence and infiltrate local social circles.

"He would drink and hand me beers in the vehicle," says [Connor's] son, who says he pleaded guilty to hunting under the influence and illegal possession of a grouse during a backwoods drive with the agent because it would have cost too much to fight the charges, even though he says he did not commit them. "Being law enforcement, you wouldn't think he could do that," [Connor's son] says.

[Rory] concurs. "The whole time he was doing this, the guy stayed drunk," he says of the covert agent. "He later claimed he was dumping beers all day, but that isn't so. This was a vacation for him, and he was partying hard."

[James] recalls Livezey arriving at his house with a 12-pack of Yuengling beer and says that the agent drank eight of them.

Of all the allegations against me in the article, I'm proud of this one. Honestly, I feel like I should take a bow. Anyone who knows me in my personal life knows that I don't drink. On the other hand, Bill Freed had to pretend that he did because it's critical for an undercover agent to fit in. I had loads of excuses to avoid doing drugs, from getting tested at work to severe headaches and panic attacks, but I played along when it came to alcohol. Bars are one of the best places to meet bad guys, and this probably comes as no surprise, but they have little interest in getting to know the guy who's drinking soda. When invited to their homes, I typically brought beer—yes, Yuengling—intended for my own "consumption." After all, nobody likes the guy who shows up and drinks their beer. They always had plenty of their own alcohol, but if a suspect of legal age asked to try one of mine, I'd oblige. Again, that's what friends do.

As for my drinking, I'd take a sip here and there to make it look good, but I didn't drink more than a couple of beers on any given night. The details matter when working undercover, and the slightest slip of the tongue can have dire consequences. If I were actually getting drunk during investigations, I wouldn't have lasted two weeks as a covert agent, let alone twenty years.

To make it appear like I'd drank eight beers instead of one, I'd dump my drink out whenever I relieved myself. I was constantly afraid that someone would catch me doing this outside or ask why I always brought my beer with me to the bathroom. I'm amazed no one ever did. The fact that so many convicted poachers came out of the woodwork after "North Woods lawless" was published to pile onto these allegations should make me a shoo-in for an Oscar. Ironically, many of them accused me of *not drinking enough* during their investigations.

You may have noticed in the previous excerpt that Woodard included my side of the story. Go back and reread it. Whenever someone is accusing me of drinking, they "say" it as a statement of fact, but I "claimed" that I was pouring out beers. Obviously, someone in that excerpt is either incorrect or lying, and with his subtle word choices, Woodard leads readers to believe that I wasn't telling the truth. This is hardly an isolated example. Throughout the article, Woodard uses a toilet-paper-thin facade of being fair and balanced to camouflage how he influences the reader's opinion. In another instance, he writes that wardens "*act* as traffic cops on snowmobile and ATV trails." The insinuation is that we aren't *real* officers of the law, even though wardens graduate from the same police academy as other law enforcement branches before undergoing additional Warden Service training.

This tilted journalism is what makes "North Woods lawless" and the *Portland Press Herald*'s numerous follow-up articles so dangerous. As the state's largest news organization, people are inclined to believe what they read in the *Portland Press Herald*. Its Wikipedia page states that "The *Portland Press Herald/Maine Sunday Telegram* has a long-standing and openly stated commitment to fair and balanced news coverage and hard-hitting watchdog journalism in the interest of the public good."

Hard-hitting, indeed. Fair and balanced? Not so much.

Many people took the bait Woodard offered—hook, line, and sinker. Not that I can blame them. He did a masterful job of painting a picture where habitual poachers with prior game and drug violations were sympathetic victims of the out-of-control Maine Warden Service. The idea that those convicted of wildlife crimes might be lying about their innocence seemed preposterous by the end of the article. If you didn't stop to ask yourself: *Why are they quoting a retired New York City police officer about the validity of an undercover operation in the Maine Warden Service? Couldn't they have gotten a law enforcement officer closer to home?* And, *Why such a focus on canned peaches? What does that matter?* Or, if you didn't know that the "facts" presented in the article were either outright falsehoods or deliberately misconstrued—you had no way of knowing better.

When the Warden Service issued a statement identifying the inaccuracies, the *Portland Press Herald* turned up the heat, publishing an additional twenty-two articles related to "North Woods lawless." This subsequent reporting is where they jumped the shark in a major way. In an article titled "Targets of another warden sting criticize conduct of investigator," staff writer Scott Dolan wrote:

> *That ruling on Livezey's undercover activities followed a 2006 decision by the Maine Supreme Judicial Court in an appeal accusing Livezey of misconduct in a separate case.* **The court ruled that Livezey's behavior in an Oxford County undercover operation might have been "repugnant,"** *but "not so outrageous" that all the criminal charges against the man targeted in that investigation should be dismissed.*

Here's the actual Maine Supreme Judicial Court ruling cited by Dolan:

*We have acknowledged that **there may be cases** in which govern-ment officers are so enmeshed in the criminal activity that the pros-ecution of another participant in that activity might be repugnant to our concept of criminal justice. The warden's activities here were clearly designed to ingratiate himself with [the defendant] and [his] friends and clients so that he could personally observe violations of the fish and wildlife laws. His testimony was replete with instances of how he attempted to avoid committing crimes personally. We are not convinced that the warden's conduct was so outrageous that due process requires dismissal of all charges.*

In no way was the court saying that my behavior "might have been 'repugnant.'" Quite the opposite—the repugnant observation is clearly referring to other cases that didn't involve me. In response to this article, the Department of Inland Fisheries and Wildlife issued a press release revealing how the *Portland Press Herald* falsely represented the 2006 rul-ing. Instead of retracting the statement, the *Portland Press Herald* turned on the spotlight and fired an even more reckless shot in an article titled "Maine Warden Service disputes latest story on sting operations." Staff Writer Edward D. Murphy wrote:

*He accused the newspaper of 'surgically' picking words from a Maine Supreme Judicial Court ruling in another case that found that the undercover warden's actions **were "repugnant,"** but "not so outra-geous" that charges against Licensed Maine Guide [the defendant] of Fryeburg should be dismissed.*

Somehow, my actions evolved from "might have been" to "were" repugnant. The only thing repugnant about this was the *Portland Press Herald's* blatant disregard of the truth. All of which begs the question: *Why?*

Why would the state's largest news organization launch a crusade against the Maine Warden Service? Why would Colin Woodard, an award-winning author and journalist, forsake his ethics to write a piece knowingly littered with misconstrued information? These questions have kept me awake on many nights. Having been in the middle of it all, I feel like I'm working on a puzzle. The pattern seems clear, but pieces are missing.

What I know for a fact is that after the Operation Red Meat arrests were made in 2014, Representative John Martin contacted the Warden Service to complain that the undercover tactics were entrapment. After getting rebuffed, he called the district attorney's office to get the cases dismissed before the arraignments. When that failed, Martin wrote a letter to the presiding judge requesting leniency for Rory, the worst offender. Martin also made it well known in political circles that he was looking for support on a bill he intended to submit to shut down covert operations in the Warden Service's Special Investigations Unit (SIU). He introduced the bill but subsequently pulled it—coincidentally after we made it known that the assistant district attorney would testify regarding Martin's interference.

It's also worth noting that Martin is a career Democrat. At this time, Maine had an outspoken conservative governor and a popular fish and game commissioner who were both Republican. An election year was on the horizon.

Around the same time that Martin was rounding up his political allies, we were tipped off that an article attacking the Warden Service was coming. Sure enough, Colin Woodard soon contacted the Warden Service asking accusatory questions about entrapment in Operation Red Meat. Another reason we didn't honor his interview requests was because the attorney general's office advised against it. By this time, Woodard's article was already widely perceived as a hit piece. When the article was published six months later, Martin was quoted prominently. *The day after* "North Woods lawless" went public, the *Portland Press Herald* published another Woodard article titled, "State senator wants answers on Maine game wardens' tactics in undercover operation." This article featured several Democratic and Republican state politicians who were troubled by the accusations that I shot the first deer and supplied guns and ammunition to entice the Allagash suspects into poaching.

As for the missing puzzle pieces, the one that gets my goat the most is this: How is it that a journalist of Woodard's stature, writing on behalf of the state's largest news organization, who is ethically bound to cover both sides of the story, and who supposedly conducted an in-depth, six-month investigation for "North Woods lawless," never once contacted the district attorney to inquire about one of the state's most influential politicians inappropriately throwing his weight around to affect a law enforcement investigation? Isn't that a story unto itself that a "watchdog" newspaper should examine? The fact that Woodard didn't follow this basic journalistic principle makes any argument that "North Woods lawless" wasn't a hit piece from the start indefensible.

Sadly, fake news has real-world implications. As I write this, the powers behind "North Woods lawless" got their way—the Colonel shut covert operations in the SIU down indefinitely. The official reason for this was officer safety, but behind the scenes, there was more to the story. For whatever reason, Representative Martin was hellbent on shutting us down. As a member of the Joint Standing Committee on Appropriations and Financial Affairs and the Joint Standing Committee on Inland Fisheries and Wildlife, he had the clout to revoke funding for the Warden Service's already approved pay increases, and our leaders were concerned about possible layoffs if they had to find an alternative path for covering this expense. My superiors did their best to shoot down the false narrative created by "North Woods lawless." Still, in the ugly political fallout, they had no choice but to sacrifice the SIU for the agency's greater good as a whole.

Now that covert operations are collecting dust on a shelf, it pains me to think about the most grievous poachers who are getting away with their crimes as a result. Ironically, those who questioned the cost of undercover operations in "North Woods lawless" have made it more expensive and challenging for the Warden Service to apprehend poachers. That's terrible news for honest sportsmen and outdoor enthusiasts who care about the way life in Maine should be.

Good guys.

Bad guys.

When respected politicians and journalists distort facts to attack game wardens, who can tell the difference?

16

THE ALLAGASH WAY

THE HOWLING WIND BEAT THE CABIN LIKE A STICK WHOPPING DIRT from a rug, and yet it paled in comparison to the raucous yammering inside. Connor McBride's parties were typically standing-room-only affairs, but on this evening, the storm had already delivered over a foot of heavy wet snow and knocked out the electricity, keeping all but his closest hunting buddies away. Undeterred, six of us played cards by flickering candlelight at the kitchen table, a nauseous blend of wax potpourris dueling the entwined cigarette and pot smoke wafting through the air.

I was up over a hundred dollars in quarters games of poker, money that aided my budget for the case. The clock was close to striking midnight, and we'd reached that inevitable point when everyone's blood was so diluted with alcohol that they ceased to remember—or care—whose turn it was to play. Oral theater had commandeered entertainment, each man competing for the most outrageous, daring, poaching story. For me, it was a lightning round of information collection.

"Check this out!" Rory Casey leaned into me. He came in hot like a teenager behind the wheel, turning the display window of a small point-and-shoot camera so I could see the nighttime image of a gigantic bonfire. The steeple flame was easily the height of a full-grown birch tree. "James torches the river island every fall. It's like, you know, Allagash fireworks."

"Wow, that's massive." I nodded my approval to James.

"The grass and weeds grow really tall there throughout the summer," he said. "They dry out and burn like paper in the fall."

"I can't believe the town lets you do that."

Everyone laughed at my naivety.

"I wouldn't say they let me," James said coyly. He took a swig of beer. The can made an empty clink when he set it down amid the flotsam of empties and chip bags littering the table.

"Billy . . ." Connor McBride said, dragging my name out in a high-pitched, half-Irish, half-Northwoods dialect that's unique to Maine and probably nowhere else in the world for that matter. "We do what we want up here. That's the Allagash way."

The *Portland Press Herald* would have you believe that these were good guys down on their luck and unfairly targeted and coerced into wrongdoing by the Maine Warden Service—i.e., me. That couldn't be further from the truth. The Allagash crew was a murderer's row of poachers known as "Moose Towners" in their small community, a moniker they flaunted with pride. Getting by on the fringe of society in the northern-most woods of Maine, some of them without electricity or running water, they viewed this hard-living sacrifice as a license to do whatever they wanted, whenever they wanted.

"Tell Bill about the other fire?" Rory said, his focus volleying between the McBride cousins, seeking permission.

James and Connor exchanged glassy-eyed, eyebrow-raised expressions that I recognized all-too-well. We'd reached a point of no return with the topic on the table. They were withholding something, and the big question at the heart of their nonverbal communication was a familiar one—did they trust me?

"What fire?" I prodded. "Was it bigger than that river inferno?"

"C'mon," Rory said, "tell him."

Connor's chair scraped the floor like nails on a chalkboard as he ceremoniously stood up from the table. A blast of wind rattled the window behind us, prompting him to note, "I sure as hell hope nobody left a window open in the Suburban." He proceeded to the fridge, discarded an empty thirty-pack box on the worn white linoleum floor, and returned with four cans of Michelob Light in his bear-paw hands, two of which were for him. He sat down with a heavy sigh, cracked one of the beers and sucked it down in a heartbeat, and looked me squarely in the eyes.

"It ain't right that they charge us to go into the Wilderness to hunt." His tone was suddenly serious and picking up steam. "I've lived and hunted here all my life—who are they to come in here and tell us that we have to pay? We weren't gonna roll over and take that, so we showed them."

To the only sober guy in the room (me), he came across as a clichéd caricature of himself, but for everyone else around the table, heads were nodding in approval as if they were taking a sermon from their preacher.

"How'd you show them?" I asked after a lengthy pause.

"You know the gatehouses where they collect the fees?"

"Yeah." The gatehouses he was talking about are nothing like the small toll booths you see when going into a state park. These are full-blown cabins with a receiving room in front for conducting business and living quarters in the back for the assigned rangers. In other words, they cost a pretty penny. "What about them?"

"When they first built 'em, we burned 'em down."

Make no mistake, the Allagash region of Maine is a special place worthy of its virgin reputation. A giant wilderness playground, its vast forests are denser than an old wool coat, its near-pristine waters are teeming with hearty fish, and the crisp air tantalizes with its sweet balsamic fragrance. Life here isn't far removed from Louise Dickinson Rich's *We Took to the Woods*, and those who choose residency forgo many modern amenities in favor of a quieter, more solitary lifestyle.

The vast majority of those I encountered in the Allagash were welcoming, salt of the earth people. But even the most pristine waters collect pollutants, and when you take the time to look past the glistening surface and dig into the sediment, the dirt comes out. There are some—the proverbial rotten apples—who live in this northern outpost of Maine to escape, cultivating a distorted *don't tread on me* mentality that blurs their sense of right and wrong. In an area with a limited supply of people, they exchange sexual partners like borrowing a chainsaw, drown themselves in drugs and alcohol, and view the abundance of wildlife as theirs for the taking.

Herein lies the rub. Go for a drive along the Allagash and St. John rivers, and you'll see sporting camps, guide services, and wilderness outfitters with the density of Dunkin' Donuts in Boston. The limited non-sporting businesses are also well aware that their bread is buttered by those who travel great distances and spend small fortunes compared to local incomes to exercise their fly rods and rifles in the storied Allagash. Excessive poaching threatens their very way of life, but in a community of fewer than three hundred people, the good guys and bad guys are commingled together as neighbors, friends, and, more times than not, family.

As a result, beneath the warm smiles, handshakes, and hugs, resentment simmers. Like a family divided by politics, very few people who disagree with the Moose Towners' mindset are willing to confront them directly or speak on the record to a *Portland Press Herald* reporter for fear of stirring a pot of disdain and incurring unpredictable retribution. If the Moose Towners are willing to burn down the gatehouses, causing tens of thousands of dollars in damage over a nominal entrance fee, what would they do to someone who rats them out? What those on the good side of the fence are willing to do when things get out of hand is whisper to their local game warden.

Their message was clear: *This has to stop.*

Because of their pleas, we enacted Operation Red Meat.

James McBride inspires fear. His cantankerous disposition and penchant for domestic disputes precede him. James always struck me as someone the Allagash wilderness chewed up and spat out in its likeness. Tall and weathered with a full beard that mixed black and white like a swirl ice cream, he was a perpetually dirty recluse who lived in a ragged trailer with no running water and at least fifteen cats that shared his bed. Believe me when I say that his place smelled worse than you're imagining.

The first time I met James, I was with a friend of his, asking questions about the best places to hunt, hoping my inquiries would lead to an introduction. My plan couldn't have worked out better. The friend and I were hanging out at the office (standing around the bed of his truck) chewing the fat when James drove into the yard.

"What's that you're drinking?" he asked me after the basic introductions.

"Yuengling," I said. "Pennsylvania's finest."

"Is it any good?"

"It'll put hair on your chest."

"Can I try one?"

"You bet."

This innocent interaction turned into me providing drinks to others in the "North Woods lawless" article, insinuating that I was feeding them beers to entice illegal behavior. The *Portland Press Herald* also charged me with failing to nab James for excessive poaching, which is technically accurate, but it doesn't tell the whole story. At forty-nine years old, James profiled as a mid-life crisis poacher, teetering between the younger man with blood in his eyes who savages wildlife without a second thought and the wise old owl who keenly calculates the risks of getting caught. Locals swore that James was poaching year-round and illegally growing marijuana in the woods for sale (as well as stealing from other growers), and my early interactions with him indicated they were right.

"Bring a gun," he told me when we went for a walk in the woods to scout hunting locations. It was October, before deer season, during my first fall working the case. "You never know when you'll see a piece of meat."

In the article, James claimed that he didn't trust me. "When he left that first weekend, he was bound and determined that I was going to shoot him a buck, and I made up my mind right there that I was going to have as little to do with the (expletive) as I could," he was quoted as saying.

The article also stated that James declined to shoot a deer for me to buy. This assertion simply isn't true. He showed me his bait pile in the woods near his trailer and told me that if the weather were cold enough to hang a deer, he'd shoot one for the next time I came up. If he genuinely didn't trust me, I doubt he would have cooked me a deer steak that he described as "an early-bird special." It was a hundred-and-forty-pound doe that he shot illegally with a rifle in September from a wildlife management district closed to the taking of antlerless deer.

While we were eating the early-bird special, his girlfriend Kami came over. James quickly hid his beer and told me to tell her it was mine. The mother of Connor's second son, Kami was considerably younger than James, and she kept him somewhat in line that first fall. However, the real reason James didn't shoot a deer for me to purchase was that he kept getting arrested by the State Police for violating his bail and threatening to kill Kami during the investigation's second year. I'd drive into town and see him leaving in the back of a squad car. The State Police also confiscated his weapons, hindering his ability to poach when he wasn't cooling off in the crowbar motel.

As an undercover warden, my job is to follow the evidence. Contrary to the spurious allegations printed by the *Portland Press Herald*, I don't conjure charges out of thin air. The statute of limitations had expired on the gatehouse arsons, and James' domestic issues and bail violations limited his fish and game infractions to closed-season hunting, exceeding the bag limit on deer, possessing an antlerless deer without a permit, hunting with a revoked license, having a loaded firearm in a motor vehicle, and violating his bail conditions. But let's not pretend that there wouldn't have been more if we'd extended the case another hunting season. If there's one thing I learned about James McBride, it's that his reputation was more fact than fiction.

"There are no malls here, no nightclubs, no strip joints—Christ, we're in the Allagash. I'm having a beer in the Maine woods. There's no ball or kids coming in the road here! Who cares!"

That's how Connor McBride described his drinking in "North Woods lawless."

"It makes no sense," Connor whined above the rowdy commotion of guys packed into his Suburban, drawing out the first syllable in *sense*. "Where's the meat?"

He swung his Browning automatic shotgun loaded with birdshot around (the safety was off), and in the split second that I was staring directly down the barrel, I was more concerned with getting a backwoods lobotomy than a soccer ball in the road. The shotgun came to a rest on his arm, pointed at Rory Casey's abdomen.

"Watch out!" Rory yelled, redirecting the barrel.

"Ha!" Connor hooted, pulling the shotgun away from Rory, his guttural laugh reverberating up from his beer-keg belly. Tall like his cousin with mostly gray sheepdog hair and a radish-red face that squeezed into a lemon-puckered expression each time he bellowed, "It makes no sense!" like a skipping record.

"Dad!" Connor's thirty-two-year-old son Johnny yelled from behind the wheel, realizing the barrel was now aimed at the back of his seat. "Cut the crap!"

Laughing more, Connor haphazardly swung the barrel around again. Seated behind him in the third row of the Suburban, I felt like I was boxing again, bobbing and weaving to keep my head intact. Needless to say, Connor was plastered. Rory kept turning the safety on when Connor wasn't looking, but he'd notice and shut it off again. Eventually, Rory unloaded the shotgun altogether.

Simply put, Connor was one of the biggest alcoholics I've ever met (don't forget, I literally grew up in a bar). The alpha male in their hunting crew, Connor wouldn't let anyone else drive his Suburban—his preferred meat wagon—unless he was so intoxicated that he couldn't keep it on the road. These hunting excursions always began with him loading a cooler filled with at least two thirty packs of Michelob Light into the back. The cooler was always empty by the end of the hunt.

I typically finagled it so that I was sitting in the Suburban's third row where I was least likely to become a shooter and could observe everyone else. Of course, this also put me closest to the cooler, so when someone yelled for a beer, I was the one to pass it up. The *Portland Press Herald* used the seating arrangement to feed the narrative that I was handing out beers to get everyone drunk. But I wasn't the one to buy the beer, fill the cooler, or put it in the Suburban. What was I supposed to say, "No, get it yourself"? That would have ended the case awful quick!

The reality is that these guys were drinking hard and hunting illegally from the Suburban whether I was with them or not. It was their pastime, and Connor's rule was that when he asked for a beer, you had to hand him two. He pounded the first one in the blink of an eye and then "savored" the second for a few minutes.

If you think I'm overselling the drinking and the danger it caused simply to refute the *Portland Press Herald* story, I submit to the court of public opinion the many bullet holes in the floorboards of Connor's Suburban from him accidentally discharging his weapons. It truly was a wonder that no one had gotten shot.

"Stop, stop, stop!" Connor yelled at the sight of an oncoming truck. "Let's see if these guys are having any luck."

Connor knew the guys in the other truck, and he got out to talk to them. I followed suit to see if they had any illegal game. The way these cases often went, the guys in the truck could end up hunting with us the next day, all of a sudden making them part of the investigation, so it was best for Connor to introduce me to gain their trust. I made the mistake of turning my back to Connor for a moment, and I was caught off guard by an explosion next to my head. I barreled over and stumbled around, nearly falling. My ears rang fiercely and my vision was blurred. When it came back in focus, Connor was standing over me.

"What did you do that for?" I yelled.

"I had to show them how the Browning fired."

"Do you have any idea how dangerous that is?"

The guy driving the truck interjected. "You gotta watch out for Connor. He's a loose cannon!"

No kidding.

Connor wasn't just the life of the party—he *was* the party. When I was there in the summer to fish, half the show was watching him stumble around bare chested like a bear in a bakery. As reckless as he was, he was a genuinely hilarious fellow with a natural aura that drew people to him. After the cooler was empty and we wrapped up hunting that day when he fired his shotgun next to my head, everyone rendezvoused at his cabin for the second round of drinking. Connor held court, telling stories deep into the night.

I was invited to stay in his cabin's loft, which was pitch black when I retired. The bed was covered with what felt like a layer of Lay's chip crumbs, but I was so exhausted from hunting all day and pretending to party half the night that I simply didn't care. I crashed on top of the bed without taking my clothes off or climbing into the covers. A couple of hours later, I couldn't take the crackling underneath me anymore, so I dug a small flashlight out of my bag that I kept for secretly documenting notes at night. It was like a scene out of a Stephen King story—thousands of dead flies plastered the bed. I've had a lot of gross accommodations working undercover, but this one takes the cake!

"That's the danger of log cabin living when it gets cold," Connor said in the morning when I told him about the flies, his eyes welling with tears he was laughing so hard.

The irony to all of this is that at fifty-six years old, Connor was cautious and calculating with his poaching. One day while road hunting in the wake of a snowstorm, we came upon a massive bull moose with a sixty-inch rack. Connor and his buddies were drunk, and one guy was so amped to shoot the moose that I thought he might pee on the carpet.

"No," Connor said, suspiciously eyeing a set of fresh vehicle tracks in the road, "we're not going to get into a mess today."

It was rare for these guys to get out of the Suburban and hunt legally, but Connor did take me out once during muzzleloader season. I typically follow the lead of the poachers I'm working, so when we got back to the Suburban, I climbed in with my gun loaded, knowing this was par for the course. To my surprise, Connor stopped to unload. He then milled around for a bit before getting in. After stalling for a few more minutes, he reloaded and then started the vehicle.

"What was that about?" I asked.

"It's a game warden trick to sit and watch a vehicle to see if you unload before getting in." He shifted the Suburban into drive. "Screw them! They catch a lot of people that way, and that's how I flush 'em out."

"Thanks for telling me. I could have been caught!"

He got a good laugh out of that.

The *Portland Press Herald* downplayed Connor's violations, saying he "was convicted of minor offenses, including taking too many trout, having his girlfriend tag a deer he'd shot, and hunting while drinking." In reality, Connor was charged and found guilty by a jury of our most severe wildlife crimes. He was convicted of three counts of hunting under the influence, three counts of exceeding the bag limit on deer, three counts of possessing a loaded firearm in a vehicle, one count of night hunting, one count of failing to register a deer, one count of going over the limit on brook trout, and two counts of theft of services from North Maine Woods by smuggling people in to hunt without paying the gate fees. Bear in mind, this is just the stuff I could prove. There was more that I wasn't privy to, I'm sure of it.

But the *Portland Press Herald* fixated on the trout, likely because the general public wouldn't see it as an egregious offense. Connor caught eleven that day on a bag limit of five, and we brought home twenty-four among three of us, but his goal was to get sixty. He attacked the stream like a greedy kid trick or treating, practically racing from hole to hole to get his line in first. The fish were biting, and I was doing things like taking the worm off my hook to keep myself from catching too many. I ended up taking seven, two over the limit, to make it look good, and we probably would have reached Connor's goal of sixty if it weren't for a string of thunderstorms and heavy rain that cut our fishing short.

Back at Connor's house, I arranged the fish together on a table and took a photo for evidence. The newspaper ran the photo with Connor's accusation that I'd taken some of the fish out of the freezer to frame him. He tried this defense in court, his lawyer arguing that some of the fish "had a distinctive different appearance because those fish had been caught on an earlier day at a different location." As I mentioned in the last chapter, that's a bunch of hogwash. Trout are like snowflakes with natural disparities in markings regardless of where they live. But the real lie was revealed during his post-conviction review when Connor admitted to freezing trout whole in water-filled Ziploc bags to best preserve them, so if we'd have taken them out of the freezer for the photo, they would have been in a block of ice.

The truth came out, but the *Portland Press Herald* preferred to peddle the lies.

Rory Casey tipped his head back and a cloud of pot smoke rolled out like steam from a paper mill's stacks. Like James McBride, he was a recluse who lived in squalor in a rundown trailer with no plumbing. The *Portland Press Herald* made him out to be an impressionable young man down on his luck, but his misfortune was his own doing. Rory was previously gainfully employed by the state Department of Agriculture, Conservation and Forestry for seven years as an assistant Allagash Wilderness Waterway ranger, a job he had to resign after a night hunting and moose poaching conviction.

Rory would get grand ideas while his thoughts were floating sky high and collect junk that rotted in his unkempt yard in the aftermath of his intoxicated delusions. He was so lazy that instead of going to the outhouse or next door to his mother's cabin to defecate, he often deposited his load in plastic bags. When the wardens raided his place, they found eight bags of feces.

Going between his mother's log cabin and Rory's trailer was like crossing between worlds. The queen of peaches kept her place clean and tidy with an immaculate lawn and quaint flower gardens, causing the illegal game that Rory shot at night and hung outside her bedroom window to stand out like a ketchup stain on a white blouse.

"Let's go for a ride," Rory said after one final bong hit.

"About time," I said, genuinely excited to get out of there.

With James' legal troubles and Connor too inebriated to keep hunting after dark, Rory became Operation Red Meat's focal point. At thirty-five years old, he was squarely in the young and dumb category of poachers who live by the mantra, *see it, shoot it.* Rory looked up to Connor and James, envious of their reputation as the Allagash's top Moose Towners, and he went to great lengths to prove he was their equal. In doing so, he far exceeded their exploits.

"Just one thing," Rory said.

"What's that?"

His bloodshot eyes looked me over for a tell. "You're shooting tonight."

We'd gone hunting five nights earlier, and the gears were grinding in his pot-fueled brain as he realized that he'd done all the shooting, wounding several deer, including a couple of does and two bucks, one of which was a young five-pointer that he'd hit in a front leg at the joint. If he really thought about it, this was the second season I'd been with them, and for someone who professed to wanting a buck, the only thing I'd shot in their presence was a partridge out the window of Connor's Suburban to make it look like I was one of them.

"I'm driving," he declared.

I knew the drill. Rory was testing me. No ifs. Ands. Or buts.

Except for one.

"No does," I told him as we drove along a woods road that he felt safe hunting at night, confident that the local warden didn't patrol it. "I'm only shooting a buck. I can get does back in Pennsylvania, and if the guys at work find out that I came all the way up here to shoot a doe, I'll never hear the end of it."

"Shouldn't be a problem."

I kid you not, as soon as I finished my bucks-only spiel, we came around a bend to find one in the middle of the road, frozen in our headlights. It was the five-pointer that Rory previously shot in the leg, in the same spot we encountered it before. Seriously. I couldn't make this up! It was just standing there as if it was a decoy deer, twenty yards in front of us, favoring its wounded leg.

"Told you it wouldn't be a problem."

I often missed shots on purpose, but this one was too easy. Missing would have confirmed Rory's suspicions. I had to shoot the deer to preserve the case. So I did.

"During these illegal night-hunting expeditions, Livezey was the first to kill a deer," Colin Woodard wrote of this encounter in "North Woods lawless," formulating an argument that Rory was following my lead.

Forget the fact that James and Connor each killed two deer over their limit earlier in the case. Never mind that Rory wounded several deer beforehand while night hunting that very week. And ignore the reality that he'd previously shot the deer that I ultimately killed—it was going to die anyway, I ended its suffering. Look closely at how Woodard worded that statement. He's talking specifically about the times that Rory and I night hunted alone together, intentionally excluding the earlier poaching by James, Connor, and others. And while the many deer that Rory shot beforehand likely died—either from the bullet wounds directly or by coyotes as a result—we had no proof.

Therefore, as far as anyone knew, Woodard's declaration that I was the first to kill a deer on solo night hunts with Rory is true—albeit a technicality predicated on Rory's poor aim. This is partly why it was near impossible for me to mount a libel defense. That said, I just don't see how a reasonable person, when presented with all of the facts, can conclude that Rory was poaching as a result of me possibly killing the first deer with him. But that's just it. Woodard didn't present all of the facts. His misleading was purposeful.

Another aspect that Woodard didn't disclose, especially with Rory, is that the so-called "scant" results were also a byproduct of me *preventing* him from committing crimes. Not all of which was against wildlife. One night, Rory took me to a Halloween party where a bunch of underage kids were drinking. Drunk, high, and wearing a rubber werewolf mask, he aggressively worked the room like he was in character at a winter deer yard. He found the weakest prey, grinding up against an intoxicated girl. Thinking of my daughters, my blood was boiling watching him work his hands over her body. I wanted to deck him and I couldn't believe that none of the other adults weren't stepping in. Statutory rape wasn't something I was willing to passively witness and document in my notebook.

"How old is that girl?" I asked him.

"Thirteen," he said, giggling behind the mask.

Rory was thirty-six at this time. *Thirty-six!*

"Dude, seriously? She's way too young. There's a bunch of underage kids here. We have to get out of here."

"She's old enough in the Allagash."

Keep in mind, this is the same guy that Representative Martin wrote a letter on behalf of to the sentencing judge requesting leniency, and he described in "North Woods lawless" as "as nice a guy as you can find." Woodard also positioned Rory as "an impressionable 36-year-old" that I coerced into committing crimes.

Fortunately, I was able to talk Rory into leaving before he got that girl off the dance floor. Of course, I also prevented him from pulling the trigger on wildlife. The crowning example was the night we encountered a federally protected lynx aside the road. People often confuse lynx with bobcat, but I knew it was a lynx by the way it stopped and eyed us, an easy target. Lynx are more docile and curious in this way than bobcat. Rory even admitted after the fact that he knew it was a lynx.

"Stop the truck," he told me, turning off his rifle's safety.

Instead of stopping, I gassed the accelerator, scaring the lynx into the woods.

"What are you doing?" he yelled.

"Sorry! I got excited and hit the wrong pedal."

"You're drunk!" he laughed.

I used the same wrong-pedal strategy the night we saw a cow moose with her calf. Rory wanted to shoot them both, so I once again hit the gas. I often wonder how Woodard's narrative would have changed if I let Rory shoot the lynx and those two moose. The lynx alone was a game-changer. Even still, if I could go back and do it over again, knowing everything I know now and the torment my family went through, I'd prevent him from shooting the lynx and those moose again. This is a fundamental part of being an undercover game warden that Woodard failed to represent. It's not a video game. My goal isn't to get the high score.

Rory Casey supplied plenty of evidence to make a case without letting him go wild. That said, we wouldn't have gotten him without an undercover operation. He'd learned from his previous moose poaching conviction with James, and he was extremely cautious, often getting out of the truck to inspect puddles in the road to see if other vehicles recently came through. After wounding a six-point buck one night—it's incredible how many deer he shot and failed to bring down with his storm-trooper aim—he spent twenty minutes searching for his shell casing in four inches of fresh snow.

"Found it," he finally said, his face beaming with excitement. "The wardens aren't going to catch me again. I always collect my shells, so there's no evidence linking me."

Then he handed me the shell. I put it in my pocket for safekeeping.

We went through the same routine of searching for his shells after he shot and killed a bull moose early one evening.

"Go get my knife bag," he told me after finding the shells.

I'll give it to Rory, he was a maestro at cutting up moose. Fast and efficient, he didn't waste a single piece of meat, even getting the inner loins. It was like watching an expert chainsaw carver at the fair turn a stump into an eagle, painfully obvious that this level of skill wasn't obtained without a serious amount of practice that couldn't possibly have come from legal kills. Rory loved showing off his ability, and he even later tried talking me into letting him shoot another moose that evening after he processed this one.

In the distance, a logging operation was at work. They were probably several miles away on a separate road system, but the shrill sound of their harvesters sawing into trees and flashing beams of light into the star-studded sky seemed too close for comfort.

"They're pretty close," I said, acting like a nervous out-of-stater before he started cutting up the moose. "Maybe we should get out of here. I can't afford to get caught."

In Rory's previous conviction for shooting a moose with James years earlier, they'd left the moose to rot, so I was curious how he'd react in this situation.

"Don't worry about them," Rory said, pulling a quart-sized freezer bag containing a rolled-up joint out of his hooded sweatshirt's front pocket. "Now we take our time, smoke a fatty, and drink some beers." He flashed me a mischievous smile. "That's the Allagash way."

17

ARE YOU AN
UNDERCOVER WARDEN?

Anticipating our destination slow boiled my nerves as I drove us along State Route 227 in Mapleton toward Castle Hill. The towns blended together like the pancaked landscape, one farmhouse and potato field after another, occasionally separated by a copse of trees—the Aroostook County version of a privacy fence. Along the horizon, the sun performed its nightly disappearing act, a brilliant ply of pink all that remained of the encore.

Headlights on, I trained my eyes—or, I should say, my eye—on the tired pavement. I looked like a one-eyed stoner, pressure building in my left eye from a severe bacterial infection I'd caught from a suspect in another case. My inflamed eye mirrored the pink hue in the sky, a mess of blood and pus escaping with each blink. It eventually landed me in the ER on Thanksgiving Day—oh, the joys of couch camping as an undercover warden!

Blurred vision was the last thing I needed on this excursion.

"This should be quick," said Scott Reddington, my literal partner in crime for this case. At thirty years old, Scott persisted as a big dumb kid that refused to grow up. His goofy smile was as well-worn as his Red Sox cap, framed by a halfhearted beard that clung to his square cinder block face like antler velvet. Only the silver runways along the sides of his dark buzzcut betrayed his age.

"Hope so," I told him, knowing his were famous last words.

This case was rooted in the false promise of being easy from the get-go. A small-scale commercial fishing investigation in Mapleton, a mere ten-minute drive from Presque Isle, Maine, near the Canadian border, it was intended as a filler between several serious cases I was already handling. Scott, and sometimes his younger brother, were selling trout and salmon for two bucks a fish to older residents of the subsidized housing complex where they lived. Simple enough. All I had to do was hang out and fish. What could go wrong?

I quickly learned that Scott's real talent was making inadvisable life decisions. In addition to catching and selling trout and salmon of any size and quantity in lieu of an actual job, he was also doing whatever drugs he could get his hands on, occasionally selling them, and conducting his grocery shopping in the fields at night with a rifle. My secret notebook quickly filled with over a hundred documented crimes from Scott and his circle of friends. The eye infection gave me a perfect excuse to maintain a spectator role since I couldn't aim a rifle, and I'd witnessed Scott shoot several deer and a moose while night hunting. At this moment, though, it was the thought of being encircled by his friends that concerned me.

This case wouldn't have landed in my lap had we known Scott was best friends with Reagan Cook and Clay Bradley. Both men were drug dealers and avid poachers from the neighboring town of Castle Hill, the latter of which was involved in a previous undercover case five years earlier. I wasn't the covert agent in that one, but I was part of the search warrant team, and I interviewed Clay's brother Shane during the takedown. That was a story unto itself. In his early twenties, Shane ran drugs with a local, self-proclaimed big shot named Errol Ayers. Coincidentally (or perhaps not), Warden Ben Drew and I had previously arrested Ayers for night hunting with his nine-month-pregnant wife two years before the undercover operation.

"Do you know who I am?" Ayers repeatedly yelled at us during that bust, adding a heavy dose of profanity and acting like he wanted to fight.

"No," I said.

"I'm Errol Ayers!"

"Never heard of him," Ben added, which further incensed Ayers. He had a violent reputation that locals feared, and Ayers somehow thought he could intimidate us.

During the takedown from that previous case, we sent separate teams to Shane's and Ayers' residences. The plan was to bring Ayers to the Houlton jail and hold him without bail, but he was accidentally taken to Presque Isle and bailed. Meanwhile, Shane was obstinate, refusing to hand over the keys to his gun cabinet, which we discovered was loaded with cocaine. Shane's tough-guy act melted into tears once he was alone in my truck hearing his Miranda rights. As I interviewed him, I caught a glimpse in the passenger-door mirror of Ayers sneaking up to us in the dark. I jumped out to intervene, but Ayers pounded on the passenger window before I could stop him, threatening Shane if he talked.

Long story short, both Bradley brothers could identify me, planting an uneasy feeling that we'd cross paths at some point during Scott's investigation. The most likely intersection was Reagan Cook's place, their trading post for drugs and illicit game. Scott had a deal going where Cook would process his deer in exchange for half of the meat. Earlier that morning, we'd dropped Scott's kill from the previous night off— fortunately, Cook was the only one there at the time—and now we were returning for the pickup. It was another roll of the dice, and as we pulled into the gravel driveway and the headlights bathed the dilapidated trailer in light, a previously unseen black Honda CRX tricked out with tinted windows and a rear spoiler stole my attention. My body turned to stone as I caught my breath in the back of my throat like a ninety-mile-an-hour fastball snapping into the catcher's mitt.

Scott looked like someone had a gun pressed to his head.

"Shane Bradley's here." He added a slew of colorful metaphors as he described at length what I already knew: Shane was bad news. In the five years since he'd broken down and confessed in my truck, Shane served his jail time and came out the other side like a rescue dog from an abusive home. "You better stay in the truck. If he doesn't know you, he doesn't trust you, and he'll pick a fight."

"Okay," I said. "I'm not looking for any trouble."

The trailer, quite literally, was a pigsty. The front had a small built-on deck and entryway that sunk into the ground like a decomposing pumpkin. In the back, an attached chicken coop and pigpen enabled the animals to come and go throughout the trailer as they pleased. The entire place smelled of rank animal feces and rotting food. And yet, watching Scott enter the trailer alone wasn't exactly cause for a sigh of relief. I obviously couldn't let Shane see me, but I'd met Cook that morning, and he knew I was with Scott. Staying in the vehicle now wasn't a good look. My concerns blossomed into full-grown panic as the minutes ticked away, exceeding an hour. I shut the truck off and cracked my window to hear if anyone came outside, and despite the near-freezing temperature, I was sweating bullets. Scott was a dimly lit bulb on his brightest day—I could only imagine what Shane and Cook were saying to pollute his thoughts against me.

As I've already disclosed, getting outed as an undercover agent was my worst fear, literally penetrating my nightmares to this very day. There were numerous close calls throughout my career, including the Thanksgiving inquisition in Damariscotta and the boning knife fiasco in Mount Vernon that could have turned deadly. Other unexpected situations, such as my son playing basketball against one of my target's kids in the state tournament, and a bear guide who posted a photo with me on Facebook, had a way of sneaking up on me. That bear guide was Facebook friends with Levi Prince from the Fryeburg case, and Levi's girlfriend commented on the post. Somehow this didn't get back to the guide I was working at the time. Maybe Levi's girlfriend didn't recognize me. Or, perhaps she did, and Levi's ego was so scarred that he let a fellow guide and purported friend get caught to save face.

Either way, I got lucky.

This situation with Scott occurred in 2009, right before the Leroux case that brought me to Pennsylvania. The conservation officers there were astounded that I'd worked undercover in a state of Maine's size for ten years. "You've got to get out soon," they told me. "It's too dangerous. Someone will recognize you."

They were right.

I've said it before, and I'll say it again, Maine is one giant small town when it comes to hunting and fishing, especially in niche communities such as bear guides where they're so close-knit that they might as well be cousins. Not only had I spent ten years getting to know bad guys as Bill Freed, but I'd served double-duty during that time as the uniformed Bill Livezey. I'd also earned my keep as a district game warden for another nine years before joining the covert Resource Protection Unit. Shoot—even my time as a corrections officer resurfaced nefarious individuals in my warden career! Altogether, that's a lot of bad guys who could identify one of the two Bills.

And yet, I continued working undercover for another ten years. It's not like I didn't recognize the danger or have the full support of Gail and my supervisors to take on a different role. Everyone knew I was playing a game of Russian roulette. Each case was another spin of the chamber, gradually increasing the odds that I'd find the bullet sooner or later. We planned my phase-out several times, and I devoted a lot of energy to training younger wardens for undercover work. But then another complicated or dangerous case came along, and I took it. I told myself that the younger guys weren't ready yet and I was doing it to protect them, but the honest-to-goodness truth is I was hanging on too tight.

Who was I, if not an undercover warden?

You might be surprised to learn that I didn't particularly enjoy working undercover. Spending hours on end hanging out in rundown trailers that reeked of urine and filth while the occupants drank, smoked pot, snorted coke—you name it—didn't exactly fit my idea of a good time as a conservative Christian. The numerous life-threatening situations I encountered, when all I could think about was whether I would see my wife and kids again, weren't exactly a perk, either. I stuck with it because I'd fallen in love with being a game warden under the wing of John Ford, getting a view into what the job was like before the bureaucracy of time cards and budgetary restrictions on overtime, and certainly, before the politics of it all turned ugly. Back then, all that mattered was saving wildlife and catching bad guys, and I was still addicted to that oath.

In this regard, perhaps John Martin, Colin Woodard, and the *Portland Press Herald* did me a favor. If it weren't for the "North Woods lawless" article dumping chum to feed a political frenzy that ultimately shut down undercover game warden operations in Maine, I might still be playing the odds, couch surfing and hunting until the wee hours of the morning with strung-out bad guys. This realization doesn't absolve them from recklessly and irresponsibly outing me as an undercover agent, which, quite frankly, was equally as dangerous. I shudder to think what would have happened if the article was published before the boning knife came out, or how a drunken joyride with Sam Gurney would have ended if he had this knowledge.

But that's all in the past. As a man of faith, I can now see the bigger picture and recognize God's greater plan at work. My life has come full circle since retiring from the Maine Warden Service amid the pandemic in the summer of 2020. Gail and I left Maine for a year and returned to Pennsylvania, where we served as house parents at the Milton Hershey School (MHS). Founded by Milton Hershey in 1909 as a home and school for orphaned boys, MHS continues its mission today of supporting families in need as a coed, private boarding school for pre-kindergarten through twelfth grade. Some of the children entrusted to our care were "only" underprivileged in the sense that they came from families living below the poverty line.

However, others encountered atrocities on their path to MHS that will break your heart. I saw my past in their confused, frightened, and outraged eyes, and I prayed daily that the Lord gave me the strength to provide them with the love, patience, and guidance that helped turn my life around. I miss being a warden, but I no longer question who I am without it. These kids gave me a new purpose.

After nearly an hour and twenty minutes, Scott finally emerged from the house carrying a plastic grocery bag filled with packaged deer meat. Before I could expel that long-held sigh of relief, a floodlight turned on. Shane and Cook followed Scott out onto the deck. The light was slow to warm up, causing their dark silhouettes to appear like looming gargoyles leering at my truck. The tips of their cigarettes flitted around as two orange fireflies with the conversation, several gestures aimed toward me.

"Let's go," Scott said the second he opened the passenger door. "Hurry, before they come over here."

He didn't have to tell me twice.

The safety of the open road did little to ease Scott's mind. For several minutes he acted like an estranged lover, unwilling to look at me, staring out his window into the darkness. Awkward silence sat between us.

"They think you're an undercover game warden," Scott eventually blurted out.

"What? Are you serious?"

"Yeah. Shane was busted before by an undercover warden, so now he doesn't trust anyone. They grilled me on how long I've known you, how we met, what we've been doing together."

"That's crazy. What did you tell them?"

Scott bit his lip, slowly shaking his head. "I told them I've known you for ten years! 'Bill's cool,' I said."

"Thanks for having my back. This thing's crazy."

Neither of us said a word for a few more minutes, allowing the awkward silence to creep back in like the cold on a winter's night after the fire dies in the cabin stove. What was Scott thinking? Did he still trust me? Had I overplayed my hand by thanking him for having my back? For his part, I'm sure he was replaying his conversation with Shane and Cook in his mind.

"You know," Scott said, once again being the one to break the silence, "there's a law in Maine that if you ask an undercover cop if they're a cop, they have to identify themselves."

"Really?"

"It's true. It's a law."

"I didn't know that."

Round three of awkward silence permeated the truck. Scott nervously rubbed his hands together, and his right knee was bobbing up and down like a jackhammer as he worked up the gumption to ask me the question we both knew he was going to ask. It was just a matter of waiting for him to get to it.

"So . . . are you . . . you know . . ."

"What are you asking me?"

"Are you . . . an undercover game warden?"

And there it was, the moment of truth. After all the times I've encountered this situation, you'd think I'd have gotten used to it. On the contrary, my insides felt like they were playing a game of Twister while I tried my darndest to project the image of Joe Cool.

"Yeah," I said, "and you're in *a lot* of trouble."

"Really . . ." If Scott were a cartoon character, his jaw would have dropped to the floor. He was full-on panicking, his eyes practically bulging out of his square Minecraft head.

You might be in disbelief at how the targets I worked with never fully figured out that I was an undercover law enforcement officer. For someone on the outside, it's easy to underestimate my secret weapon. You see, my success and longevity were entirely due to the fact that I was good at making friends. It was that simple. The good Lord blessed me with the gift of gab, and it opened doors for me.

Whenever they questioned it, guys like Scott Reddington, Levi Prince, Tucker Leroux, Todd Walsh, Jamie D'Ambrosio, Sam Gurney, Randall Jones, and Connor McBride didn't think I was a warden because they wanted to believe I was their friend. Scott had already shown his hand in this regard by lying to his actual friends about how long he knew me. It was a double-edged sword because he and many others would give me illicit game meat for free, refusing to sell it on the grounds of our friendship.

The bond of friendship also weighed heavy on me. Gail always noted how my mood soured before I went undercover. Mentally, I was preparing myself to become Bill Freed. To stay in the homes of bad guys, eat from their tables, and josh around with their kids. Judas is a psychologically challenging role to play, and it's not easy to betray those who trust you, even when they deserve it. Working undercover played games with my mind and arrested my thoughts. Twenty years of it is a long, pretzeled journey I wouldn't recommend to anyone.

Stopping the truck in the middle of the road, I wound up and gave Scott a hard five-star slap across the chest.

"You dummy! If I was a game warden, do you think I'd be coming up from Pennsylvania to go hunting with you every night?"

"No." He snorted at himself for the foolishness of it all. It was as if a dam broke, releasing the tension. His body relaxed, and his goofy smile returned. "Oh my God, you had me there for a minute. I thought I was in so much trouble."

"I know!"

We both laughed it off.

And then we went night hunting.

He had no idea what was coming.

But I did.

ABOUT THE AUTHORS

Bill Livezey retired from the Maine Warden Service as an investigator in July of 2020 after a thirty-year career. Having served twenty years in the elite Special Investigations Unit, Bill is the longest-tenured undercover operative in the history of the Maine Warden Service. A graduate of Unity College, his dedication to protecting people and defending wildlife earned him recognition as Warden of the Year in 2004, along with six Exemplary Service Awards and one Meritorious Service Award from the Maine Warden Service; recognition from The National Association of State Boating Law Administrators (NASBLA) in 1995; and the "Living Legend Award" as an Officer of the Month from the National Fallen Officers Memorial in 2005.

After retiring from the Maine Warden Service, Bill and his wife, Gail, served as house parents at the Milton Hershey School in Hershey, Pennsylvania. They are currently seeking their next great adventure. Sherman, Maine, remains their home base.

Daren Worcester is the author of *Open Season: True Stories of the Maine Warden Service* (2017). He has also been published in *Backpacker* and *Down East* magazines. A native of Hanover, Maine, and a graduate of the University of Maine, Daren lives in New Hampshire with his family. A sportsman who enjoys hiking, hunting, and fishing, he has never gone for a ride. Read more of his stories at www.wardenstories.com.